KT-873-237

Communication, Public Opinion, and Globalization in Urban China

As China is increasingly integrated into the processes of economic, political, social, and cultural globalization, important questions arise about how Chinese people perceive and evaluate such processes. At the same time, international communication scholars have long been interested in how local, national, and transnational media communications shape people's attitudes and values. Combining these two concerns, this book examines a range of questions pertinent to public opinion toward globalization in urban China: To what degree are the urban residents in China exposed to the influences from the outside world? How many transnational social connections does a typical urban Chinese citizen have? How often do they consume foreign media? To what extent are they aware of the notion of globalization, and what do they think about it? Do they believe that globalization is beneficial to China, to the city where they live, and to them personally? How do people's social connections and communication activities shape their views toward globalization and the outside world? This book tackles these and other questions systematically by analyzing a four-city comparative survey of urban Chinese residents, demonstrating the complexities of public opinion in China. Media consumption does relate, though by no means straightforwardly, to people's attitudes and beliefs, and this book provides much needed information and insights about Chinese public opinion on globalization. It also develops fresh conceptual and empirical insights on issues such as public opinion toward US-China relations, Chinese people's nationalistic sentiments, and approaches to analyze attitudes toward globalization.

Francis L.F. Lee is Associate Professor and Head of Graduate Division at the School of Journalism and Communication, Chinese University of Hong Kong.

Chin-Chuan Lee is Chair Professor in the Department of Media and Communication at the City University of Hong Kong

Mike Z. Yao is Associate Professor in the Department of Media and Communication at the City University of Hong Kong

Tsan-Kuo Chang is Professor in the Department of Media and Communication at the City University of Hong Kong

Fen Jennifer Lin is Assistant Professor in the Department of Media and Communication at the City University of Hong Kong

Chris Fei Shen is Assistant Professor in the Department of Media and Communication at the City University of Hong Kong

Routledge Studies in Rhetoric and Communication

Communication, Public Opinion, and Globalization in Urban China

Francis L.F. Lee, Chin-Chuan Lee,
Mike Z. Yao, Tsan-Kuo Chang,
Fen Jennifer Lin, and Chris Fei Shen

Routledge
Taylor & Francis Group
NEW YORK   LONDON

First published 2014
by Routledge
711 Third Avenue, New York, NY 10017

Simultaneously published in the UK
by Routledge
2 Park Square, Milton Park, Abingdon, Oxon OX14 4RN

*Routledge is an imprint of the Taylor & Francis Group,
an informa business*

© 2014 Taylor & Francis

The right of Francis L.F. Lee, Chin-Chuan Lee, Mike Z. Yao, Tsan-Kuo Chang, Fen Jennifer Lin, and Chris Fei Shen to be identified as authors of this work has been asserted by them in accordance with sections 77 and 78 of the Copyright, Designs and Patents Act 1988.

All rights reserved. No part of this book may be reprinted or reproduced or utilised in any form or by any electronic, mechanical, or other means, now known or hereafter invented, including photocopying and recording, or in any information storage or retrieval system, without permission in writing from the publishers.

Trademark Notice: Product or corporate names may be trademarks or registered trademarks, and are used only for identification and explanation without intent to infringe.

Library of Congress Cataloging-in-Publication Data
Lee, Francis L. F. (Francis Lap Fung)
  Communication, public opinion, and globalization in urban China / by Francis L.F. Lee, Chin-Chuan Lee, Mike Z. Yao, Tsan-Kuo Chang, Fen Jennifer Lin, and Chris Fei Shen.
    pages cm. — (Routledge studies in rhetoric and communication)
  Includes bibliographical references and index.
  1. Sociology, Urban—China. 2. City dwellers—China—Attitudes. 3. Globalization—Social aspects—China. 4. Mass media and globalization—China. 5. Public opinion—China. I. Title.
  HT334.C6L44 2013
  307.760951—dc23
  2013016264

ISBN13: 978-0-415-71320-7 (hbk)
ISBN13: 978-1-315-88344-1 (ebk)

Typeset in Sabon
by IBT Global.

SUSTAINABLE FORESTRY INITIATIVE
Certified Sourcing
www.sfiprogram.org
SFI-01234
SFI label applies to the text stock

Printed and bound in the United States of America by IBT Global.

Contents

Figures

Tables

Preface

In *2012*, the Hollywood blockbuster about a group of people running for their lives during a set of catastrophic events constituting "the end of the world," the world's governments collaborated to build a number of huge ships that would save at least those people who are rich enough to pay for the limited places on board. Responsible for constructing the ships is China. At one moment in the movie, a character opined that only China can complete the building of the gigantic ships on time.

It is probably not a mere coincidence that this "China as savior" theme would appear in a movie that was shown about one year after the global financial turmoil in late 2008. Yet the line uttered by the character in the movie is not necessarily meant to be a compliment. For people outside China, the line could readily be interpreted as a sarcastic statement, a veiled attack on the authoritarian nature of the Chinese state, an allusion to how many workers would have to suffer if such a project were to be completed within a very short period of time. Nevertheless, movie-goers in some cinemas in mainland China did reportedly take the line literally and applauded.

This anecdote points to many of the basic issues involving the inter-section of China, globalization, and media communication. As the most populous country in the world, China is, first and foremost, a huge and expanding market in the eyes of multinational corporations. This point is certainly not lost on people in the media industries. Yet entering the China market is complicated. Entry barriers are formidable in the form of import restrictions and quotas—the film *2012* was one of the 20 foreign films allowed to be shown in China's cinema in 2009. In some cases, severe content censorship is assumed or imposed. Then there is the need to develop the contents in ways that would appeal to the Chinese audience. Finally, it is important to figure out what meanings Chinese audiences would derive from the media contents.

These issues point to the structural and individual-level barriers that exist between the Chinese people on the one hand, and foreign media and cultures on the other. Even in cyberspace, the Chinese government has erected barriers to forbid people inside China to access numerous prominent websites such as *Facebook* and *YouTube*. However, the presence of such barriers is only part of the much more complicated story about global media and communication in China these days. Looking at the situation from another perspective, people in mainland China may actually be having better and more ready access to the world's media when compared to people in, say, the international metropolis of Hong Kong. Take ppstream as an example. The website provided internet users with access to a wide range of television dramas, movies, animations, comics, television variety shows, etc. from both within China and around the world. The point worth noting here is that, if one tries to access ppstream from Hong Kong, one would find almost no American and Japanese movies and television dramas available on the site. Yet these contents would become available when one accesses the site from within China. In fact, just based on personal experience, most of the Japanese movies available on ppstream within mainland China would simply be unavailable anywhere in Hong Kong—not on the internet, not in DVD shops, not in libraries.

Making such access possible in China is a confluence of factors and conditions: the lack of copyright protection, the presence of overseas Chinese who have immediate access to foreign media materials, the collective endeavor of the so-called "subtitle groups" organized by ordinary people themselves, the presence of a huge and diverse population such that all kinds of non-mainstream and alternative contents would have their followings, etc. In any case, it is nowadays not uncommon for movie lovers in Hong Kong to get pirated DVDs of foreign movies from across the border in China, not necessarily because they do not respect copyright, but simply because DVDs of non-mainstream foreign movies are often unavailable in the small market of Hong Kong and can be found only by crossing the border.

These types of phenomena and issues have existed in China for many years. Our fascination with these and other related issues and phenomena was one of the main reasons behind our decision, back in 2005 and 2006, to conduct a large-scale survey study of Chinese people's attitude toward globalization. To our knowledge, ours is the first large-scale and relatively comprehensive survey examining how mainland Chinese perceives the world and understands the processes of globalization, and how such perceptions and understandings relate to their basic value and attitudinal orientations on the one hand, and patterns of media consumption and social communications on the other. Our survey questionnaire encompasses questions about people's local, national, and foreign media use, traveling experiences and transnational social connections, interests in foreign affairs, cultural values and nationalistic sentiments, attitude toward foreign countries, perceptions of the United States, awareness of the discourses of globalization, and perceptions of the impact of globalization on their country, their cities, and themselves, among others. In the extant literature there are, of course, the occasional studies by interested scholars on more narrowly defined aspects of the problematic. Those studies provide us with valuable information and insights about some of the issues we are interested in. But our survey should remain unique in its scope and scale.

Certainly, survey research has its own inherent advantages and limitations. The nuances in how people make sense of their environment, their experiences, and the media contents they consume, the complex interactions among personal life trajectories and communication behavior in shaping one's attitudes, and how people actually make use of media contents as cultural resources in their everyday lives are just some of the issues that survey research may not be particularly good at tackling. But what a well-conducted survey can provide is the broad and representative picture of the basic patterns of how Chinese people communicate with each other and with the world and how they perceive their local and global environment. A survey study can also allow us to examine whether there are solid empirical evidences supporting a range of oft-made claims, such as claims about the influence of foreign media consumption, claims about the relationship between nationalistic sentiments and attitude toward globalization, and claims about how Chinese people evaluate the United States. On the whole, our survey study provides a baseline for other types of research and analyses focusing on more specific issues and phenomena.

Our survey constitutes the baseline also in the sense that, admittedly, the data came from a study conducted a number of years ago, before numerous happenings such as the global financial turmoil and the Beijing Olympics in 2008, the World Expo in 2010, and so on. Nevertheless, we believe that the data remain valuable not only because they can serve as points of reference and comparison for any current and future studies, but also more fundamentally because of the continual and generalizable significance of the themes and questions generated by our analysis. For example, the analysis of urban Chinese residents' national, local, and foreign media consumption in Chapter 3 has generated the paradoxical finding that residents in the more internationally connected coastal cities of Beijing and Shanghai reported lower levels of foreign media consumption when compared to residents of the inland cities of Xi'an and Chengdu. This paradoxical situation, however, is quite similar to the above-mentioned case that people in Hong Kong may, in a sense, be considered as having more limited access to certain types of foreign media products when compared to people in mainland China. This particular paradox should be a meaningful theme that can guide future research on globalization and media consumption not only within China but also around the world. For another example, Chapter 4 presents an analysis of Chinese people's nationalistic sentiments and how such sentiments related to media communication and to feelings toward foreign countries. In the analysis, we differentiated between developmental nationalism from cultural nationalism, and we found both similarities and differences between how the two kinds of nationalistic sentiments relate to other factors. The distinction between developmental and cultural nationalism and their differential impact on public opinion should be another theme deserving continual research attention.

Certainly, the Chinese economy and society are developing at a rapid pace, and some of the concrete findings from our survey may have changed if we are to conduct the survey again today. The proportion of Chinese people who have the experiences of traveling abroad, for example, should have been increasing rapidly. More broadly, the continual economic growth of the country, combined with the economic troubles the world is seemingly facing, and in addition China's successful hosting of world mega-events such as the Beijing Olympics and Shanghai World Expo, should have given urban Chinese residents new found self-confidence about their own country and ways of life. The implication of such a development is unclear though. When Chinese people become more confident about their own country, the sense that China needs to learn from the West may weaken. Some Chinese may come to the conclusion that the political and social institutions in China do "work" after all. However, a more self-confident population may also be less defensive and thus more open toward foreign cultures. In any case, the status of public opinion in China can continue to change. As China is expecting to recognize its new national leader, Xi Jinping, in 2013, the world is paying close attention to Xi's approach to world affairs, which can have significant influence on how mainland Chinese thinks about the world and about globalization. After all, the Chinese state, as a main part of our analysis in this book suggests, does have substantial influence on public opinion within the country. Yet it is exactly because public opinion can be continually in flux that it is often more important to grasp the underlying themes and questions that one should focus on. We hope our book can contribute to the literature in this regard.

Acknowledgments

We are indebted to the City University of Hon g Kong for providing a grant to the Center of Communication Research for conducting this research. Since its inception in 2005, the Center has been taking advantage of Hong Kong as a focal institutional and cultural base for studying the forces, processes, and issues of technological convergence and media globalization in the whole Greater China and Asian contexts (Lee, 2011). This project was initiated and led by Professor Chin-Chuan Lee, the director of the Center. When we began the survey project in 2005 and 2006, the team included three of the present authors (Dr. Francis L. F. Lee, Professor Chin-Chuan Lee, and Dr. Michael Yao) as well as Dr. Zhou He and Dr. Wanying Lin, who also contributed substantially at the early stage of the project. When the Department of Media and Communication at the City University of Hong Kong was established in 2008 (with Professor Lee as the founding Head), Professor Tsan-Kuo Chang, Dr. Fen Jennifer Lin, and Dr. Fei Shen, who became members of the Department, were invited to join the team. Dr. Francis Lee took up the coordinating role and brought this manuscript to fruition. Dr. Charles Man, research associate at the Center of Communication Research, coordinated the process of survey administration and did initial data analysis.

We thank *Pacific Affairs* for permitting us to use a published article as the basis for Chapter 7 of the current volume. That publication was titled "Urban Chinese's attitudes towards globalization: A survey study of media influence" and appeared in volume 82, issue no. 2 of the journal (pp. 211–230). We owe a thank you to acquisition editor Liz Levine at Routledge for helping this book see the light of the day. As the book is about to enter into the public domain, we delight in participating in the discourse on the media-globalization nexus. We also bear the blame for the limitations that remain.

1 Introduction

It is often claimed that we are living in the era of globalization. Anthony Giddens (1991) defined the term more than 20 years ago as "the intensification of worldwide social relations [that have linked] distant localities in such a way that local happenings are shaped by events occurring many miles away and vice versa" (p. 64). Theorists have debated about the point of origin of globalization, with some seeing it as a relatively recent phenomenon, as a "consequence of modernity," and others seeing it as having started six centuries ago, coterminous with the emergence of the capitalist world system (Wallerstein, 1999; Waters, 2001). But no matter when the process began, most scholars would agree that increasing global interdependence is a continuing process that speeded up in the last decades of the twentieth century. Today national borders are becoming increasingly porous for the flow of money, commodities, media, technologies, ideas, people, images, and viruses. Our lives are indeed increasingly affected by events happening afar, matters over which we usually have little control and about which we may have little knowledge.

Besides the "objective reality" of increasing global interdependence, globalization also involves a subjective component. Roland Robertson (1992), for example, defined globalization as referring "both to the compression of the world and the intensification of consciousness of the world as a whole." Marshall McLuhan (1964) used to describe the rise of television as a harbinger of an emerging "global village." A more apt metaphor would indeed be what Saskia Sassen (1991) calls global cities, with international metropolises serving as the key nodes in the global capitalist system. For the residents of global cities, the reality of globalization can be easily felt in everyday lives, through encounters with tourists and migrants, exposure to foreign media, purchases of foreign commodities, working for or dealing with multinational corporations, and so on. The signs of global capitalism—ranging from Nike, Coca-Cola, and McDonald's to Prada, Apple, Microsoft, Google, and Giorgio Armani—are ubiquitous, and international nongovernmental organizations, such as Greenpeace, Oxfam, the Red Cross, and others often play important roles in linking domestic policies to global concerns.

Of course globalization is also an uneven process. Influences in some directions are much stronger than in others, and different countries are drawn into the processes of globalization in different ways and to different extents. Although the amount of time needed to travel from one place to another continues to shrink, some places remain much more difficult to get to as compared with others. As the common saying goes, when America sneezes, the whole world gets a cold. The European debt crisis is also having a significant impact on economies and stock markets throughout the world. One can only imagine, however, whether and how things happening in the world at large are affecting people living in societies such as North Korea and Burma.

Obviously China is somewhere in between the extreme self-enclosure of North Korea and complete openness to the outside world. On the one hand, capital flows are still under heavy control, as continual debates between China and the United States on the valuation of *Renmenbi*, China's currency, remind us. The household registration (*hukuo*) system continues to place severe limits on Chinese people's mobility even within the country, not to say in terms of traveling abroad. The media system in China remains tightly controlled by the state. In a seminal article in the early 1990s, communication scholar Joseph Chan (1993) described China's media scene with the phrase "commercialization without independence," and the phrase is as applicable today as it was 20 years ago (see Zhao, 2008). In addition, the Chinese government had a history of seeing foreign media as a threat, as agents bringing "spiritual pollution" to the Chinese people and society (Lee et al., 2011). Despite China's entrance into the World Trade Organization (WTO) in 2001, the Chinese government still imposes significant barriers, such as import quotas for movies, to the entrance of foreign media.[1] Even in cyberspace, Internet users in China may find it hard to access many foreign websites, ranging from the websites of some Hong Kong newspapers that are regularly critical toward the Chinese government to some of the most prominent websites in the era of Web 2.0, including Facebook and YouTube.

On the other hand, there is no question that Chinese citizens are increasingly connected to the outside world. In order to engage with global capitalism, the Chinese government has created numerous zones of "exceptions" (Ong, 2006)—the coastal metropolises, the Special Economic Zones, and the Hong Kong and Macau Special Administrative Regions—in which foreign capital, foreign people, and foreign media can circulate and move *relatively* freely. Meanwhile, China's international travelers may constitute only a small proportion of the whole Chinese population, but their sheer number is significant. And with their new-found spending power, their presence is now keenly felt by shopkeepers in places near and afar.

Many Chinese people are also active in defying state control in order to come into contact with the outside world. Despite restrictions on the import of foreign media, American and European films, television dramas, and popular music are widely available online. Many Chinese students study-ing in the United States, for example, are actively engaged in the practice of copying and "subtitling" the entertainment contents on American televi-sion and then sharing them with others back in China (Chu, 2012).[2] They do so through file sharing software and several highly popular Chinese websites (such as tudou.com). Their work is so speedy that today pirated copies of Hollywood movies are often available to Chinese people online even before the movies are shown in cinemas in China. The young and technically sophisticated Internet users within China can also "get across the firewall" and reach the banned websites. Even politically sensitive con-tents from abroad are often circulated through online channels and arenas such as *weibo* (microblogs). People who circulate such contents in China use various methods to evade official censorship, most notably by "recod-ing" whatever sensitive keywords may be involved.

For Chinese people, foreign media and commodities can be of consider-able significance to their lives and cultural identities. In some cases, Chinese people make use of foreign media and cultural products to develop, con-struct, and/or fulfill their dreams of being modern and cosmopolitan "world citizens." Here, "foreign media" can include media products coming from Hong Kong, the former British colony. As Eric Ma (2011) has shown, Hong Kong has served as a "satellite" in the processes of cultural globalization, relaying and refracting western modernity into China. But with the continual economic growth of China, Chinese people are nowadays looking directly to the West. Take cultural studies scholar John Erni's (2008) analysis of China's reception of *Harry Potter*, for example. By mid-2007, the Chinese editions of the *Harry Potter* novels reached a combined sale of about 10 million. Although the translated versions of the novels often illustrate the logics of hybridization and localization, Erni argues that the urban Chinese reception of *Harry Potter* should also be understood in relation to the background of the "myth" of the rising Chinese elite middle class:

> If the "Chinese middle-class" today is in part a self-generating myth as well as a global dream, then *Harry Potter* provides a clear case of cul-tural interface of the production of that global-local fantasy. Chinese youth who engage with *Harry Potter* give off a visible impression of a growing middle-class society capable of enjoying and performing a translation of cultures; in other words, they are (self-) positioned as the cultural intermediaries of globalization. (p. 144)

But China is also a country with a rich cultural tradition of its own. Chi-nese people take pride in being descendants of Emperor Huang , a member of an ancient civilization with a history of five thousand years. The intru-sion of "western" and/or "global" culture can also result in backlashes. An illustrative controversy surrounded the case of the Starbucks coffee shop in the Imperial City. In January 2007, famous Chinese Central Television

(CCTV) anchor Rui Chenggang criticized the presence of Starbucks within the old Imperial Palace in Beijing, arguing that Starbucks represents American "lowbrow food culture." Rui's argument received support from many people in China, and public pressure finally led to the closing of the shop in July 2007.

The controversy demonstrated not only the possibility of a backlash but also the fundamental unpredictability of when, where, and how it would happen. After all, that particular Starbucks opened in 2000. For years, the coffee shop did not seem to be generating any discontent. Rui Chenggang, meanwhile, was far from being a narrow-minded old man clinging to the ancient culture of his own country at all costs. In fact, he was an anchor for the English channel of CCTV-9, a Yale World Fellow in 2005, and is a journalist who had interviewed many of the world's important political and economic leaders. He is not only a member of the rising middle-class elite in China but, if there is an emerging global elite (Castells, 2000; Davidson, Poor and Williams, 2009; Sklair, 2002), he is definitely also a member of it. The controversy, therefore, is more a matter of taste in the global cultural field than an outbreak of xenophobic nationalism—Rui was criticizing Starbucks not so much as representing lowbrow culture *from* America than as lowbrow culture *in* America. His statement was also a criticism of crass commercialism encroaching on what is supposedly a sacred symbol of imperial pride.

On the whole, under the conditions of continual political control, economic and social reform, media commercialization, and the general processes of globalization, many Chinese people today are engaging in what Norris and Inglehart (2009) labeled "cosmopolitan communications" in their own unique and complex ways. At the same time, Chinese people's reactions to foreign media and culture are also complex and at times contradictory. However, there have not been many studies examining Chinese people's attitude toward the processes of globalization and their perceptions of foreign countries, and there are even fewer studies addressing the questions of how media consumption, transnational experiences, and social connections may relate to such attitudes and beliefs.

Against this background, this book provides a systematic examination of Chinese public opinion toward globalization and the world at large, with a specific focus on the impact of media and social communications. This endeavor is important given the rising influence of China. Although the country is not a democracy, public attitudes remain a constraining force on the parameters of what the government can and cannot do. An understanding of public opinion in China is far from irrelevant to an understanding of the roles China is likely to play in world affairs.

This book aims at achieving three goals. First, it aims to provide a descriptive overview of urban Chinese people's connections with and perceptions of foreign countries and globalization at a specific historical juncture. The survey data analyzed in this book came from a survey conducted in late 2006 and early 2007. Although the data may not fully reflect the most current situation in the country, they should still be valuable because of their relative rarity. A look into the scenario of early 21ˢᵗ century China should provide information and insights that can help to clarify the more current scene, and the data can also serve as an important basis for future comparisons. In any case, we have just argued above that Chinese people are increasingly drawn into the orbit and processes of globalization. But to what degree are they really exposed to the influences from the outside world? How many transnational social connections does a typical urban Chinese citizen have? How often do the Chinese consume foreign media? To what extent are they aware of the notion of globalization? Have they developed a "consciousness of the world as a whole"? If yes, what do they think about the processes of globalization? Do they believe that globalization is beneficial to China, to the city where they live, and to them personally? Various researchers may have addressed some of these questions separately, but this book analyzes all of them and therefore presents a relatively more comprehensive overview of Chinese people's "global outlook" at a specific historical moment.

Second, our analysis also examines how social positions and psychological orientations influence Chinese people's attitude toward the world and globalization. People located differently in the social structure are connected to the processes of globalization to different extents and in different ways (Bauman, 1998). They are likely to have different amounts of transnational experiences and social connections, to consume national and foreign media to different extents, and to perceive foreign countries and the processes of globalization differently. In addition, people's value orientations should also play an important role in determining individual attitudes. Our analysis in different chapters will examine the social and psychological determinants of Chinese people's connections with, attitudes toward, and perceptions of the world at large. Through such analyses, the significance of many findings in this book goes beyond the time and place of the survey; many findings should contribute to research on the formation of public opinion regarding globalization in general.

Third and most important to the authors, this book examines the significance of media and social communications in shaping people's attitudes and perceptions of the world. Walter Lippmann (1922) pointed out almost a hundred years ago that people rely on the media to transform "the reality out there" into "pictures in our heads," and in the process journalists have to resort to the imperfect construction of "steoreotypes" as interpretive categories. In articulating his theory of public opinion against the background of the nationalization of politics in the United States, Lippmann in effect argued that the media would become more important when public matters could no longer be fully understood within a local context and on the basis of personal observations. It follows that the significance of the media in shaping people's understanding of the world at large would only be even higher. Early modernization literature (Katz and Wedell, 1977; Lerner, 1958; Schramm, 1964) all pointed to the media as a key catalyst of national integration and cultural expression. Lerner (1958), in particular, theorized the media as the "magic multiplier of empathy," or a capacity to break off from the yoke of fatalism and to imagine beyond immediate roles and contexts; such a modernizing personality was deemed essential to the "passing of traditional society" into the threshold of modernity. Now our activities, identities, and imaginations may go far beyond national borders. Borrowing the famous argument of Benedict Anderson (1991), any idea of a global society can only be a product of imagination, and the media should be the most important sources of materials on the basis of which people can construct their own global imaginations. At the same time, as people start to develop more transnational social networks, these networks may provide interpersonal sources of information that are perceived to be more credible and trustworthy. And as people have more chances to go abroad to travel, work, and study, they can experience and see "the world" by themselves. Their personal experiences and observations may confirm or deny the images from the media. The various chapters of this book will empirically examine whether and how media consumption and social communications matter to people's attitudes toward their own country and the outside world. Again, such an analysis not only gives us an understanding of the formation of public opinion in China but also has broader theoretical implications for our understanding of the impact of communications on how people see the world.

In sum, by addressing the issues stated above, this book should make important contributions to the study of contemporary Chinese societies and public opinion as well as to our understanding of the effects of media and communications on people's attitudes and beliefs related to globalization. Whereas the previous pages have sketched a rough background of the relationship between globalization and the Chinese public, a brief discussion of the problematic of communication effects should also be useful.

ON THE SIGNIFICANCE OF "COSMOPOLITAN COMMUNICATIONS"

There have been many studies on the influence of the media on people's values and attitudes within the field of international communications research. Most of these past studies focus on a rather narrowly defined aspect of a person's psychological profile. For example, some research has looked into the impact of foreign media on cultural values in an attempt to test (often quite inadequately) the media or cultural imperialism thesis—that is, the question of whether the consumption of foreign media would lead to acceptance of the cultural values and behavioral norms presumably encoded into the foreign media texts (e.g., Salwen, 1991; Willnat et al., 2002). Nisbet and colleagues (2004) examined the influence of television news on anti-American perceptions and sentiments among people in nine predominantly Muslim countries. Meanwhile, De Vreese and Boomgaarden's (2006) analysis of media effects on public opinion regarding the European Union touches upon issues of national and supra-national identities (for additional studies, see Antecol and Endersby, 1999; Disdier, Head, and Mayer, 2010; Kern and Hainmueller, 2009). Most recently, in two earlier articles based on the current survey project, we examined the influence of national and foreign media consumption on Chinese people's attitudes toward globalization and political and cultural values respectively (Lee et al., 2009; Lee et al., 2011).

Not many scholars have attempted to examine the effects of transnational communications on a range of social, political, and cultural values and behavior comprehensively. One exception is Norris and Inglehart (2009). Their book-length treatment of the impact of what they labeled "cosmopolitan communications" is an ambitious effort. Although this book is by no means restricted to an analysis following or testing their theory, a focused discussion of their book can help clarify some of the conceptual issues involved in the analysis of communication effects. It will also help us explicate the approach undertaken by our study.

We may begin by recapitulating their major arguments and findings. In the most general sense, Norris and Inglehart defined cosmopolitan communications as "the way that we learn about, and interact with, people and places beyond the borders of our nation-state" (p. 9). Yet what they actually emphasized through the concept is the growth of transnational communications of all kinds, driven by media deregulation in many countries, the increasing power and reach of multinational media conglomerates, the advance of deterritorialized new media technologies, the increasing level of people's geographical mobility, and other processes of globalization at large. Putting aside the question of whether people are attitudinally and behaviorally "cosmopolitan," more and more people in the contemporary world do find themselves embedded in dense transnational networks of communications.

Given this background, the empirical research question they posed is: What would be the impact of cosmopolitan communications on people's attitudes and values? This research question is not fundamentally different from the one that has long been posed by scholars interested in testing some components of the cultural imperialism thesis. If there is a difference, it resides in the distinction between the influence of "foreign media," which is the concern of media scholars interested in the cultural imperialism theorists, and that of "cosmopolitan communications," which is not equivalent to foreign media use. This is a distinction we will soon return to. But at this point, it is more important to note that instead of predicting that cosmopolitan communications would lead to the emergence of cultural homogeneity across countries, Norris and Inglehart (2009) proposed a "firewall model" of media effects. They argued that cosmopolitan communications may not influence everyone to the same extent and in the same way because of fire-walls erected both at the societal level and at the individual level. At the societal level, countries vary in terms of degree of media freedom and policies regarding foreign media and cultural imports. The former established internal barriers to information, whereas the latter can constitute external barriers to integration in cultural markets. At the individual level, people are socialized within their own cultures. They hold deep-rooted values and beliefs which constitute the lenses through which they receive and interpret media images and messages. Moreover, people do not have equal access to all kinds of media. Universal access to radio and television is far from being achieved in the less developed countries in the world, and Internet access is by no means universal even in the advanced nations. Therefore people may not be influenced simply because they may not really be heavily exposed to cosmopolitan communications in the first place.

None of these main arguments is new. For instance, the idea that local audiences would receive and interpret foreign media through the lenses of their own culture is a well-established argument in cultural analysis of audience reception of foreign media (e.g., Liebe and Katz, 1988). Media economists also talk about "cultural discounts," arguing that media products are often "discounted" when they travel abroad because foreign audiences lack the requisite cultural knowledge and background to fully appreciate the contents (Hoskins and Mirus, 1988; Lee, 2006, 2008, 2009; Wildman and Siwek, 1988). An implication is that the influence of foreign media is likely to be weaker than that of local media. Regarding media access, Norris herself is among the most prominent scholars on the problem of the "digital divide" (Norris, 2001). But Norris and Inglehart (2009) did manage to meld various arguments together into a systematic and relatively parsimonious analytical framework.

They then utilized the data from the ninety-country World Values Survey to empirically verify a number of hypotheses derived from the theory. Specifically, they hypothesized that news media consumption, which is the variable standing in for cosmopolitan communications in their empirical analysis, would relate to values and attitudes such as higher levels of tolerance toward foreign lifestyles, a more positive attitude toward global capitalism, more liberal and secular attitudes toward gender equality and sexuality, higher levels of support for democracy, and acceptance of individual success as an important value. This set of "main effect" hypotheses still largely points to the range of effects that conventional cultural imperialism theorists might presume to exist. However, consistent with the idea underlying the firewall model, they also hypothesized that use of different news media would differ among social sectors (i.e., the unequal-access firewall). More interestingly, they hypothesized that cosmopolitan communications would have the strongest effects in the most "cosmopolitan" societies—that is, those societies which are most economically developed—so that people have wide access to the media, are most integrated into global markets and communication networks, and have the highest levels of media freedom. In other words, the effects of cosmopolitan communications should be strongest in places with the fewest and weakest firewalls.

So what did they actually find? Not surprisingly, the hypotheses regarding differential access to and consumption of different types of media by different social groups are largely supported. People who are located in the more privileged positions in the society—educated people with higher levels of income—are more involved in cosmopolitan communications. More importantly, media use—captured by an index composed of people's self-reported weekly use of newspapers, radio/TV news, the Internet, books, and magazines—does have a range of main effects on the dependent variables. Media use is positively and significantly related to trust in outsiders, support for individual success values, support for right-wing economic policies, higher levels of civic engagement, higher levels of secularism, and more liberal sexual and moral values.

Moving one step further, Norris and Inglehart (2009) demonstrate some support for the hypothesis regarding the conditioning influence of a society's degree of cosmopolitanism. The positive relationship between media use and trust in outsiders, as well as that between media use and liberal moral values, is stronger in more cosmopolitan countries. Meanwhile, although there are apparently no main effects of media use on support for democratic values, the interaction effect between media use and the degree of a society's cosmopolitanism on support for democratic values is positive and significant. This pattern of findings suggests that media use does have positive effects on support for democratic values in cosmopolitan countries.

Nevertheless, some findings are contrary to expectation. Although media use does relate positively to support for individual success values and for right-wing economic policies, the interaction effect between media use and degree of cosmopolitanism of the social context is contrary to expectation: the influence of media on individual success values and support for right-wing economic policies is stronger in less cosmopolitan societies. Besides, although Norris and Inglehart did not set up a specific hypothesis about the relationship between media use and nationalistic sentiments, we would have expected a negative relationship between the two if media use were indeed an indicator of cosmopolitan communications. What they actually found, however, is a positive relationship between the two.

In one sense, Norris and Inglehart were most concerned with demonstrating the falsity of simplistic arguments regarding the influence of media on cultural homogenization. Their findings, highlighted in the above paragraph, though unexpected, do not contradict their most general conclusion: that media effects are not always powerful and straightforward because of the presence of various firewalls.

Nevertheless, the mixed findings do point to certain limitations of Norris and Inglehart's analysis that are relevant to our present research. Most fundamentally, one major limitation of Norris and Inglehart's analysis is that the primary analysis presented in most of their chapters uses a single media-use variable to represent "cosmopolitan communications." This methodological limitation has huge conceptual implications. As mentioned earlier, the two scholars treated cosmopolitan communications as a broad concept, or in their own words, "far broader and more comprehensive than the idea of transnational media" (p. 9). Hence we can argue that there is a substantial gap between the concept and the measure. Most specifically, by using a singular media use index based on people's consumption of five different media types, there is no distinction between consumption of foreign and domestic media and also a conflation between media consumption and social communications. Notably, as mentioned earlier, the range of possible "media effects" of concern to theorists of cultural imperialism are all supposed to be effects of foreign media consumption. Yet in the contemporary world, even in the most cosmopolitan cities equipped with a full range of transnational media, people in general still consume their domestic media most frequently. In other words, part of Norris and Inglehart's analysis was essentially using a measure of domestic media consumption to test the supposed effects of foreign media use.

Of course some may question whether the distinction between domestic and foreign media remains important in the contemporary world. James Carey (1998) discussed the end of the national communication system before the turn of the century. In fact, the concept of cosmopolitan communications itself implies a blurring between the local and the global. When movies increasingly involve international coproduction (Miller et al., 2005) or what some scholars have called transculturation (Wu and Chan, 2007), when the copying of program formats is so common that people all over the world are watching their local versions of *Who Wants to Be a Millionaire* or *The American Idol* on television (e.g., Cui and Lee, 2010; Meng, 2009; Moran, 2009), when people get an increasing proportion of information from websites, when hybridity and deterritorialization are central features of the contemporary cultural condition (Tomlinson, 1999), the significance of the distinction between domestic and foreign media may indeed be declining.

However, the blurring between domestic and foreign media is a matter of degree, and the significance of the distinction certainly varies according to contexts and to topics concerned. Whereas it is arguable that, at least in highly cosmopolitan societies, national and local media have become a conduit of cosmopolitan communications, one cannot ignore the fact that national and local media remain *primarily* the conduits for national and local communications. As research on international news in the past two decades has shown, news media in different countries often do not cover the same set of foreign countries and events. And even when they do, domestic news media tend to localize foreign news so that foreign affairs will become more relevant to, understandable to, and/or resonant with the local audience (e.g., Clausen, 2004; Cohen et al., 1996; Lee, Chan, and

Zhou, 2011). In other words, the "cosmopolitan communications" as delivered by domestic media are often tainted by national perspectives (Lee et al., 2002).

In fact, by keeping in mind that the influences of domestic and foreign media may be the same on some issues and in some contexts but different on others, we can better understand the full set of Norris and Inglehart's empirical findings. For the most obvious example, the positive relationship between nationalistic sentiments and media use becomes readily understandable if we recognize that the media use index represents primarily domestic media consumption. Besides, an explanation can also be ventured regarding why the positive relationship between media use and support for right-wing economic policies would be weaker in more cosmopolitan societies—it is possibly because most governments in the contemporary world (with the few exceptions such as Cuba and North Korea, which are not in the World Values Survey dataset anyway) are supportive of neoliberal globalization regardless of their levels of economic development. In less cosmopolitan societies, which are likely to have lower degrees of media freedom, the domestic media are more likely to reflect or even promote the state's policy goal. Hence the use of national media is likely to produce support for right-wing economic policies. In contrast, in "cosmopolitan" societies, where there are generally higher degrees of media freedom and journalistic professionalism, the voices of the "antiglobalization movement" would have a relatively better chance to be heard through the media. Therefore the relationship between media use and support for right-wing policies would be less positive or even negative in these places.

Meanwhile, by recognizing the potential difference between domestic and foreign media and the former as a carrier of "national communications" instead of cosmopolitan communications, we have an additional reason to expect social contexts to moderate the effects of media use on attitudes and values. For example, consumption of national media may lead to stronger support for liberal moral and political values in cosmopolitan societies for an obvious reason: Cosmopolitan societies are more likely to be western liberal societies and their media tend to cultivate liberal values among the populations. (As a matter of fact, the fourteen countries scoring highest on cosmopolitanism in Norris and Inglehart's analysis are all European or North American countries, with Japan being the fifteenth.) In other words, the contents of domestic media tend to be more similar to those of foreign media in cosmopolitan societies. In less cosmopolitan societies, in contrast, the contents of domestic and foreign media may differ more radically.

Instead of undermining the value of the analysis provided in Norris and Inglehart, we find ourselves in broad theoretical agreement with their basic claims on the likely impact of media communications. Media consumption is likely to lead to the acceptance of "foreign" values, attitudes, and norms only under certain societal conditions, and such media effects are also likely to be moderated by certain firewalls at the individual level. Such firewalls include the gaps in access to various forms of media, the tendency for people to interpret and receive media messages selectively and in line with their preexisting values and beliefs, and the availability of alternative sources of information. We differ from Norris and Inglehart, however, on a key point: Instead of assuming that cosmopolitan communications pervade all kinds of media and nonmedia communication channels, we propose a more differentiated analysis about how different forms of communications may affect citizens. Domestic media, in particular, should be considered as carriers of primarily national and/or local communications.

Such a more differentiated analysis is also necessitated by the fact that we will be focusing on only one country instead of conducting a cross-national comparative analysis. Certainly comparative analysis is extremely important to the building and testing of theories. It can help us to examine the generalizability of certain findings and directly tackle the problematic of how contexts affect people and shape the relationships among different variables. However, cross-national comparative analyses often necessitate the simplification of "national contexts" into a few dimensions for the sake of parsimony. In Norris and Inglehart's (2009) analysis, for example, "contextual variations" are ultimately reduced to the overarching concept of degree of cosmopolitanism in a society. Although this can be a valid and important step in analyzing a cross-national survey dataset, the analysis inevitably misses many of the nuances and specificities of the contexts of specific nations. In the case of China, the contextual factors that may influence people's attitudes toward the world as well as the effects of communications on such attitudes would include, among others, the social formation of the Chinese society, the environment of specific Chinese cities where people reside, the rise of strong nationalistic sentiments since the 1990s, the historical relationship between China and individual foreign countries, the processes of economic and media reform, and the government's policy toward and rhetoric related to globalization, and so on. Paying attention to these various contextual factors will help formulate our expectations and interpret our findings more appropriately and adequately.

THE FRAMEWORK AND CHAPTER OUTLINE

To recapitulate, Norris and Inglehart (2009) presented a very meaningful analysis of the impact of cosmopolitan communications on a wide range of people's attitudes, beliefs, and behavior. They have shown that media communications are related to an arguably more "cosmopolitan" outlook, but the relationships between communications and attitudes can vary across contexts. Nevertheless, their findings are not unequivocal and contain at least two limitations. First, there was no distinction between domestic media consumption and foreign media consumption, and the main independent variable in their empirical analysis embraces a mixture of national, local, and cosmopolitan communications. Second, their cross-national analysis, while powerful for examining certain general theoretical arguments, tends to oversimplify the contexts of specific countries.

Pointing out these two limitations is not to contest the overall value of their work but to highlight how a single-country study, such as the current one, remains important in the study of the effects of global communications. In the analysis of this book, we will make more detailed differentiations between the different types of communications that contemporary Chinese citizens engage in, and we will pay closer attention to the complexities of the Chinese context. More specifically, Figure 1.1 presents the conceptual framework that guides our empirical analysis. This framework begins with the recognition of the fact that people are located differently in the social and economic structure of a society. Beyond the basic demographic factors such as age, gender, education and family income, our analysis also pays particular attention to differences among the four Chinese cities where our survey was conducted. They include two coastal metropolises (Shanghai and Beijing) and two inland cities (Xi'an and Chengdu).

We expect structural locations to explain Chinese citizens' media consumption and their "foreign experiential connections." Media consumptions encompass national, local, and foreign media uses, which are dealt with as separate variables in the analysis. Meanwhile, foreign experiential connections refers to people's personal experiences and social connections with the outside world. In concrete terms, it includes people's experiences

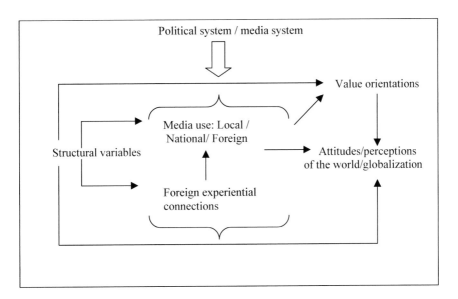

Figure 1.1 Analytical framework.

of traveling, studying, and working abroad, the number of friends and relatives living in foreign countries, and the frequencies with which people communicate with their friends and relatives abroad. Foreign experiential connections is also expected to relate to media use in specific ways. Foreign media consumption, for an obvious example, is likely to relate positively with foreign experiential connections.

Media use and personal experiential connections are shaped by the features of the political and media system in place. The political and media systems are contextual parameters instead of variables in this study, but we include them in the figure to highlight the importance of contextual considerations.

Both mass and interpersonal communications are posited as agents of shaping people's attitudes toward globalization and perceptions of the outside world. More concretely, we will examine Chinese people's overall likes and dislikes toward a set of countries around the world, their attitude toward different aspects of the United States, their awareness and conceptions of globalization, and their perceptions of the negative and positive impact of globalization on themselves.

At the same time, this set of attitudes and perceptions should be explained not only by communication behavior but also by other social and psychological factors, including people's location in the society and their value orientations. For value orientations, the following chapters will examine people's support for western liberal values, their support for traditional values, and their orientation toward the opportunities of moving abroad. More importantly, we pay particular attention to nationalism, not only because nationalistic sentiments may crucially shape how people look at the world at large but also because of the background of the rise of nationalism since the early 1990s in China (Zhao, 2004). Obviously, while various value orientations may shape people's attitudes toward the world, the value orientations themselves can also be partly the product of social structural locations and communication behavior.

Notably, this framework does not radically differ from that of Norris and Inglehart (2009). Figure 1.1 can be taken as a revised version of their analytical framework to suit our own data and analytical purposes. Compared with their work, we will pay more attention to the differentiation between domestic and foreign media consumption, and we will directly examine whether and how people's personal experiences and social connections affect the way they see the world. But because ours is a single-country analysis, we will not directly examine how societal-level firewalls affect people's attitudes and beliefs.

It should also be noted that although we have been using the language of "media effects" in the previous pages, our ability to demonstrate causal relationships is fundamentally limited by the cross-sectional nature of the survey reported in this book. Theoretically speaking, one may also challenge Figure 1.1—as well as the framework in Norris and Inglehart (2009) and even most traditional media effects studies for that matter—as being too linear in positing people merely as audiences responding to messages communicated to them rather than as critical citizens engaging actively in the negotiation and reproduction of meanings. We acknowledge such limitations, but we believe that our survey analysis still provides many valuable findings and insights to people interested in the problem of public opinion regarding globalization.

Indeed, we must emphasize that our analysis is not restricted to being a test of the theory of cosmopolitan communication. Figure 1.1 is meant to be a general heuristic guide for our analysis instead of a theory to be formally tested. It provides a broad framework that helps us organize the analysis of issues such as Chinese people's attitude toward foreign countries and nationalistic sentiments. Therefore, Figure 1.1 also explains the organization of the chapters in this book. After this introductory chapter, Chapter 2 provides a descriptive overview of Chinese people's foreign experiential connections. It illustrates how people located differently in the social structures are connected to the outside world. At the same time, the chapter presents an analysis of whether and how experiential connections explain people's interests in foreign countries.

Chapter 3 then presents an analysis of Chinese people's media consumption. It will provide an overview of the media system in China and people's overall access to different types of media. The analysis will demonstrate how media use is related to sociodemographic factors. Of particular conceptual and empirical interest is the analysis regarding the predictors of foreign media consumption. We will examine whether foreign experiential connections explain foreign media use, and we will show that, contrary to usual expectations, Chinese people living in the two coastal cities of Beijing and Shanghai are not those with the highest levels of foreign media use.

Based on its social and theoretical significance, we devote a chapter to the notion of nationalism. Chapter 4 develops a conceptual distinction between developmental and cultural nationalism for Chinese people. It presents an overview of Chinese people's nationalistic sentiments and the factors that explain the formation of such sentiments, including the impact of media and foreign experiential connections. The last part of that chapter will also begin the analysis of Chinese people's attitude toward the outside world by examining how nationalistic sentiments, communication behavior, and other factors relate to people's feelings regarding a range of countries around the world.

Chapter 5, then, focuses sharply on Chinese people's attitude toward the United States. As the world's most powerful country and the architect of the post-Cold War global order, the United States both inspires admiration and attracts severe criticisms from the Chinese public. The analysis emphasizes the multidimensionality of and ambivalence in Chinese people's attitude toward the United States. It analyzes how value orientations—such as what we will label global adventurism, support for liberal and traditional values, and the nationalistic variables developed in Chapter 4—explain the valence and ambivalence of Chinese people's attitudes toward America. Overall, the chapter will develop an argument that America constitutes an "ambivalent other" for the Chinese public.

Chapters 6 and 7 will tackle Chinese people's awareness, understanding, and perceptions of "globalization." Although globalization has been one of the buzzwords in academic discourse for the past 20 years, there is no guarantee that common citizens in China are familiar with the term and its associated discourses. Chapter 6 thus analyzes Chinese people's awareness and understanding of globalization by focusing on respondents' answers to two questions: (1) a question asking if they have heard of the term "*quan-qiu-hua*" (i.e., globalization) or not, and (2) for those who reported having heard of the term, an open-ended question asking them to explicate the meanings of the term. We will differentiate between "global" and "local" conceptions of globalization, and we will examine whether media consumptions and city contexts play any roles in shaping people's understanding of *quan-qiu-hua*.

Chapter 7 then analyzes Chinese people's perceptions of the impact of globalization. Making use of a set of thirty-two survey items, we examine whether Chinese people would agree on different statements about the positive as well as negative impact of globalization on politics, economics, society, and the environment. The perceived impact is also differentiated in terms of impact at the country, city, and individual levels. The analysis of the predictors of Chinese people's perception is grounded in a contextual discussion of the Chinese government's official policy and rhetoric about globalization. We will show that there is indeed a close correspondence between official policy and rhetoric on the one hand and Chinese people's attitude toward globalization on the other.

Finally, Chapter 8 will conclude the book by summarizing the findings and discussing their major social and theoretical implications. We will discuss how some of the findings may allow us to understand more recent developments in China's engagement with globalization, as well as how some of the findings may change in the future in light of recent developments.

A NOTE ON THE SURVEY

As already mentioned, this book comes out from a large-scale survey project conducted in four urban cities in China—Beijing, Shanghai, Chengdu, and Xi'an—in late 2006 and early 2007 under the auspices of the Center for Communication Research at the City University of Hong Kong. The four cities were selected based on the generally acknowledged argument that globalization is an uneven process affecting different parts of China in different ways. As the nation's capital, Beijing is undoubtedly the political, educational, and cultural center of China. Shanghai is the "economic capital" of China, widely regarded as the symbol of China's modernization and its foremost commercial and financial center. Situated in the inland provinces, Xi'an and Chengdu are less developed than large coastal metropolises. Xi'an was the capital of Ancient Chinese civilization for many centuries and the eastern terminus of the "Silk Road," which connected China to the West in ancient times. Millions of overseas tourists go to Xi'an every year to visit the famous "Terracotta Soldiers" and other cultural treasures. Although Chengdu has less international exposure relative to the other three cities, it is an important industrial center and a communication and transportation hub domestically. Certainly there are other cities that are worth examining, such as the southern metropolis of Guangzhou. Resource constraints forbid us to cover more cities, and the four cities included, taken as a whole, should allow us to capture a range of urban contexts in contemporary China.

A translated version of the complete questionnaire is available in the appendix. Here, a note about the survey method is in order. The surveys in the four Chinese cities were conducted in December 2006 and January 2007 by commissioning a reputed commercial research firm in China. There are both practical and substantive reasons for the survey to focus only on urban cities. Practically, conducting survey research in rural areas in China is extremely difficult and costly if one insists upon representative sampling. The infrastructure for conducting survey research with representative sampling is much better developed in urban cities in China. Substantively, as compared with rural areas, urban cities are more directly engaged in the processes of globalization, and urban residents are exposed and/or connected to the outside world to a greater extent. Questions on feelings toward foreign countries and those about the benefits and dangers of globalization should be more pertinent to urban residents.

The target respondents of the survey were Chinese-speaking residents of the four cities between the ages of eighteen and sixty-five. People over age sixty-five were excluded because the questionnaire is lengthy and interviews with the elderly would be difficult to complete. A multistage probability sampling approach was adopted. The commercial firm first delimited the geographical areas under study, which are largely those near the city center (i.e., the outer districts were not included). It then randomly selected "residential committees" within each administrative district in each city. Trained interviewers were instructed to follow a systematic sampling procedure to select households from residential committees. Finally, the most-recent-birthday rule was used to select a respondent from a household. This sampling procedure means that all people living in a housing unit under a residential committee would be included in the sampling frame regardless of whether they were born in the city or were part of the mobile population.

The sample size is 500 in each city and thus 2,000 in total. The maximum response rates ranged from 30.3 to 36.9 percent in the four cities and the minimum response rates ranged from 24.8 to 28.9 percent.[3] The response rates of the present survey are certainly not optimal. But it should be noted that the research firm has already put in place a stringent procedure for "revisits," so the low response rates were not the result of inadequate design. Recent discussions of survey research in China have pointed to the trend toward increasing nonresponses, particularly in urban cities (see Li and Hao, 2004), even on noncontroversial topics. In any case, the samples in all four cities do not differ hugely from the populations in terms of income and education. But there are some sample-population discrepancies in age and gender, as females and young people were overrepresented. The dataset was therefore weighted according to the age-gender distributions of each of the four cities.

2 Profiling the Urban Chinese

About eight decades ago, when the Chinese writer Lin Yutang worried about how the world understood China, he did not trust Europeans who spoke Chinese too well, because they "might develop certain mental habits akin to the Chinese and are regarded by their compatriots as queer" (Lin, 1935, p. 14). Nor did he trust Chinese who spoke English too well, because they might develop western mental habits and become "denationalized." The only way, for him, to survey and understand his own country and people was to look at China by searching "not for the exotic but for the common human values, by penetrating beneath the superficial quaintness of manners and looking for real courtesy" (Lin, 1935, p. 14), which exists in the real Chinese living their daily experiences.

An examination of Chinese people's personal experiences certainly remains an important basis for understanding their attitudes and behavior despite the radical differences in context between China in the early twentieth century and in the early twenty-first century. Where globalization is concerned, Starbucks, McDonald's, Nike and Coco-Cola are not just companies or brand names that have entered the country's market. They have entered Chinese people's daily lives in different ways and to different extents, possibly leading some Chinese to change their habits and consumption patterns.

For communication researchers and public opinion analysts, an emphasis on personal experiences also echoes the long debate on the nature of media effects. Since the late 1940s, scholars have found mass media to be exerting only limited effects on shaping people's opinions (Lazarsfeld, Berelson, and Gaudet, 1944). Personal experiences, however, might alter the influence of mass media. Social relations can also filter, reinterpret, and/or reinforce the effects of the mass media through the mediation of opinion leaders (Katz and Lazarsfeld, 1955), who may be regarded as exerting a more direct influence on the individual's perceptions and behavior. After all, besides being exposed to the media, Chinese people today are connected to the outside world through migration, traveling, and working and studying abroad.

The influences of mass-mediated information and those of personal experiences and interpersonal communications should not be considered as a competitive and zero-sum game (Ball-Rokeach and DeFleur, 1976; Mutz, 1994). The mass media can contextualize individual personal experiences (Lane, 1962) by weaving discrete events into a continuing story (Lang and Lang, 1981). The media expose people to similar experiences of others, thus enabling individuals to understand their experiences and concerns within a broader social spectrum (Mutz, 1994). An urban Chinese citizen might not perceive globalization as important to him or her personally just because the news says so, but she or he might see globalization as particularly relevant when both the media and personal experiences point to its importance (Hawkins and Pingree, 1982). In other words, personal experiences and media images can work together to generate specific perceptions and attitudes on the part of individuals.

Therefore we begin our analysis of the urban Chinese's "global outlook" by examining personal experiences and patterns of social connections. How many transnational social connections and overseas experiences does a typical urban Chinese resident have? To what extent can transnational social communications help translate the giant societal transition of globalization into a "common sense"—that is, how can these help individuals to make sense of in their daily routines?

This chapter explores such questions. The following sections first further discuss the relevant concepts and contexts underlying this chapter's analysis. Our data analysis then begins by providing a profile of our survey respondents' demographic features, value orientations, personal experiences with the outside world, and transnational social connections. We then investigate how demographic characteristics and personal experiences affect Chinese people's interests in the affairs in foreign countries. In a nutshell, this chapter offers a brief portrait of the urban Chinese in the global era.

CONCEPTS AND CONTEXTS

From a sociological perspective, it is difficult for individuals to fully comprehend social transitions without breaking these transitions into microevents of which they can make sense (Collins, 1981). After all, social norms, values, and conceptual schemes about time, space, and social order are embodied in and enacted by the routines and scenarios of everyday life (Ortner 1994). The waves of national mood and intellectual debates on the relationship between China and the world would not have emerged without the many accumulated changes in the daily experiences of Chinese people in the global era. Specifically, the abstract and general process of "globalization" can be experienced by urban Chinese people through their concrete traveling experiences as well as their transnational social connections. These two make up the analytical focus of this chapter. Hence it would be useful to first provide some background discussion related to these phenomena.

Personal Experiences with the Outside World

In communication research, personal experiences are often considered to be more powerful than mass-mediated information in shaping people's beliefs, attitudes, and behavior (for a review of this literature, see Chaffee and Mutz, 1988). Watching an African safari on the Discovery Channel seems like a fundamentally different experience from joining a safari tour. Traveling can be a secular pilgrimage in search of authenticity for some and can be simply a form of leisure activity for others; in either case, traveling is a means to both obtain and display status, education, and style. Recent sociological analyses of tourism as commercialized hospitality have discussed the phenomenon of traveling from many aspects, ranging from the representation of culture involved in tourism to the relationship between tourism and social change and/or economic development (cf. Apostolopoulos, Leivadi, and Yiannakis, 1996).

At the individual level, tourists/travelers as strangers and outsiders are temporarily assigned certain social roles and statuses in the places they visit. Such a process reconstructs the guest-local/host-tourists relationship (Cohen 1984). These changing dynamics lead to further social and economic and even political changes in the places tourists visit. Meanwhile, the experience tourists bring back to their native lands might modify their native fellows' perceptions of the outside world.

In the case of China, the development of outbound tourism has gone through different stages in the past decades. In the early 1980s, the government allowed only a limited number of organized tours to Hong Kong and Macau. These tours were supervised by the China National Tourism Administration and were intended only for visiting friends and relatives. In the early 1990s, the Chinese government signed bilateral agreements with Singapore, Malaysia, and Thailand, opening up a door for self-funded Chinese leisure tourists through the then newly established Chinese Travel Service.

Yet China's outbound tourism did not take off until the mid-1990s. In 1995, China adopted a selective outbound tourism policy and formalized the Approved Destination Status (ADS) system, under which Chinese citizens could travel in organized group tours to countries approved by the government. In 1997, the government signed its first bilateral agreements with Australia and New Zealand, creating an opportunity for Chinese to experience western culture at first hand. By late 2011, a total of 140 destinations around the world had signed agreements with China regarding the ADS scheme.[1] Certain popular locations witnessed substantial growth in the number of tourists from China. Japan, for instance, received 1.4 million tourists from China in 2010, as well as 201,000 Chinese tourists in the first two months of 2011 (before the earthquake struck in March).[2] For foreign countries receiving Chinese tourists, more significant than the sheer numbers of tourists from China is probably the spending power of these tourists. According to the World Tourism Organization, Chinese tourists spent $54.9 billion overseas in 2010; only German and American travelers spent more money that year.[3]

At its present rate of growth, China is expected to have 100 million tourists traveling abroad by 2015 (Department of Foreign Affairs and Trade, 2005); by 2020, outbound Chinese tourists will constitute 6.4 percent of all international travelers, which will make China the fourth largest provider of outbound tourists globally (Keating and Kriz, 2008). As the Chinese proverb goes, "Seeing it once is better than hearing it a hundred times," opening up the venues for Chinese citizens' exposure to the outside world and contact with it may result in changes in national self-image and bring new input into the ways in which the Chinese people perceive others.

Interpersonal Influence via Social Connections

Interpersonal relations influence attitude, taste, and behavior through various mechanisms. Social relations prompt audiences to consume the media fares in a self-selective way and thus would moderate the effects of the media. As interpersonal relations tend to be consistent and stable over time, the stable microenvironment thus created may reduce individuals' susceptibility to media influence (Baron and Kenny, 1986; Hardy and Scheufele, 2005). Social relations can provide their own persuasive influence through social norms and pressures toward conformity. Individuals tend to conform to others in order to make accurate and valid judgments, to seek social approval, or from fear of being isolated from the majority (Deutsch and Gerard, 1955; Noelle-Neumann, 1983). In addition, social networks help to translate mass-mediated messages into meaningful individual actions (Baron and Kenny, 1986; Hardy and Scheufele, 2005). Influence through social relations is almost invisible and often occurs through informal everyday contacts. It is "casually exercised, sometimes unwittingly and unbeknown, within the smallest grouping of friends, family members and neighbor" (Katz and Lazarfeld, 1955, p. 138). It has pushed scholars to rethink the meaning of "mass" in the communication process (Scannell, 2006; Williams, 1958).

To further explore the flow of influence from social communication through social relations, we borrow Granovetter's (1973) seminal idea and define "strong-tie" communication as the communication among family members, close friends, and relatives. Studies reveal that individuals are more likely to be persuaded when they are approached via strong-tie communication, especially when they encounter new issues at the personal level. For example, regarding skin cancer, researchers found that mass media are more influential in shaping individuals' perceptions of third-party risk, whereas interpersonal communication plays a more significant role in shaping their perceptions of self-risk (Morton and Duck, 2001). In addition, individuals are more likely to change their opinions to achieve greater attitudinal congruence while socializing with close relations than with strangers (Davis and Rusbult, 2001). Research also indicates that mass media are powerful in diffusing information but that interpersonal ties are more influential at the decision-making stage (Rogers, 2003). Whereas globalization has brought new experiences into the lives of the Chinese people, people's perceptions of novel phenomena might be significantly shaped by their communications with their friends and families.

Transnational Social Connections

The communication patterns with family members can be further elaborated by taking family structure into consideration. Globalization has called for new definitions of private life, family, gender, and identity (Giddens, 2000). Broadly speaking, the rise of the information society, the global economy, evolutionary changes in human reproduction technology, the surge of women consciousness and the feminist movement combine to challenge the patriarchal nuclear family (Castells, 1997). More specifically, processes of globalization have led to the emergence of the transnational family (Ziehl, 2003; Yeoh, Huang, and Lam, 2005). Transnational families then serve as important "building blocks" of transnational communities. For instance, emphasizing the individual agency in the transnational flow of people, images, and cultural forces, Aihwa Ong (1999) outlined how the experience of intensified travel, family communication, and mass media has created a transnational Chinese public. Among many overseas Chinese, the family provides an institutional context and a web of power within which Chinese subjects relocate and realign themselves as they traverse global space. In other words, an individual's perception on the outside world might be affected by whether he or she is more in contact with what may be called a localite or cosmopolitan family. As defined by Merton (1957), "a localite largely confines his interests to this community" (p. 447), while cosmopolitans orient significantly to the world outside of the local community but still maintain at least minimal relations within the community.

China has a long history of emigration. From the late nineteenth century to the late 1940s, Southeast Asia was a popular destination for Chinese emigrants. After 1949, the emigrants mainly comprised students setting off to the Soviet Union and workers going to various developing countries. From the late 1970s to the early 1980s, half a million Chinese entered Hong Kong. Hong Kong was not only a popular destination for mainland Chinese emigration during the period but also an important midway station for Chinese emigrants going to Southeast Asia, Europe, and North America. Since the late 1990s, North America and Australia have become the more preferred destinations. In numerical terms, the World Bank has ranked China as the fourth largest country of emigration in the world. In 2010, there were 8.3 million China-born people living outside China's borders, which includes 3 million who were born in China and living in Hong Kong and Macau (World Bank, 2011).

Meanwhile, it should be noted that studying abroad has become one of the major channels of emigration for young Chinese. From 1978 to 2003, the total number of Chinese students living overseas reached over 0.7 million. But the number continued to grow at a fast pace. According to statistics from the Ministry of Education, China had the largest number of overseas students in the world by the end of 2010, as 1.27 million Chinese students were studying abroad at the time and more than 20 percent of them were "new students" who went abroad in the year 2010.[4]

PROFILES OF THE URBAN CHINESE

Basic Demographics

The above discussion provides the contextual background for our empirical analysis. But before analyzing the foreign experiences and transnational social connections of the urban Chinese, it will be useful to first provide a basic profile of the urban Chinese in our survey. Table 2.1 provides a summary of the relevant statistics.

Table 2.1 Basic Demographic Characteristics

	Beijing	Shanghai	Chengdu	Xi'an	Total	F/χ^2
Age	39.0	42.7	41.3	41.5	41.1	6.78***
% Male	50.5	50.2	50.7	51.6	50.8	0.22
% with religion	4.6	10.6	4.4	7.6	6.7	20.25***
% Monthly income						268.53***
< 1,000	2.8	1.2	11.0	13.2	7.1	
1,000–5,000	82.2	72.4	87.2	83.8	81.6	
5,000–10,000	14.8	24.2	1.2	1.8	10.5	
> 10,000	0.2	2.2	0.6	1.2	1.1	
% Occupation						
Private	27.8	26.6	30.0	21.6	26.5	9.75*
State	28.5	17.6	13.6	34.2	23.4	77.26***
Foreign/Joint	3.2	9.0	1.2	2.6	5.0	46.11***
% University	13.2	12.0	8.2	13.2	11.7	8.21*
% Father u-grad	4.8	4.6	1.8	5.4	4.2	9.71*
% Mother u-grad	2.0	2.2	1.2	2.0	1.9	1.63

Note: Entries for age are mean scores. All other entries are percentages. For monthly income, differences across cities were tested by cross-tabulating the city variable with the four-category family income variable. For occupations, differences across cities were tested by cross-tabulating the city variable with three dichotomized variables—working for private enterprise vs. others, working for state enterprise vs. others, working for foreign companies or joint ventures vs. others—separately. * $P < .05$; ** $P < .01$; *** $P < .001$.

As noted in Chapter 1, females and young people were overrepresented in our samples. Hence the samples were weighted according to these two demographic characteristics for the analysis. After the weighting procedure, 50.8 percent of our respondents were male, and the median age was 41, corresponding to the official figures on the age and gender distributions of the populations in the four cities. Average age varies by city though: the respondents from Shanghai, taken as a group, were oldest (mean age = 42.7) and the respondents from Beijing were youngest (mean age = 39.0). The between-cities differences in age are statistically significant in a one-way ANOVA analysis.

The majority of our respondents—93.3 percent—claimed that they had no religious beliefs. About 4.9 percent believed in Buddhism, 1.1 percent were Christians, 0.5 percent believed in Islam, and 0.2 percent were Catholic. Females were slightly but significantly more likely to believe in some kind of religion than were males (7.9 percent vs. 5.6 percent, $\chi^2 = 4.19$, $P < .05$). Compared with the other three cities, Shanghai has a higher percentage of people who had a religious belief.

Most respondents (81.6 percent) in the survey had monthly household incomes between 1,001 and 5,000 Renminbi (RMB). About 7.1 percent of them lived in families earning less than 1,000 RMB per month, while 10.5 percent of the respondents had monthly household incomes between 5,001 and 10,000 RMB. This leaves only 0.7 percent of our respondents having a monthly household income of more than 10,000 RMB. In terms of occupation, 26.5 percent of respondents in our sample were either managers or staff in private enterprises, whereas 23.4 percent were either managers or staff in state enterprises. Notably, 4.0 percent of our respondents were either managers or staff in foreign companies or joint ventures. Not surprisingly, in comparing the cities with each other, Shanghai had the largest proportion of respondents working in foreign companies or joint ventures (9 percent). Only 3.2 percent of the respondents in Beijing were employees of foreign companies or joint ventures. The corresponding percentages were even lower in the two inland cities: 2.6 percent for Xi'an and 1.2 percent for Chengdu.[5] The between-cities differences are highly statistically significant in a cross-tabulation analysis.

As the bottom of Table 2.1 shows, about 11.7 percent of our survey respondents had university degrees. At the same time, 58.5 percent of them had senior high school or senior vocational school diplomas, and 29.8 percent had junior high school education or less. Chengdu had the lowest percentage of respondents with university education, whereas the proportions of university graduates in the other three cities are highly similar. Yet the respondents' overall educational levels were already much better than those of their parents. As the last two rows of the table show, when the four cities are combined, only about 4.2 percent of the respondents' fathers and about 2 percent of their mothers had university degrees.

Predictably, parents' educational levels had a significant impact on their children's educational attainment. Using the original seven-category education variables (ranging from no education to university degree), the correlation between personal educational level and father's educational level is at $r = .48$ ($P < .001$), whereas the correlation between personal educational level and mother's educational level was also the same at $r = .48$ ($P < .001$). Notably, at least among the respondents' parents, highly educated people tended to marry highly educated people, as father's and mother's educational levels are very highly correlated at $r = .71$ ($P < .001$).

Foreign Language Skills

Beyond basic demographics, the present survey also explored the respondents' foreign language capabilities. English is arguably the "world language" of the late twentieth and early twenty-first centuries owing to colonial expansion in earlier centuries, the growth of international capitalism, and the relatively recent advance of cultural globalization (Pennycook, 1994). In China, since the reform and opening-up policies began in 1978, English education has gradually gained legitimacy and become increasingly popular (Hu, 2005). In the 1990s, with the growing need for China to be incorporated into the world community, English education was not only regarded as important for individual advancement but also seen as an essential part of national development. Likewise, English is no longer taught just as a subject but also as a means of communication (Hu, 2005; Wang and Lam, 2009). As Pan (2011, p. 252) put it, "the significance of English learning is not restricted to its linguistic and communicative usefulness, but is elevated first to a national level and connected to social development, and then to an international level, and boosted to relate to the importance of gaining a stronger foothold in the world-system."

The Chinese state's education policy has officially embraced the idea that an adequate command of English by the Chinese people is necessary and important for modernization and the country's sustained development (Pan, 2011; Ricento, 2000). For example, the 2003 version of *English Curriculum Requirements at Compulsory Education Stage* (below age 16) justified the importance of English learning on the basis of the increased information of social and economic globalization. The 2003 version of *English Curriculum Requirements at Senior High Education Stage* (ages 16 to 18 in general) also emphasized that "with the globalization of social and economic activities, foreign language competence has already become a basic requirement for people around the world. Therefore, learning and mastering foreign languages, especially English, is of critical importance."

However, the enthusiasm of the state education policy for embracing English, given its pragmatic utility, has been tempered by the concern that English learning might pose threats to Chinese culture and identity. The global spread of English has given the United States and the United Kingdom unrivaled cultural, economic, and political dominance (Pennycook 1994; Phillipson 1992; Crystal 1997). As a result, has China tried to distance its foreign language education policy from any particular cultural model and not to specify any particular variety of English as the legitimate form in China. In other words, the official policies try to neutralize the role and the function of the language and especially its cultural associations. But to what extent learning about a language can be separated from learning about a culture is another issue.

At the individual level, English proficiency is increasingly recognized as a passport to better education, employment, and success. In the survey, we asked respondents to evaluate their own fluency in English. About 46.3 percent claimed that they don't know English at all, while 29.9 percent knew a little bit English and 19.0 percent said their English was "so-so." Only 4.4 percent claimed to be fluent in English, and 0.5 percent claimed that they were at the level of native speakers.

People from the four cities varied substantially in the self-evaluation of their English ability. Yet the differences do correspond to our basic understanding of the degree to which the four cities are "internationalized." The two coastal cities' respondents reported higher levels of English ability. Only 32.1 percent of our Beijing respondents said they did not know any English at all, while 7.2 percent claimed that they were fluent or at the level of native speakers. In Shanghai, the two corresponding percentages were 43.1 percent and 4.8 percent respectively. In contrast, 59.6 percent of respondents from Chengdu and 50.1 percent of respondents from Xi'an reported that they did not know English at all, and only 4.4 percent in Chengdu and 3.2 percent in Xi'an claimed they were fluent or better than fluent. In general, younger people had better English proficiency than the older generation. At the bivariate level, the five-category English ability variable and age are correlated at $r = -.43$ ($P < .001$). This relationship reflects the development of English education in China over the past few decades. Certainly English ability is also related to education and social class, such that more educated people and people with higher levels of family income would report having better English ability ($r = .62$ between education and English ability, $P < .001$, and $r = .27$ between income and English ability, $P < .001$). Not surprisingly, people working in foreign companies or joint ventures also reported much higher levels of English proficiency. Only 11.3 percent of those who worked at a foreign company or joint venture said they did not know any English at all, in contrast to 47.7 percent for all other respondents. Notably, these bivariate relationships all remain statistically significant in a multiple regression analysis.

Value Orientations

Globalization suggests the possibility of not only an expanded consciousness of the world but also a salient transformation of behavior and value orientation (Knight, 2006). As "an enduring belief that a specific mode of conduct or end-state of existence is personally or socially preferable to an opposite or converse mode of conduct or end-state of existence" (Rokeach, 1973, p. 5), traditional values have encountered new competition coming from the "Coca-colonization" or "McDonaldization" of daily lives. Some evidence in past research around the world has indicated a deep-rooted tension between tradition and modernity and between collectivism and individualism. In advanced industrial societies, the past decades have also witnessed a shift in people's value orientations from materialism to postmaterialism, from deference to authority to self-expression, and from treating cultural diversity as threatening to treating it as interesting (Inglehart, 2000).

Although we do not have longitudinal data to examine whether there have been similar trends in China, our survey allows us to provide a snapshot of Chinese people's value orientations at a time when the country became much more engaged with the world at large. The present survey asked the respondents to evaluate two sets of values on a five-point Likert scale, ranging from very unimportant to very important. The first set is composed of a number of *society-oriented* values: harmony, stability, prosperity, democracy, freedom, equality, and strong nation. The second set is constituted by *self-oriented values*: wealth, reputation, ideal, leisure, health, and education.

All these values were, not surprisingly, favorably regarded. But as Table 2.2 shows, differences existed in the extent to which specific values were rated as highly important. Among all society-oriented values, urban Chinese treated a "strong nation" as by far the most important. It is followed by "stability" and

Table 2.2 Chinese People's Value Orientations

		Very Important	Important	Neutral
Society-oriented	Harmony	58.3	37.9	3.2
	Stability	62.4	34.2	3.2
	Prosperity	50.9	42.9	5.5
	Democracy	45.3	44.2	9.9
	Freedom	45.9	43.8	9.8
	Equality	54.4	40.2	5.2
	Strong nation	75.2	22.2	2.2
Self-oriented	Wealth	37.8	51.0	8.8
	Reputation	28.1	43.4	21.0
	Ideal	30.2	45.9	18.4
	Leisure	19.9	47.4	25.9
	Health	76.8	21.1	2.0
	Education	54.0	39.7	5.6

Note: Entries are percentages. Answers were recorded by a five-point Likert scale ranging from "very important" to "very unimportant." The two categories "unimportant" and "very unimportant" are excluded from the table because very few respondents chose the two categories for most of the values. The percentage distribution across the three options included in the table should give a good sense of the *relative* importance of the values in the eyes of the respondents.

"harmony," two values actively promoted by the state through its emphasis on "harmonious society." Comparatively, among the society-oriented values, freedom and democracy received the least recognition.

Among all individual-oriented values, Chinese people rated health as the most important, with 76.8 percent saying that it is "very important." Only 37.8 percent endorsed wealth and 28.1 percent rated reputation as "very important." But in these two cases, we have to be aware of the possibility of people giving "socially desirable" answers rather than expressing their true feelings.[6] Culturally, an emphasis on wealth and reputation may be seen as a sign of greed and as conflicting with the traditional ideal of modesty. Nonetheless, it is notable that the least important self-oriented value for our urban Chinese respondents is "a relaxed and leisurely life."

Further correlation analysis (Table 2.3) reveals how Chinese people perceived the relationships between the values. For society-oriented values, the correlations between "harmony," "stability," and "strong nation" are generally high, whereas the correlations between "democracy," "freedom," and "equality" are also relatively high. In fact, in an exploratory factor analysis, the seven values would be clustered into two factors. Interestingly, prosperity is split across the two factors. It seems that "prosperity"" serves as a bridge to connect the two factors in the Chinese context.

The patterns of correlation should be understood in relation to how the idea of democracy was introduced into the Chinese context: The contemporary Chinese discourses on the "D word" have tangled with the discussion

Table 2.3 Correlations among Values

	1	2	3	4	5	6	7
Society-oriented							
1 Harmony	1.00						
2 Stability	0.59	1.00					
3 Strong nation	0.36	0.29	1.00				
4 Prosperity	0.35	0.42	0.29	1.00			
5 Freedom	0.32	0.33	0.34	0.37	1.00		
6 Equality	0.31	0.32	0.19	0.29	0.53	1.00	
7 Democracy	0.32	0.34	0.21	0.54	0.62	0.42	1.00
Self-oriented							
1 Wealth	1.00						
2 Reputation	0.43	1.00					
3 Ideal	0.24	0.45	1.00				
4 Leisure	0.26	0.30	0.41	1.00			
5 Health	0.17	0.06	0.15	0.16	1.00		
6 Education	0.21	0.25	0.33	0.21	0.35	1.00	

Note: Entries are Pearson correlation coefficients. All coefficients are statistically significant at $P < .05$.

of national survival since the very beginning. When Mao Zedong and Deng Xiaoping (and other non-communist modernists) invoked the term "democracy," they invariably regarded it not as an end in itself but as a means to achieve a thriving nation (Thornton, 2008). Even though the current political leaders have been talking about democracy with increasing frequency and detail (for instance, President Hu Jintao has called democracy "the common pursuit of mankind," and Premier Wen Jiabao, in his address to the 2007 National People's Congress, declared that "developing democracy and improving the legal system are basic requirements of the socialist system"), democracy is still constructed in party terms as a method to achieve national prosperity and modernity. In fact, some political scientists have pointed out that Chinese people may tend to understand democracy in terms of a good and benevolent government that would consult the opinion of the people rather than a government that is ultimately and institutionally controlled by public opinion through periodic elections (Diamond, 2010; Shi and Lu, 2010).

The bottom panel of Table 2.3 shows that the correlations between the self-oriented values are generally weaker than the correlations between the society-oriented values. The relatively stronger correlations include the relationship between wealth and reputation and that between ideal and reputation. When the six values are put into an exploratory factor analysis, a two-factor solution emerges, with reputation, wealth, ideal, and having a relaxed and leisurely life constituting one factor and with education and health constituting the other. Such findings suggest that many respondents were interpreting the idea of "ideal" (*li xiang*) and "having a leisurely life" as something related to the material well-being of an individual. In this sense, the type of "ideal" that people had in mind may have stronger linkages with more materialistic things such as career ambitions than with non-materialistic values such as self-realization or self-expression.

To analyze the correlates with value orientations, we created four indices based on the factor analysis results mentioned above. Traditional value

Table 2.4 Demographic Correlates of Value Orientations

	Traditional	Liberal	Material	Nonmeaterial
Gender	-.02	.02	.03	.03
Age	-.04	-.02	-.14***	.04
Education	-.12***	.03	-.02	.03
Household income	-.01	-.00	.04	.05*
English ability	.12***	.02	.02	.05
Work in state enterprise	.02	.04	-.04	-.03
Work in foreign companies	-.02	-.04	.01	.01
Adjusted R²	-0.9%	0.1%	2.4%	0.6%

Note: Entries are standardized regression coefficients. * $P < .05$; ** $P < .01$; *** $P < .001$.

orientation is the average of people's rating of harmony and stability, whereas liberal value orientation is the average of democracy and freedom. Materialistic value orientation is the average of wealth and reputation, whereas nonmaterialistic value orientation is the average of health and education.[7] We then conducted a multiple regression analysis using a number of demographic factors as the independent variables. The multiple regression analysis can give us information about how the value orientations relate to the demographic factors when the influences of different demographic factors are controlled against each other.

Table 2.4 shows, in general, very little and weak relationships between value orientations and other demographic factors. People with higher levels of education tended to rate the traditional values of harmony and stability as less important. Surprisingly, when other variables are controlled, people with better English tended to rate the traditional values more highly. No matter what contributes to this positive relationship, this finding at least reconfirms the point already made in Chapter 1 that those contemporary urban Chinese people who are most globally connected are not necessarily antitraditionalists.

The set of demographic factors included in the regression analysis of Table 2.4 does not relate to rating of liberal values at all. Meanwhile, younger people tended to rate the materialistic values of wealth and reputation as less important. Interestingly, if the same finding appears in developed economies, it could be readily taken as a sign of a shift toward postmaterialistic thinking among the younger generation (Inglehart, 1990). The finding here, therefore, may be interpreted as suggesting that the same generational shift toward "postmaterialism" may be happening, if only in limited ways and to limited extents, in the more developed urban centers of China.

TRANSNATIONAL PERSONAL EXPERIENCE

As discussed in the background section, traveling abroad is no longer a novelty for at least part of the urban Chinese public. In the survey, we first asked respondents to identify how frequently they traveled and worked in various overseas locations: Hong Kong/Macau/Taiwan, Japan/Korea, Southeast Asia, United States/Canada, Europe, and Middle East. We consider visiting Hong Kong, Macau, and Taiwan as a part of mainland Chinese's "overseas" experience because mainland Chinese need special visas to visit these locations, and the societies and cultures in these cities and places can be substantially different from the society and culture in mainland China. In fact, the "cultural differences" between Hong Kong and mainland China are so significant that, combined with a complex set of historical, economic, and political factors, a backlash against mainland tourists has happened most recently in Hong Kong (from late 2011 onward and extending into early 2013, when the manuscript for this book was finalized).

Nevertheless, we found from our survey that, by 2006 and 2007, the percentage of Chinese who actually had traveled abroad was very small. Only 3.1 percent of the respondents claimed that they sometimes or frequently visited Hong Kong, Macau, or Taiwan. For each of the other overseas regions, less than 1 percent of the respondents had had the experiences of traveling there. The percentages of people who had had working experiences in the different overseas region are even smaller. At most, only 0.6 percent of our respondents claimed that they had worked in Hong Kong, Macau, or Taiwan sometimes or frequently.

Given the frequency distributions, we created an index for foreign traveling experiences by averaging people's frequencies of traveling to the six different regions. The working experience variables were not included in the index because of the total lack of variance in some of these variables. Since the resulting variable is highly skewed, we applied the square-root transformation to the variable to reduce the skewedness.

With the index, we can more efficiently examine the demographic correlates with Chinese people's foreign traveling experiences. First, traveling experiences do vary across cities. People in Chengdu had the least foreign traveling experiences (M = 1.0011 in the index), whereas people in the other three cities had more or less equal levels of foreign traveling experiences (Ms = 1.0065, 1.0068, 1.0063 for Beijing, Shanghai, and Xi'an respectively). The between-cities differences are statistically significant in a one-way ANOVA analysis (F = 5.57, P < .01).

At the bivariate level, foreign travel is not significantly related to age or gender. But it is significantly and positively related to income, education, and English ability (Pearson r for the three correlations is .16, .14 and .12 respectively, P < .001 for all three). That is, traveling is the experience enjoyed primarily by the privileged and those who have higher levels of cultural capital. Moreover, foreign travel is significantly related to working for a foreign company or joint venture. Employees of foreign companies or joint ventures had on average more foreign travel experiences than other people (Ms = 1.0161 vs. 1.0047, t = 2.25, P < .03 in an independent-samples t-test).

When the demographics are put into a regression model, education and income remain significant predictors of travel experiences. But the relationship between foreign travel and working in foreign companies or joint ventures became insignificant. At the same time, a significant though weak relationship between age and foreign travel emerges—older people tended to travel overseas relatively more frequently when other demographic factors were controlled. One possible reason for the latter relationship is that, when financial and cultural resources are equal, older people may have more time and freedom in their lives to enjoy travel.

As indicated above, at the time of our survey overseas experience was limited to a very small circle of elites. Therefore, for the Chinese population at large, travel experiences might not be the main channel through which they perceive the global community. However, although the common Chinese's overseas experience might be constrained by the individual's economic situation, the subjective willingness to travel and work in other places might present a different picture. In the survey, we asked respondents to indicate on a five-point Likert scale whether they agreed with the statement that "to move to another place to seek development is a good thing." We label this variable "adventurism," which can be defined as an attitudinal inclination toward living outside the comfort zone of a familiar place. It is worth noting here that this attitudinal orientation variable will appear as an independent variable in the analysis in some of the later chapters.

Nearly 9 percent of our respondents strongly agreed with the statement, whereas another 38.9 percent agreed. In other words, close to half (47.9 percent) of our respondents were willing to seek career development in other places. At the other end, only 9.4 percent of the respondents disagreed or strongly disagreed with the statement. Overall, at the time our survey was conducted, although many urban Chinese people still did not have much chance to travel abroad, they were nonetheless longing for such opportunities.

Degree of adventurism varied across the four cities. Beijing residents scored highest on the variable ($M = 3.86$), whereas the residents in the other three cities scored substantially lower ($Ms = 3.38, 3.22$, and 3.39 for Shanghai, Chengdu, and Xi'an respectively). The between-cities differences are statistically significant in a one-way ANOVA analysis ($F = 64.63$, $P < .001$).

At the bivariate level, adventurism related to the demographic factors in almost exactly the same way as did foreign travel experience. Adventurism related positively and significantly with education, income, and English ability (Pearson r coefficients = .05, .09, .07 respectively, $P < .03$ in all cases). Moreover, workers in foreign companies and joint ventures also exhibited higher levels of adventurism ($Ms = 3.65$ vs. 3.46, $t = 2.14$, $P < .04$ in an independent-samples t-test). Therefore those who were socially and economically privileged were more likely to regard living abroad as a good thing.

But when put into a multiple regression analysis, only income related significantly to adventurism. The lack of relationships between adventurism and other demographic factors suggests that the subjective willingness to travel abroad was rather evenly distributed across the various social positions (as opposed to the actual opportunities for traveling abroad, which were more unequally distributed across different social groups). The urban Chinese were generally interested in seeking development in other places, no matter whether they were men or women, young or old, or highly educated or not.

Transnational Social Connections

In the survey, we asked respondents how many overseas relatives or friends they had in six overseas locations: Hong Kong/Macau/Taiwan, Southeast Asia, Japan/Korea, the United States and Canada, western Europe, and the Middle East. The answers were recorded using a four-point scale ranging from 1 = none to 4 = many. Similar to foreign traveling experiences, although the absolute number of overseas Chinese can be substantial, the actual proportions of urban Chinese with some relatives overseas were actually small. Only 3.2 percent of the respondents indicated that they had at least some relatives in Hong Kong, Macau, or Taiwan. Historically speaking, Southeast Asia used to be the most popular destinations for Chinese migrants, especially from the southern provinces of Guangdong and Fujian, but in our four-city survey, only 0.8 percent of respondents reported having relatives or friends in that region (of course this low percentage might stem from the fact that we did not have respondents from the Guangdong and Fujian provinces). In contrast, urban Chinese had somewhat more relatives or friends in the developed western world: 2.7 percent of the respondents indicated that they had at least some relatives in North America, and the corresponding percentages were 1.6 percent for Japan and Korea and 1.1 percent for western Europe. Almost no urban Chinese had relatives or friends in the Middle East (0.1 percent). Overall, we found that 92.7 percent of the respondents did not report having any relatives living in any of the six regions. In terms of proportion, this would suggest that urban Chinese had limited transnational social connections. But of course the sheer number of people being connected to other countries through personal connections would still be substantial, as 7.3 percent of citizens in the four cities in 2006 would mean a total figure of about 4 million people.

Having relatives and friends living abroad does not imply receiving information about the outside world from them. Actual communication between Chinese citizens and their overseas acquaintances can be important only to the extent that such social connections become channels of images and information. Therefore we also asked our respondents how frequently they contacted their relatives and friends in each locale. The results show that 2.6 percent of the whole sample reported contacting their relatives or friends in Hong Kong, Macau, or Taiwan at least "sometimes." Given that only 3.2 percent of the respondents had relatives or friends in these places, the figure of 2.6 percent with contact means that most people who had relatives or friends in Hong Kong, Macau, and Taiwan did keep some contact with such overseas acquaintances. The same applies to other regions as well: 1.4 percent of the respondents kept contact with friends or relatives in Japan/Korea and 2.2 percent kept contact with friends or relatives in North America at least "sometimes." The corresponding percentages for Europe and Southeast Asia were 0.9 percent and 0.6 percent respectively. All these figures are just slightly lower than the percentages of people with at least some relatives or friends in the respective regions.

To examine the demographic correlates with transnational social connections, we first created two separate indices. We averaged the number of friends and relatives people had in the six regions to form an index of overseas contact; then we also averaged the amount of communications people had with overseas acquaintances to form an index of overseas communications. We further multiplied the two indices to form yet another overall index of transnational social connections. As with travel experiences, we adjusted for the skewedness of these three indices by applying square-root transformations.

In the multivariate analysis in the last part of this chapter as well as the remaining chapters of this book, only the multiplicative index of transnational social connections were be employed. But here it would be useful to examine the demographic correlates of all three indices for illustrative purposes.

Degree of transnational social connections varied significantly across cities. Not surprisingly, as China's international financial center with a past history of multinational semicolonial ties, Shanghai provided the most transnational social connections. Shanghai residents' scores on the overseas contact, overseas communications, and transnational social connection indices were 1.0157, 1.0129, and 1.0303 respectively. The mean scores were 1.0017, 1.0016, and 1.0034 only for Chengdu. In fact, among the four cities, Chengdu residents had the fewest transnational social connections.

For the other demographic correlates, Table 2.5 shows the results of the relevant multiple regression analyses. All three indices perform in almost exactly the same way. Transnational social connections are positively related to education, household income, English ability, and age. In other words, older people who were located in more privileged positions in society tended to have more transnational social connections. However, it is noteworthy that age is not strongly and significantly related to the three indices at the bivariate level. This is because older people in China tend to have less education and weaker English ability; this affected the number of transnational social connections they had. Yet simply because they were older, their longer life histories would have allowed them to develop more connections inside and outside of the country. At the bivariate level, these two implications of age cancel each other out; hence age does not seem to

Table 2.5 Demographic Predictors of Transnational Social Connections

	Overseas Contact	Overseas Communication	Transnational Social Connections
Gender	.02	.02	.02
Age	.15***	.19***	.18***
Education	.10***	.12***	.11***
Household income	.09**	.14***	.12***
English ability	.12***	.13***	.14***
Work in state enterprise	-.03	-.03	-.04
Work in foreign companies/ joint ventures	-.01	-.01	-.01
Adjusted R^2	4.1%***	6.5%***	6.1%***

Note: Entries are standardized regression coefficients. * $P < .05$; ** $P < .01$; *** $P < .001$.

LIVERPOOL JOHN MOORES UNIVERSITY
LEARNING SERVICES

relate to transnational social connections at all. But as Table 2.5 shows, when education and income are kept constant, the positive impact of age on transnational social connections emerges.

Interest in Foreign Countries

Having provided a basic profile of the urban Chinese in our survey, we now examine the extent to which such demographic factors, together with transnational social connections and foreign travel experiences, would relate to Chinese people's interests in foreign countries. The survey asked the respondents to indicate, by means of a five-point Likert scale, whether they were interested in seven types of issues in each of five regions. The seven types of issues are politics, economics, society, education and science, popular culture, lifestyle, and sports. The five regions are Hong Kong/Macau/Taiwan, Japan and Korea, the United States and Canada, Europe, and the Middle East.

We averaged the respondents' interest scores by location and by issue domains respectively. Figure 2.1 presents the results graphically. The urban Chinese, on the whole, did not express a strong interest in what happens around the world. In fact, it is notable that all mean scores except one shown in both the top and bottom panels of Figure 2.1 are below the midpoint of the scale (that is, 3) substantially. Even the "exceptional" case of "interests in Hong Kong, Macau and Taiwan" has a mean score of only slightly above the midpoint of the scale ($M = 3.05$, $SD = 0.72$).

Comparatively speaking, among the five overseas locations, urban Chinese were most interested in the outer regions of "Greater China": Hong Kong, Macau, and Taiwan. Their interest in Japan and Korea was comparable to interest in the United States and Canada; they were relatively less interested in Europe and the Middle East. The results probably reflect the importance of proximity in determining people's interests in foreign countries. The Greater China regions and Japan and Korea are both geographically and culturally close to China. The United States, meanwhile, remains the most powerful country in the world and hence many Chinese people would be interested in what is happening there.

Among the seven issue domains, urban Chinese were most interested in sports, society, lifestyles, and education and science. They were less interested in foreign politics and economics. Generally speaking, it seems that the urban Chinese were more interested in "soft topics" rather than "hard topics" where foreign countries are concerned, although the difference is not huge.

But what explains Chinese people's interest in foreign affairs? To undertake a multiple regression analysis, we further averaged people's interest in the seven issue domains to construct an overall index of people's interest in foreign affairs as the dependent variable. The independent variables include the basic demographics (age, gender, income, education) in addition to the three demographic factors that we have been analyzing throughout this

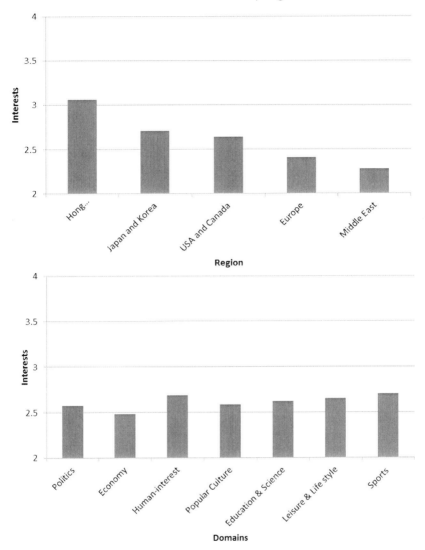

Figure 2.1 The interest of urban Chinese in foreign affairs by region and issue domain.

chapter: English ability, whether working for state enterprises, and whether working for foreign companies or joint ventures. A set of three city dummies, with Beijing used as a reference category, were also included in the model to capture between-cities differences. Finally, we incorporated into the model foreign travel experiences, adventurism, and transnational social connections. The results are summarized in Table 2.6.

Age is significantly and negatively related to interest in foreign affairs. It is not surprising that the younger generation was more interested in global

Table 2.6 Regression Analysis on Interests in Foreign Affairs

	Dependent Variable: Interests in Foreign Affairs
Age	-.06**
Gender	-.09**
Education	.15***
Household income	.05*
English ability	.02
Work in state enterprise	-.06**
Work in foreign companies/joint ventures	.03
Shanghai	-.15***
Chengdu	-.35***
Xi'an	-.25***
Adventurism	.08***
Foreign traveling experiences	.06**
Transnational social connections	.04
Adjusted R^2	21.3%

Note: : Entries are standardized regression coefficients. * $P < .05$; ** $P < .01$; *** $P < .001$.

affairs than the older generations. Besides, males, better educated Chinese, and the middle class also had stronger interest in foreign affairs. Somewhat surprisingly, English ability does not relate to interests in foreign affairs when all other factors are controlled. But this is actually understandable because of the development of English education in China. When English is taught and learned at school simply as part of the formal curriculum, English ability may simply reflect a person's intellectual quality rather than a specific type of attitude or orientation toward the outside world.

More interestingly, workers in state enterprises were significantly less interested in foreign affairs, although workers in foreign companies or joint ventures were not significantly more interested in foreign affairs. This suggests that there may be a degree of parochialism within the state enterprises and among their workers.

Residents in Beijing, which serves as the reference category in the regression analysis, displayed the highest level of interest in foreign affairs. Comparing among the regression coefficients for the three other cities reveals that the Chengdu residents were the least curious. Such regional variations can be understood in relation to general perceptions of the "city personality" of the different places: Chengdu is famous for its own laid-back lifestyle, whereas Beijing has a more vibrant intellectual environment.

Moreover, both foreign travel experience and the subjective sense of adventurism relate positively and significantly to interests in foreign affairs. Transnational social connection also has a positive regression coefficient but it does not reach the conventional level of statistical significance.

SUMMARY AND DISCUSSION

This chapter provides a general profile of our survey respondents, with a focus particularly on their foreign experiences and transnational social connections. In sum, despite the advance of globalization, the urban Chinese, by 2006 and 2007, remained somewhat "parochial" and "not globalized" in a number of ways. First and foremost, they were not particularly interested in foreign affairs. Comparatively, they were more interested in sports or other "soft topics" than hard topics (such as politics and economics), and more interested in Hong Kong, Macau, and Taiwan than other more "remote" countries.

Official statistics and foreign news reports suggested that Chinese people have been traveling abroad more often. However, the percentage of Chinese who could afford overseas travel and work experiences was still quite small when this survey was conducted. Nevertheless, our analysis does show that those who were well traveled were also more interested in foreign affairs. Whether travel experience would have other implications on how urban Chinese see the world is examined in later chapters.

Similarly, the findings show that not many urban Chinese had extensive transnational social networks, although most did communicate with their friends and relatives overseas when they had such transnational social connections.

Individuals' connections with the outside world—no matter through personal travel experience or through transnational social connections—were distributed unevenly across society. Education, household income, and age were all significantly related to both travel experience and transnational social connections. Consistent with findings from other countries, people who occupy privileged positions within society are also better connected to the world at large.

Moreover, city contexts were also important in shaping the general outlook and degree of transnational experience that people had. The relevant findings in this chapter do not always fall neatly and clearly into the conventional dichotomy of coast vs. inland city. But Chengdu residents did consistently illustrate characteristics that mark them as relatively less "cosmopolitan," whereas residents in Shanghai, and to a lesser extent Beijing, tended to be better connected to the world at large.

Nonetheless, one finding that defies the portrayal of a rather parochial Chinese is our respondents' willingness to seek life or career development in other places. The multivariate analysis presented further shows that this attitudinal orientation of adventurism is spreading quite evenly across social classes and age groups. Therefore it is also likely that, as Chinese society continues to develop, as people become more capable of overcoming financial obstacles, and if regulatory and policy constraints loosen, the personal experiences and transnational connections that Chinese people have with the outside world are likely to increase substantially. This could already have happened in the few years since the survey was conducted and is likely to continue in the future.

3   Media Use

The role of the media in human societies can be broadly understood in three ways. First, media texts (e.g., books, newspapers, films, etc.) are records of various aspects of human lives. By studying these texts, we can gain knowledge about major social events and notable human accomplishments; media texts may also reflect the beliefs and values of individual authors and/or of a whole community. Second, the creation, diffusion, and adoption of media technologies are themselves important markers of the development of specific civilizations (cf. McLuhan, 1964; Rogers, 1995). They are important indicators of human societies' technological advancements, social and political changes, and cultural heritages. Third, both media texts and the related technologies can influence a society and its people. Such "media effects" may be microscopic and direct. For example, exposure to media content can lead to changes in individual users' beliefs, emotions, and behavior through various social and psychological processes (see Bryant and Oliver, 2008, for a comprehensive review). The influence of media can also be macroscopic and indirect. For instance, freedom of information expressed through mass communication is believed to be contributory and necessary to the social and economic development of a nation (Schramm, 1964); unequal access to media and information in a society can lead to social stratification and instability (Tichenor, Donohue, and Olien, 1970), and media exposure can help cultivate conventional cultural beliefs and consciousness (Gerbner et al., 2002).

Whether the focus is on the media texts, media technologies, or their psychological and social effects, knowledge about how people interact and use media should be a central concern. Without understanding who uses what media, how often and for what purposes, discussions about specific media texts, technologies, and/or effects would be idiosyncratic at best and meaningless at worst. Specifically related to this book, it is therefore essential to first discuss patterns of media usage among Chinese people in the context of globalization if the reader is to gain a contextualized understanding of the research questions addressed in later chapters.

The past few decades saw a period of historic changes and rapid developments in China's social, political, and economic systems. Such changes have led to dramatic shifts in Chinese people's media consumption, both in terms of contents and access. At the same time, the invention and diffusion of digital media and the Internet have significantly changed the ways in which people access media content. New media technologies have allowed richer information to be delivered faster to a wider population than ever before. To some extent, new technologies have provided an unprecedented ability and opportunity for a segment of the population to circumvent or bypass strict official censorship on traditional media. Together, the unique social changes that have taken place in China and the broad technological revolution in media and communication systems worldwide have combined to give researchers a great opportunity to explore and examine the role of the media in shaping Chinese people's beliefs and attitudes related to globalization.

At the heart of the intellectual discussion about globalization is the notion that a nation's power is reflected not only in its military and economic resources (i.e., its "hard power") but also in its dominance in values, culture, policies, and institutions (i.e., what American political scientist and foreign policy advisor Joseph Nye [1990] has called its "soft power"). Because popular culture and the mass media are regularly identified as important sources of soft power, it is no surprise that the internationalization and marketing of China's media industries—and the influence of foreign media on the nation's social, cultural, political, and economic systems—have been the subjects of many intellectual discussions (cf. Chan, 1994; Lee, 1980; Lin, 2004; Zhao, 2004). Although knowledge about these macrolevel issues is both important and necessary, a comprehensive view of the impact of globalization on China should also include analyses at the micro and individual levels, because changes in a social system are likely to be caused by both sociostructural forces and individual actions (Giddens, 1984). Specifically, in examining the social impact of globalization through media and cultural goods, Lukes (1974) cautioned against the "vehicle fallacy"—an erroneous assumption that one could use the resources that may produce behavior (e.g., the availability of media products) to measure the behavior itself (e.g., changes in values and beliefs as influenced by the cultural and media artifacts). To this extent, several studies in the literature of media and public opinion research have examined the impact of western media exposure on Chinese people's worldviews (Willnat, He, and Hao, 1997; Willnat et al., 2002) and cultural values (Wei and Pan, 1999; Zhang and Harwood, 2002).

Although a great deal of intellectual focus has been placed on media texts and effects related to globalization and its influence on China, few studies have closely examined individual Chinese people's media usage and interests, particularly in the context of globalization. This void has left many interesting questions unanswered. For example, how does the tension between domestic and foreign media at the structural and institutional levels (Zhao, 1998, 2000) affect the media consumption of individual Chinese people? What are Chinese people reading, watching, and/or listening to today? Through which channels? From what sources? How frequently are Chinese people exposed to nondomestic media and cultural products? Who are those Chinese who frequently come into contact with foreign media? How many of them are there? Are there regional differences? With these questions in mind, this chapter aims to provide a snapshot of urban Chinese people's media use habits and interests.

Here a note about terminology is needed. Throughout this chapter, we will use foreign media and nondomestic media interchangeably; in later chapters mainly the notion of foreign media will be used. Strictly speaking, however, there can be a distinction between the two—the key issue is the status of media products from Hong Kong and Taiwan. Mainland Chinese may not consider these media products "foreign," but the styles and contents of Hong Kong and Taiwan media are certainly very different from those of mainland Chinese media. In later analysis, we will include media from Hong Kong, Macau, and Taiwan in the nondomestic media index. But for simplicity, we will apply the label "foreign media consumption" to it.

This chapter places more emphasis on foreign than on domestic media consumption for two reasons. First, the use of foreign media can be seen as an important indicator of the tension between global media conglomerates' efforts to dominate a developing country's market and the growth of this country's own domestic media industry in the larger context of globalization (i.e., a measure of the influence of soft power). Second, despite the Chinese government's restrictions on nondomestic media companies to operate independently within China, foreign popular culture and entertainment media products are widely available to Chinese consumers through various legal as well as illegal channels. In a media market where pirated and/or unregulated products are widely available, official and conventional indicators of media usage (e.g., ratings, market share, and subscription rate) are highly inaccurate and unreliable. Therefore a separate and focused analysis of foreign media use by individual Chinese people is highly important.

The discussions and analyses in this chapter are organized in three sections. The first discusses the development of the media system in China after 1979 and paints an overall picture of the contemporary media scene. The second and main section draws upon the findings from our present survey to provide a detailed description of media usage and interests among urban Chinese. It also presents an analysis of the social and motivational factors that would contribute to the consumption of local, national, and foreign media products. The final section briefly examines the relationship between urban Chinese people's domestic and foreign media consumption and some of the value and attitudinal orientations examined in Chapter 2.

A LANDSCAPE OF CHINA'S MEDIA ECOSYSTEM

In the last 30 years, after nearly a century of political and social instability, the Chinese have experienced an unprecedented period of economic growth. Such prosperity, coupled with a population of over 1 billion people and a previously underdeveloped domestic media market, created an enormous demand for popular culture and media products. China's old media system, which primarily functioned as a mouthpiece and propaganda machine for the Chinese Communist Party (CCP), could no longer satisfy people's thirst for information and entertainment. Although the national state-run media outlets such as *Xinhua*, *CCTV*, and *People's Daily* continue to control a large share of China's media market, the provincial and local media industries—particularly in less politically sensitive areas such as sports, finance, and entertainment—experienced exponential growth and have become increasingly commercialized. For example, the number of television channels has grown from 12 in 1965 to now more than 700 broadcast channels and over 3,000 cable channels nationwide. CCTV, which operated 21 public channels and 19 pay channels as of early 2012, remains the most powerful television network in China[1]; but regional media giants such as Shanghai Media Group (SMG) and the Hunan Broadcasting System are quickly catching up.

In addition to the dramatic growth of the domestic media industry, foreign media companies also heavily influence the Chinese media market. In the early 1980s, China loosened its iron fist on cultural and media products by selectively importing popular culture products from non-communist countries. In 1983, *The Legendary Fok*, a 20-episode Hong Kong TV drama series about a patriotic Chinese martial artist, became China's first imported TV series from Hong Kong, then a colony under the control of the United Kingdom. At a time when less than 5 percent of the Chinese population owned television sets (Lee, 1994), *The Legendary Fok* started a feverish obsession nationwide. Many families, sometimes even entire neighborhoods, would gather in front of the only available television set within a few blocks to watch the show every week. Between 1980 and 1990, the percentage of imported programs shown on Chinese TV grew from 10 percent to 30 percent. In the same period, the number of imported programs increased by more than 800 percent, from 21 programs from 11 countries to 174 programs from 23 countries (Wang and Chang, 1996).

Into the 2000s, with the proliferation of new television channels, DVD players, and Internet-based video sharing services, imported programs continued to play the important role of filling up the airtime. In addition to the omnipresent music and entertainment programs from Hong Kong, Taiwan, and the United States, television entertainment in China also arguably came from a wider range of sources with the growing popularity of Korean and Japanese popular culture. In the print media market, foreign capitals also found ways to enter China through various joint ventures and partnerships

(To and Yep, 2008). For instance, Feng and Frith (2008) found the women's magazine market in China to be heavily infiltrated by western and Japanese media conglomerates through licensing agreements and advertising revenues. Six out of the top ten magazines with the highest advertising revenues in China are international women's magazines.

The proliferation of nondomestic cultural and media products in China did not occur without resistance. For the Chinese government, the task of modernizing and marketing China's media system is an intricate balancing act. On the one hand, the government needs foreign media products to help ease the monstrous demand from its domestic market; it would also have to rely on the financial resources, domain expertise, and technological innovations of foreign media companies to develop and nurture the previously anemic domestic industry. On the other hand, the government would like to maintain tight control over its media industries and market for cultural, political, and economic concerns. Culturally, there is a fear of cultural imperialism—the idea that the one-way flow of western media products would bring in undesirable foreign values and erode indigenous cultures (Boyd-Barrett, 1977; Lee, 1980; Schiller, 1976, 1989, 1991; Tunstall, 1977). Politically, the state-owned mass media in China have historically been served as a mouthpiece for the Communist Party's agenda and policies. Although, in a market-oriented economy, this function of the mass media has become less obvious in recent years, the Chinese government is still concerned about losing its grip on citizens' ideological "purity" and the role of western media in fostering democratic movements (Zhao, 1998, 2000, 2003). Economically, the government wants to protect the interest and profitability of China's domestic companies against the much more powerful and well-developed global media conglomerates.

Prior to China's ascendency to the World Trade Organization (WTO), there was tremendous concern that multinational media conglomerates would come in to gobble up China's domestic media outlets or to terminate the latter's monopolistic advantages; thus domestic media outlets were organized by official decree into ever-larger "media groups," presumably to meet potential foreign competition (Lee, 2004). After joining the WTO in 2001, China was able to protect its media groups from foreign threat because the WTO, under French pressure, excluded cultural fare from its "open market access" rules. As a result, multinational media conglomerates have made very limited inroads directly into the Chinese market, especially in terms of owning news production companies. The influence of foreign media companies was largely limited to injections of capital, joint ventures, partnerships, and special licensing. For example, the Chinese government granted limited TV broadcasting rights to Viacom, News Corp, and AOL Time Warner in the Guangdong Province and the Pearl River Delta Economic Zone in southern China. Viacom started a joint-venture TV deal to produce children's programming in Mandarin with Shanghai Media Group (SMG), and Warner Brothers started the first foreign joint venture to produce films in China in 2004. Direct access to foreign TV channels, such as HBO and CNN, is permitted only in hotels and apartment compounds where foreigners live. Meanwhile, China's domestic media groups, despite their cultural rhetoric to the contrary, have concentrated their efforts on maximizing profits without offending the authorities (Lee, He, and Huang, 2006, 2007).

Furthermore, although the Chinese government permits foreign investment in local media companies, foreigners are allowed to invest in only one authorized business entity, with total foreign investment not exceeding 49 percent under the regulation of China's General Administration of Press and Publication. The government also closely monitors and censors foreign media content. All imported media products are subject to a strict censorship process. The Chinese government routinely suspends foreign media when sensitive political issues arise. The Chinese government also conducts strict censorship on the Internet. More than 60 Internet regulations have been enacted, and censorship technologies are vigorously implemented by state-owned Internet Service Providers (ISPs), business companies, and organizations (OpenNet, 2005). Some of the most popular websites in the world, such as Youtube.com and Facebook.com, are blocked in China. Google, the world's largest Internet search engine in terms of market share, was forced out of the Chinese market in 2010 because of the company's unwillingness to comply with China's strict Internet censorship. Users of Wikipedia maintain a comprehensive list of banned foreign websites in China. Ironically, the popular online encyclopedia itself was among the victims of government censorship. In the broadcasting scene, the State Administration of Radio, Film and Television (SARFT), the government department in charge of regulating the broadcast media in China, may also put forward specific measures from time to time limiting the use of imported programs by Chinese television stations. One of the most recent measures was put forward in February 2012, as SARFT banned all imported programs during prime time. The new rules also asked all stations to limit imported programs to no more than a quarter of each day's programming.[2]

However, as mentioned earlier, the Chinese government also has to make strategic concessions from time to time to allow more foreign media to enter China. For example, just a few days after SARFT implemented the new regulations restricting broadcasting of foreign imported programs on Chinese television, China agreed to open its movie market to U.S. movies by permitting 14 premium formal films to be exempt from the existing import quota of 20 films per year. This move effectively enlarged the import quota from 20 to 34.[3] Of course where the presence of U.S. movies in China is concerned, it must be noted that the import quota may mean nothing to technologically savvy (or actually not-so-savvy) urban Chinese, since pirated versions of U.S. movies are now widely available online, a point we will soon return to below.

The complex interdependency and tension between the foreign and domestic media creates a blurry picture of China's media system. On the one hand, the influence of foreign cultural and media products is heavily regulated and controlled through macro and structural means by the Chinese government, what Norris and Inglehart (2009) called societal-level "firewalls." On the other hand, however, many foreign media products can still be accessed by average Chinese through informal and/or illegal means. As such, traditional market research tools such as rating share, subscription rate, and sales statistics are highly inaccurate. Moreover, although it is relatively useful to find macrolevel proxies, such as the aggregated data on media ownership and revenue, it might be problematic for foreign media to use these indicators of media use at the individual level.

Furthermore, media internationalization is a "diffusion process" (Rogers, 2003) by which all aspects (e.g., ownership, structure, production, distribution, and content) of a country's media market is infused by foreign media interests (Chan, 1994). The role and influence of foreign media in China's domestic market as a whole are often invisible to the average person. Foreign media companies might produce many seemingly local media products, while local media producers may create programs with a "foreign" flavor. It is therefore difficult to disentangle and differentiate the localized foreign media products from those globalized local media products. Although such distinctions may be important to media economists, they are not critical in examining the media consumption of ordinary users and the societal and cultural impact of globalization.

Finally, at the same time when foreign media are trying to penetrate the Chinese market, the mainland Chinese are also actively and aggressively pursuing a global interest. In 2010, the Chinese government invested more than 45 billion RMB (over $9 billion) to form the China Xinhua News Network Corporation with plans to distribute Chinese news programs worldwide. In 2011, the Alibaba Group, a Chinese investment company that specializes in Internet-based services, started aggressively pursuing a takeover of Yahoo!, its former U.S.-based investor. As such global influence from China becomes more and more visible, it becomes even harder to discuss the effects of globalization and foreign media at the individual level.

Let us use television, the most widely used media outlet, to further illustrate the point. Legally imported programs are widely available to Chinese viewers on their local TV channels. These programs are most often screened, censored, and dubbed by domestic production companies and broadcasters. They can be widely viewed by average Chinese regardless of their income, education, or foreign language proficiency. In addition to these "koshered" foreign media products, some people can also directly view a number of preselected foreign television channels if they stay in high-end hotels or if they live in luxury residential compounds that cater to foreign residents. Other than these government-approved means of viewing nondomestic TV programs, many Chinese also have access to foreign channels that are not technically permitted to air within the country. For instance, millions of Chinese families have installed satellite dishes with direct access to hundreds of TV channels worldwide even though the government does not permit Chinese citizens to have satellite dishes and receivers at their homes. This is because the restriction on satellite dishes is difficult for local authorities to enforce when it applies only to Chinese citizens but not foreigners living in China or the returning overseas Chinese. Moreover, many "illegal" satellite dishes are manufactured by subsidiary companies operated by the Chinese government, such as the Ministry of Electronics, the Chinese Army, and the Ministry of Radio, Film and Television. Banning these dishes would mean a loss of revenue for these state-run businesses (Severin, 1994). As such, use of satellite dish is "illegal" only in the most superficial sense, yet no one would want to lift the thin veil to reveal the real picture. Finally, despite the introduction of copyright laws, media piracy is so common in China that pirated foreign TV programs and movies are for sale at nearly every streetcorner.

To make things even more complicated, as already mentioned in discussing movie imports, the widespread access to broadband Internet and online video sharing would allow computer users to download, view, and circulate foreign TV shows through new technologies such as file-sharing software and Internet Protocol Television. Although no reliable statistics are available, most observers would agree that pirated foreign movies and TV shows are now a part of many Chinese people's regular media diet. An anecdote would support this view. In 2008, Wentworth Miller, the star of the American hit TV show *Prison Break*, was one of the most popular celebrities in China, with millions of fans. Thousands of fan groups, forums, and discussion groups about Miller, and the TV series could readily be found in the Chinese web sphere. Miller was received by hundreds of screaming fans at the airport when he visited China that year. Interestingly, however, *Prison Break* was never officially aired in China; the only way an average Chinese citizen could have viewed this show within China would have been through pirated DVDs or Internet file sharing.

As discussed earlier, an understanding of globalization's impact in China through cultural and media products must consider both structural as well as individual-level effects. Such effects must be contextualized by Chinese people's interests and habits of media use, particularly as related to the use of foreign culture and media products. Individuals' media consumption not only reflects the general development of a country's media market but can also be seen as an important indicator of the social changes taking place in a country as a result of globalization. However, as the case of television viewing in China clearly illustrates, China's media system is complex and irregular. In the absence of reliable means and official statistics to accurately track domestic and foreign media use, it is difficult to gauge the true impact of globalization on Chinese society and its people. Given this background, the following analysis can be seen as an attempt to fill this void in current research.

MEDIA USE IN FOUR CHINESE CITIES

Domestic Media Use

Our survey included a battery of 42 items asking the respondents to self-report the number of times they had consumed six forms of media from seven geographical regions in the week prior to the survey interview. The six forms of media were newspapers and magazines, books, radio programs, television programs, movies, and websites. The seven regions were local; national; Hong Kong, Macau, and Taiwan; Japan and Korea; the United States and Canada; western Europe; and the Middle East.

Our findings show that television is still by far the most frequently consumed media platform by the urban Chinese. In our study, nearly everyone (98.7 percent) had watched TV in the week prior to the survey. Not surprisingly, almost everyone watched both national and local TV programs across all four cities. In terms of frequency, the respondents watched programs on their local television channels 7.22 times in the week prior to the survey interview—that is, more than once per day. This is somewhat higher than viewing of national television (6.48 times in a week). Interestingly, however, residents of Shanghai and Chengdu watched local TV programs more frequently than national TV programs, whereas residents of Beijing and Xi'an watched more national TV programs. Particularly, as Table 3.1 shows, the respondents in Shanghai watched local TV programs 8.66 times in a week, which was significantly more often than residents in other cities (the mean frequencies are 6.28, 7.55, and 6.38 times for Beijing, Chengdu, and Xi'an residents respectively. The differences among the mean scores are statistically significant in a one-way ANOVA analysis, $F = 49.80$, $P < .001$).

Data from our survey also show that 83.2 percent of the respondents reported reading a newspaper and/or magazine at least once in the previous week. In terms of frequencies, when all respondents were counted, they read a local newspaper or magazine on average of 4.84 times in the week prior to the interview. In contrast, our respondents read national newspapers and magazines only, on average, 1.58 times in a week. Compared across cities, national and local newspaper reading was more frequent among the two coastal metropolises. Beijing residents read a local newspaper or magazine 5.04 times in a week, whereas Shanghai residents read a local newspaper or magazine 5.41 times in a week. The figures are only 4.45 and 4.47 for Chengdu and Xi'an respectively. The same pattern applies to national newspapers and magazines. The mean numbers for reading a national newspaper or magazine in a week are 1.84 and 2.12 times for Beijing and Shanghai, whereas the figures are only 1.18 and 1.19 for Chengdu and Xi'an. For both local and national newspaper/magazine reading, the between-cities differences are statistically significant in a one-way ANOVA analysis ($F = 10.90$ and 18.60 respectively, $P < .001$ in both cases).

Table 3.1 Summary of Domestic Media Consumption (Times Per Week)

	Beijing	Shanghai	Chengdu	Xi'an	Overall
Local					
Newspaper	5.04	5.41	4.45	4.47	4.84
Book	0.64	1.37	0.50	0.53	0.76
Radio	2.09	2.84	1.14	2.08	2.04
Movies	0.45	0.13	0.12	0.34	0.26
TV	6.28	8.66	7.55	6.38	7.22
Web	1.40	2.62	1.03	1.13	1.54
Total	15.91	21.03	14.79	14.93	16.66
National					
Newspaper	1.84	2.12	1.18	1.19	1.58
Book	0.71	0.81	0.47	0.57	0.64
Radio	1.65	1.42	0.69	0.85	1.15
Movies	0.42	0.19	0.24	1.00	0.44
TV	6.52	6.62	5.97	6.82	6.48
Web	1.92	2.94	1.24	1.72	1.96
Total	13.08	14.01	9.79	12.15	12.26

Note: Entries are mean scores representing the number of times a respondent has consumed a specific of medium in the week prior to the interview. Between-cities differences in the mean scores are statistically significant at $P < .001$ in one-way ANOVA analysis in all cases.

As compared with newspaper reading, only about 30 percent ($n = 597$) of our respondents had read a book in the week before our survey. Again, a difference between the coastal cities and inland cities was found when frequencies of book reading are concerned, with Shanghai residents reading books most frequently, followed by Beijing residents and then residents of the two inland cities.

Web usage and radio consumption follows a similar pattern of between-cities differences, with residents in Shanghai and Beijing consuming these media more frequently than people in Chengdu and Xi'an. Movies, however, constitute an exception. Surprisingly, the frequency of movie watching was relatively low among the Shanghai respondents, probably because of the availability of other leisure alternatives. In contrast, Xi'an respondents reported the highest frequencies of watching "national movies"[4] in the week prior to the interview.

Without overinterpreting the descriptive statistics, some interesting patterns emerged from these findings as a whole. First, there is a clear difference between coastal cities and the inland cities in terms of media use. With the exception of movie watching, people in Beijing and Shanghai used almost all forms of media more frequently than their counterparts in the two inland cities; most of them watched TV almost every day; more than half of the people in these two cities read newspapers on a weekly basis;

many of them frequently read books and used the Internet. In contrast, fewer residents in the inland cities read newspapers or listened to the radio. They also used the Internet less frequently.

Second, our data also point to a strong region-centrism in Shanghai. As the economic center of China, Shanghai has a strong local media industry. Even though people in Shanghai used media as often as did those in Beijing, they were much more interested in local issues across all media types. As Table 3.1 shows, on adding all types of local media consumption together, the difference between Shanghai and Beijing residents in their overall level of local media consumption is quite substantial. In fact, the mean frequency of local media consumption in Beijing is close to the mean frequencies of local media consumption in Chengdu and Xi'an. In contrast, when all types of national media consumption were added together, the difference between the mean scores of the two cities is relatively small, although Shanghai residents also exhibited a higher level of national media consumption as compared with Beijing residents.

To further explore the patterns of domestic media consumption, the influence of various social and demographic factors on media usage were considered. Specifically, we examined the influence of gender, age, household income, education, occupation, English proficiency, and city contexts on both local and national media consumption. Regression analyses were conducted with the total local and national media consumption as the dependent variables. In multivariate analysis, the local media consumption index and the national media consumption index were both square-rooted to reduce the skewedness of the variables. It should be noted here that these two indices were also used in subsequent analyses and chapters in analyzing the relationship between media consumption and various social and political attitudes and beliefs.

Table 3.2 Predictors of Local and National Media Consumption

	Local Media	National Media
Gender	-.07**	-.09***
Age	.14***	.08**
Education	.18***	.26***
Household income	.03	.09***
English ability	.10**	.08***
Work in state enterprise	.01	-.00
Work in foreign companies	-.04	-.02
Shanghai	.23***	.01
Chengdu	-.02	-.14***
Xi'an	-.06*	-.02
Adjusted R^2	13.0%***	6.1%***

Note: Entries are standardized regression coefficients. * $P < .05$; ** $P < .01$; *** $P < .001$.

As Table 3.2 shows, the demographic predictors of local and national media consumption are quite similar to each other. Where local media are concerned, males, older people, more educated people, and people with higher levels of English proficiency were more likely to have consumed local media more frequently. Similarly, males, better-educated people, people with better English ability, and older people were also more likely to have consumed national media more frequently. Besides, household income also had a separate and positive relationship with national media consumption.

Regarding the between-cities differences, as already noted in Table 3.1, Shanghai residents tended to exhibit higher levels of local media consumption than Beijing residents, while Xi'an residents exhibited significantly lower levels of local media consumption than Beijing residents. For national media consumption, Table 3.2 shows that there is no significant difference between Shanghai and Beijing residents when other variables are controlled, nor is there a significant difference between Beijing and Xi'an residents. Chengdu residents, however, constituted a group of people who consumed national media particularly less frequently.

Use of Nondomestic (Foreign) Media

More than half of our respondents (61.2 percent) reported that they had used nondomestic media at least once in the week prior to the survey. When all forms of nondomestic media from all regions were added together, our respondents accessed nondomestic media almost 4.15 times during that week on average. However, the disparity of nondomestic use in terms of frequency was very high (SD = 5.62). If we further combine foreign media use, national media use and local media use to form an index of total media use and then calculate the proportion of foreign media use out of total media use for each individual, we will find that the average proportion is 0.1124 for our respondents. That is, 11.24 percent of people's overall media consumption was constituted by consumption of nondomestic media. This figure is by no means insignificant considering that people everywhere in the world would tend to use their domestic media much more frequently.

The numbers reported thus far do not tell the whole story, though. In comparing different types of media, we found that the respondents consumed foreign television programs most frequently. On average, the respondents watched foreign television programs 2.9 times in the week prior to the interview. By comparison, they used other types of media less than 0.60 times per week. This points to the vital importance of considering the illegal or semi-legal access to foreign TV programs discussed earlier in this chapter. The reach of foreign TV programs in China may be far beyond what the official statistics of licensed and/or important programs would suggest.

In looking at nondomestic media use in terms of geographic regions, we found that urban Chinese consumed media products from Hong Kong, Macau, and Taiwan relatively more frequently. An urban Chinese had, on average, consumed such media products 2.04 times in the week prior to the interview. These are followed by Japanese and Korean media products, then by media products from United States and Canada. These findings are not surprising. Media products from Hong Kong, Macau, and Taiwan are accessible as well as culturally and linguistically familiar. At the same time, even though language might constitute a significant barrier, media products from Japan and Korea might also be preferred by Chinese consumers because of cultural and geographic proximity. Of course, it is also worth noting that the survey was conducted at a time when the "Korean Wave" (Kim, 2007) in East Asia was arguably near its peak.

The implications of our findings for the "soft power" of American media are therefore mixed. On the one hand, Chinese people did consume U.S. media regularly, but the reach of these media could not match that of the regional media. This is in line with research indicating that the global media system cannot be simply bifurcated into a western/American center and a global periphery. Instead, the continual prominence of American media is often intertwined with regional dynamics of media flow, constituting a more complicated picture of people's foreign media consumption (Thussu, 2007).

As Table 3.3 shows, significant cross-city differences were found. When all nondomestic media consumption was added up, residents in Shanghai exhibited the lowest level of foreign media consumption. An average Shanghai resident consumed foreign media only 2.12 times in a week. Beijing residents also consumed foreign media relatively less frequently. In contrast,

Table 3.3   Summary of Non-Domestic Media Consumption

	Beijing	Shanghai	Chengdu	Xi'an	Overall
By type					
Newspaper	0.05	0.16	0.35	0.18	0.18
Book	0.19	0.06	0.09	0.14	0.12
Radio	0.03	0.03	0.15	0.05	0.06
Movies	0.47	0.09	0.29	1.33	0.55
TV	2.16	1.34	3.93	4.17	2.90
Web	0.16	0.43	0.40	0.36	0.34
By region					
HK/Taiwan	1.05	1.28	2.42	3.38	2.04
Japan/Korea	0.84	0.47	1.71	1.51	1.13
US/Canada	0.60	0.24	0.69	0.94	0.62
Europe	0.41	0.10	0.25	0.29	0.26
Middle East	0.15	0.03	0.13	0.12	0.10
Total	3.05	2.12	5.21	6.23	4.15

Note: Entries are mean scores representing the number of times a respondent has consumed a specific type of medium in the week prior to the interview. Between-cities differences in the mean scores are statistically significant at $P < .001$ in one-way ANOVA analysis in all cases.

Chengdu and Xi'an residents consumed foreign media 5.21 and 6.23 times a week respectively. The between-cities differences are highly statistically significant in a one-way ANOVA analysis ($F = 62.15$, $P < .001$).

At first glance, these findings may appear to be somewhat counterintuitive, because one would expect that coastal metropolises such as Shanghai and Beijing would be deeply penetrated by foreign culture and media products. However, the data can be interpreted from a different perspective, which might help to explain the seemingly counterintuitive finding.

First, there may be an accessibility issue. Because they are the two most important political and cultural centers of China, Beijing and Shanghai are subject to much tighter government regulation and control. Millions of people leave or enter the country through these cities every year, and a large community of foreign expatriates resides there. The Chinese government devotes much of its resources to controlling the flow of undesirable foreign influence in these two cities. Therefore illegal access to foreign media, such as the use of unauthorized satellite dishes, may be less pervasive.

Second, the counterintuitive finding of low nondomestic media exposure in "more globalized" cities may be due to the strong presence of local media industries. To counter foreign influence in China's domestic media industries, China is trying to create its own media conglomerates. In 2001, Shanghai Media and Entertainment Group (SMEG) was formed, becoming the largest media conglomerate in China. It is one of the biggest media content and cultural product providers in China. Its main subsidiary, Shanghai Media Group (SMG), operates 11 analogue TV channels, 90 digital paid cable TV channels, a full broadcasting Internet TV service, and with 10 analogue and 19 digital radio services. The group also operates and owns 5 sports centers and 14 cultural art centers. According to a survey of AC Nielsen in 2003, 11 of the group's TV channels achieved a market share of 76 percent during prime time. These numbers may help explain the curiously low frequency of foreign media use in Shanghai, one of the world's largest cities.

These statistics clearly show that a portion of Chinese society frequently accesses media content from nondomestic sources in spite of government control. These findings further illustrate the danger of using structural-level indicators to measure individual-level effects. Whereas most media scholars would agree that the media markets in Shanghai and Beijing are much more internationalized when they are measured by macrolevel indicators such as number of joint ventures and licensing agreements, amount of foreign investment, and/or import/export statistics, our data clearly show that the individual-level effects of foreign media can be less straightforward and even contradictory.

Predicting Nondomestic Media Use

What predicts urban Chinese residents' consumption of foreign media? As in the case of domestic media consumption, a multiple regression analysis was conducted. The dependent variable was total foreign media consumption. The index was square-rooted to reduce its skewedness. The independent variables include the factors used in Table 3.2 for explaining domestic media consumption. In addition, since foreign media consumption is concerned here, we also include people's foreign travel experience, transnational social connections, interests in foreign affairs, and adventurism into the model (the operationalization of these variables was discussed in Chapter 2).

The first column of Table 3.4 summarizes the results. What is notable is that the city dummy variables seem to be the strongest predictors of urban Chinese residents' foreign media consumption. As Table 3.3 has already shown, residents in the two inland cities actually consumed moe foreign media products than did the residents of Beijing, whereas Shanghai residents consumed even fewer foreign media products than did Beijing residents. These findings suggest that, by knowing where people live in China, we can relatively accurately predict how often they are likely to use non-domestic media and cultural products. This was the case at least when the survey was conducted.

Predictably, younger people, better-educated people, and people with better English ability also tended to consume more foreign media. There is simultaneously a weak but significant relationship between gender and foreign media consumption, with females consuming foreign media slightly more frequently. In addition, foreign media consumption is positively related to interest in foreign affairs. More importantly, even after controlling for all other factors, a significant relationship still exists between foreign media consumption and transnational social connections. Urban Chinese who had relatives and friends abroad and regularly communicated with them were more likely to have consumed more foreign media. However, there is no relationship between foreign travel experiences and foreign media consumption. There is also no significant relationship between adventurism and foreign media consumption. People who have traveled abroad and those who wished to go abroad to seek development were not more avid consumers of foreign media. These latter findings suggest that the consumption of foreign media can be simply a means for urban Chinese people to entertain themselves. The "foreignness" of the foreign media consumed may be meaningful in terms of signifying certain qualities of the media products, yet it may not be associated with an interest in knowing more about the outside world.

In comparing the findings in Tables 3.2 and 3.4, however, we can see there are several shared predictors as concerns domestic and nondomestic media consumption. More educated people, for example, are understandably more likely to consume media of all kinds owing to their presumably higher levels of both economic and cultural capital. To examine the "uniqueness" of the predictors of foreign media consumption, we conducted an additional analysis by using the ratio of foreign media consumption to total media consumption (i.e., foreign plus domestic) as the dependent

Table 3.4 Regression on Non-Domestic Media Consumption

	Foreign Media	Foreign Media / Total Media
Gender	.04*	.07**
Age	-.08**	-.10***
Education	.08**	.03
Household income	.04	.02
English ability	.08**	.05
Work in state enterprise	.02	.02
Work in foreign companies	-.00	.01
Shanghai	-.13***	-.16***
Chengdu	.23***	.22***
Xi'an	.29***	.28***
Foreign traveling experience	.03	.02
Transnational social connections	.06**	.05*
Interests in foreign affairs	.13***	.09***
Adventurism	.04	.02
Adjusted R^2	18.9%***	18.1%***

Note: Entries are standardized regression coefficients. * $P < .05$; ** $P < .01$; *** $P < .001$.

variable. The second column of Table 3.4 illustrates the results, which show that education and English ability are no longer significantly related to the dependent variable. In other words, the influence of English ability and education on foreign media consumption merely represents their influence on media consumption in general.

Nevertheless, all other factors that significantly predict foreign media consumption in the first column remain significant predictors in the second analysis. In other words, younger people not only consumed foreign media more frequently but foreign media consumption also constituted a higher proportion of their total media diet. By the same token, in terms of their total media consumption, females, residents in Chengdu, residents in Xi'an, people who were interested in foreign affairs, and people who had more transnational social connections were all seen to consume a larger proportion of foreign media media products.

Taken together, the results of our analysis point to two different types of nondomestic media users in urban China. The first are the Chinese media consumers who frequently use both domestic and nondomestic media products. Highly educated adults are particularly likely to belong to this type. To these users, media use, both domestic and nondomestic, may be highly functional; that is, they acquire useful information from these media outlets to facilitate professional and leisure activities.

Unlike the first type of media consumer, the second type do not often use domestic media; nondomestic media products are more dominant in their total media consumption. As compared with the first type of user, the second type is younger. These more frequent users may not have extensive overseas traveling experience but nevertheless have some friends or family in foreign countries. They are also more interested in foreign affairs in general. To these users, the use of nondomestic media may reflect an active imagination about the world outside of China and/or a sense of dissatisfaction with media products produced domestically.

MEDIA CONSUMPTION AND VALUE ORIENTATION

In the conceptual framework presented in Chapter 1, we posited that media consumption and personal experiential connections with the outside world may influence people's value orientations. In Chapter 2, we examined the value orientations of urban Chinese in terms of their rating of both traditional values such as harmony and stability and liberal values such as democracy and freedom. We have shown that demographic factors have limited relationships with value orientations. Here, it would be relevant to examine whether and how media consumption and personal experiences with the world at large relate to such value orientations.

As discussed earlier in this chapter, the influence of foreign media on an audience's attitudes and values has long been an important concern among scholars in the field of international communication. In the 1970s, concerns with foreign media influence were often articulated with the theoretical perspective of cultural or media imperialism. To put it briefly, some early accounts of cultural imperialism hold that the transnational flow of media products is highly unbalanced. Audiences in developing countries consume many imported media products from the developed West (especially the United States). The unidirectional character of transnational media flow is a cause of worry for the developing countries, not only because the dominance of foreign media imports may hamper the development of the local media industries but also because foreign media can present a cultural challenge. Media products are not just economic goods; they are also containers of cultural values and ideas. They portray alternative models of behavior and social interaction, and they provide images of different lifestyles to which people can aspire. Repeated consumption of western media products may lead audiences in the developing countries to acquire the embedded ideas and values and/or adopt the portrayed lifestyles and behavioral models.

The description of the types of media effects presented above may admittedly represent a rather simplified account of cultural imperialism, or "westernization effects." It is conceptualized to be a form of direct impact of foreign media consumption. The more people consume western media, more likely they are to become westernized in their values, beliefs, and behavior. Over the years, however, empirical survey evidence supporting such straightforward westernization effects has been mixed at best. It is important to note that, safe in the settings of laboratory experiments, the imputation of direct cause and effect is hard to find in media studies elsewhere. It is very difficult to achieve conceptual exactitude and measurement robustness in survey research for as complex an issue as "cultural imperialism," thus necessitating other types of evidence (such as historical study or anthropological observations). We present the analysis of our survey data with this caveat in mind.

In the Chinese context, Willnat and colleagues (1997) found that people in Shenzhen who had higher levels of total western media consumption indeed had more positive views and feelings about Americans. But when total western media consumption was broken down into the consumption of different media types, more mixed findings were discovered. Positive images and feelings were apparently promulgated only by the consumption of western newspapers, radio, and cinema, whereas the consumption of western television actually led to more negative attitudes and feelings toward Americans. Similarly, Zhang and Harwood (2002) found that, among a sample of college students, total viewing of imported programs, imported movies, and imported sports programs was related negatively to perceived importance of the traditional Chinese value of interpersonal harmony. These findings apparently support the argument that foreign media consumption may undermine traditional cultural values. Yet the study actually also showed that perceived importance of interpersonal harmony was negatively related to viewing of Chinese children's programs and Chinese music performance.

Theoretically, there are a number of major reasons why there seems to be no strong and straightforward "westernization effects" of foreign media consumption. In Chapter 1, we discussed Norris and Inglehart's (2009) argument about the presence of "firewalls" insulating people from the influence of "cosmopolitan communications." To elaborate further, at least three points can be raised. First, national governments often adopt various kinds of gatekeeping policies aiming at curbing the reception and thus influence of foreign media in their countries. These policies may include screen quotas for foreign movies and television programs, restrictions of foreign ownership of media operations, licensing requirements for satellite broadcasts, laws against private ownership of satellite dishes, and so on. Second, media economists have long argued that a media product is likely to suffer from a discount in value when it travels from one culture to another because a foreign audience may not have the background knowledge and cultural cues to fully appreciate the product (Hoskins and Mirus, 1988). The implication of this argument is that a local audience is likely to prefer media materials that are culturally more proximate to them if the other qualities of the media materials are more or less the same. In response, transnational media corporations, on entering different markets, often attempt to localize their products. That is, it is held that the phenomenon of media localization should reduce the extent to which "western values, ideas, and behavioral models" are present in the contents of imported western media.

Third, no matter what "the dominant readings" of the imported foreign media are, local audiences may interpret the meanings of the media products according to existing cultural schema. Since the 1970s, the audience's ability to generate negotiated or even oppositional readings of media texts was widely demonstrated in a range of "reception analyses" inspired by British cultural studies. Some of the classic analyses have dealt explicitly with audience's reception of foreign media (e.g., Liebes and Katz, 1988). The image of the audience as cultural dopes was challenged and replaced by an image of the audience as creators and appropriators of meanings. Therefore, as Chanda and Kavoori (2000) have argued, "while transnational media organizations constitute an undeniable and often aggressive presence in the [Asian] region, their domination is restricted by the interplay of national gate-keeping policies, the dynamics of audience preference as well as the forces of local competition" (pp. 442–443).

Related to these arguments, we can employ our data and analyze whether the consumption of local, national, and foreign media would relate significantly to people's rating of the two types of society-oriented values discussed in Chapter 2 (i.e., traditional values and liberal values). If we follow the conventional logic of "cultural imperialism," we might expect foreign media consumption to relate negatively to the rating of traditional values and positively to liberal values. Multiple regression analysis was conducted to test these relationships. The regression model included the demographic factors included in Table 2.5 in the previous chapter plus city dummies, media consumption indices, foreign travel experience, and transnational social connections.

Table 3.5   Relationship between Media Consumption and Value Orientations

	Traditional Values	Liberal Values
Shanghai	.18***	.13***
Chengdu	.21***	.18***
Xi'an	.17***	.13***
Foreign travel experience	.00	.03
Transnational social connections	.07**	.06**
Local media consumption	-.00	-.07*
National media consumption	.01	.05
Foreign media consumption	-.00	.04
Adjusted R²	4.6%***	3.0%***

Notes: Entries are standardized regression coefficients. The full model includes the above variables as well as seven other demographic factors: age, gender, education, household income, English ability, working for state enterprises, and working for foreign companies or joint ventures. The regression coefficients and the adjusted R² values refer to those in the full model. * $P < .05$; ** $P < .01$; *** $P < .001$.

As Table 3.5 shows, the findings are consistent with the critiques of the idea of simplistic "media effects." Foreign media consumption does not relate significantly to either value orientation. And in fact national and local media consumptions also have limited relationships with the dependent variable. The only significant relationship is a negative one between local media consumption and liberal value orientation. Interestingly, transnational social connection is related significantly and positively to both rating of traditional values and rating of liberal values. In other words, although significant relationships exist, there is also no simple and straightforward relationship between transnational social communications at the interpersonal level and the adoption of a more "westernized" value orientation.

SUMMARY AND DISCUSSION

There is no doubt that China's media landscape is changing rapidly. Both domestic and external forces have contributed to a dramatic growth in the past 30 years. On the one hand, the domestic media industries have expanded exponentially since the beginning of China's economic reform in 1979. More content and more channels are available to an average Chinese media user than ever before. An average Chinese can access a diversity of domestic media content from hundreds of TV channels, dozens of newspapers and magazines, and the Internet. Although the central government maintains tight control over ideologically and politically sensitive content in the media, other domains—such as sports, finance, leisure, and entertainment—face little regulation from the government. Regional and local media companies have also grown bigger and stronger in order to compete with the national media outlets. Parallel to such a growth of the domestic market, the influence of nondomestic media is also self-evident. Largely motivated by economic factors, scores of joint ventures and collaborations have been established between Chinese domestic media producers and global media conglomerates at the national and local levels. In addition, pirated and illegally accessed foreign media products have widely penetrated the Chinese market.

Against this backdrop, this chapter has examined individual people's media consumption in China's globalizing cities. Our analyses show that most Chinese people used domestic media for information and entertainment purposes. Education and cultural capital such as English proficiency are significant predictors of both domestic and nondomestic media consumption. The various age groups, however, are differentiated from each other more clearly in terms of their relative preference for domestic vs. foreign media.

Transnational social connections do relate to foreign media consumption, although foreign traveling experience does not. But the most interesting finding in this chapter is that people living in the two coastal metropolises, as compared with people living in the two inland cities, were actually less likely to have directly consumed foreign media. It shows that the dynamics driving people's foreign media consumption at the microlevel can be complicated and paradoxical. People living in "global cities" may in the end consume local media the most because of the strength of the local media organizations in such cities.

Finally, this chapter provides an analysis of the relationship between media consumption and two society-oriented values. The results show that expectations about the direct and straightforward impact of media consumption on value orientations can be misguided. Firewalls established at the societal and individual levels can successfully neutralize possible media effects.

However, despite the apparent lack of "media effects" shown in this chapter, two qualifications are needed. First, because it is difficult to tackle the issue of media effects empirically, we must admit to not to having enough evidence to dismiss the "cultural imperialism" theme. Looking back over the past several decades, we can appreciate the unequivocal trend in which the cultural tastes, values, and consumption patterns of urban Chinese have, in many ways, been moving rapidly closer to what can be seen as the western-cum-capitalist way of life. The popularity of McDonald's, Starbucks, fashion stores, and expensive cars is a far cry from the antimaterialism of the bad old days. It would be hard to believe that media do not play a role as carriers of such values, but media effects may be embedded as part and parcel of the process of capitalist transformation. Furthermore, the transfer of foreign norms and consumption values may proceed through domestic media, not necessarily through public exposure to foreign media directly. The fact that the *Global Times*, a prominent and popular subsidiary of the *People's Daily*, proudly boasts of having the Fortune 500 companies as its main advertisers (Lee, 2010)—an indicator of success and prestige—should be a case for reflection.

Second, this chapter's results should not be taken to mean that media effects on any values and attitudes do not exist. As the remaining chapters will illustrate, various relationships between media consumption (or personal experience) and people's attitudes and beliefs may indeed exist, especially when the attitudinal variables are better explicated and measured in a more differentiated manner. Hence the next chapter will continue to tackle the relationships between communications and people's value orientations—more specifically the highly important value orientation of nationalism..

4 Nationalism and Affect toward Foreign Countries

As a product of the rise of modern states (Gellner, 1981), nationalism can be defined as the consciousness and sentiment regarding one's relation to the nation. This chapter intends to explore three major issues related to nationalism in the Chinese context. First, we seek to gauge the intensity of nationalistic sentiments in four different mainland Chinese cities. Among the many types of nationalistic sentiments, this chapter pays special attention to one's affective evaluation of the shared Chinese cultural legacy (i.e., cultural nationalism) and one's psychological commitment to having a thriving and strong nation (i.e., developmental nationalism). The former hinges upon one's ties to the past, whereas the latter speaks to the country's future.

Second, mass media and popular culture are considered powerful forces to be reckoned with in creating and sustaining nationalistic sentiments (Billig, 1995; Hajkowski, 2010). From both political and economic motivations, the media under state control in mainland China constantly seek to reinvigorate the party's governmental legitimacy by embedding narratives of patriotism into everyday media discourses. The nationalism-patriotism discourse in the Chinese context contains both cultural melancholy and materialistic appeals. With individual-level survey data at hand, this chapter investigates the extent to which various types of media use (local, national, and foreign), transnational social connections, and the experience of foreign travel are connected with the intensity of one's nationalist sentiments. In particular, we ask an important question: Will exposure to national-level media content, which is most strictly controlled by the party, lead to higher levels of nationalism in mainland China?

Third, people's affect toward their own nation has profound implications for their evaluation of other nations based on the in-group versus out-group distinction. How do Chinese people evaluate other countries? How are their feelings toward foreign countries related to their levels of nationalistic sentiment? Do cultural nationalism and developmental nationalism have different implications for the ways in which urban Chinese people evaluate other countries?

Answers to these three clusters of interrelated questions will provide meaningful cues for understanding the formation of nationalistic sentiments in China as well as part of their impact. But before the analysis is considered, more contextual and conceptual discussions of nationalism in China will be offered.

THE DIVERSE MEANINGS OF NATIONALISM

Nationalism has been a widely studied topic in the social sciences (e.g., Anderson, 1991; Billig, 1995; Gellner, 1983; Guo, 2004; Smith, 1993). Although efforts of conceptualization abound, nationalism seems to be a mushy concept, as it can mean many things to many people. The discussion of nationalism first requires a solid definition of the term "nation." According to Smith (1993), "nation" refers to "a named human population sharing a historic territory, common myths and historical memories, a mass, public culture, a common economy and common legal rights and duties for all members" (p. 14). "Nation" is distinctive from "state," which designates a set of political institutions having sovereignty over a territory. Some scholars have stressed the need to separate loyalty to the nation from loyalty to the state (Billig, 1995), although the two overlap to varying degrees in different social and geographic contexts. Identification with the state is conceived as state nationalism (Guo, 2004) or political nationalism (Hutchinson, 2003), whereas identification with a nation is viewed as cultural nationalism.

The existence of a nation is contingent upon both objective and subjective antecedents and current practices. Shared language, territory, and cultural norms are products of historic forces beyond the individual's control. But a nation must be imagined. Theorists such as Gellner (1983), Anderson (1991), and Giddens (1985) all stress the role of "subjective" criteria in the construction of a nation and the formation of national consciousness. At root, nationalism involves self-categorization, which, according to social identity theory (Tajfel, 1974, 1981, 1982a), is a common psychological phenomenon.

Nationalism is not a single entity but comes in a multitude of forms and shapes. Particularly, official nationalism as defined by the government and popular or grassroots nationalism do not necessarily share the same connotations. In some contexts, such as the city of Hong Kong after the handover, official nationalism as imposed by the Chinese government and grassroots nationalism as generated from within the local society can be in tension (Ma, 2011). Official nationalism contains a particular ideological stance of the ruling power. Back to the case of mainland China, the Chinese Communist Party (CCP) has been preaching its own theories of nationalism in line with party ideology, serving its existential purposes. But nationalism in the eyes of ordinary people can mean nothing related to the party or the state. Some scholars (e.g., Guo, 2004) equate state/political nationalism with official nationalism, which may be inaccurate. The official version of nationalism in China, as argued in the next section, is a mixture of political, developmental, and cultural nationalism. It bundles the cultural elements of ancient China with the materialistic accomplishment of the CCP, which aims to "modernize the country."

This brief discussion on the concept of nationalism lays the groundwork for the ensuing survey data analysis. The Chinese conception of national identity is complicated in many ways (Townsend, 1996). Unlike European nation-states, whose political territories largely coincide with a single national group, the boundary of the People's Republic of China is ascribed to a wide range of ethnic groups, such as Hans, Manchus, Tibetans, Uighurs, and Mongolians, and so on. Despite persistent ethnic tensions between the Hans and the other groups, such as the Uighurs, the Mongolians, and Tibetans, frequent cultural, political, and military exchanges in the long history of China have facilitated the convergence of different ethnicities. Fitzgerald (1996) even claimed that the Chinese state is a "nationless state." In addition, the contemporary experiences of civil war and colonization in the twentieth century add much complexity to the identity of being Chinese. Residents in Hong Kong and Macau, for example, after being ruled by the British and the Portuguese respectively for more than a century, unavoidably took on a unique collective identity (Lee and Chan, 2005; Ma, 1999; Mathews, Ma, and Lui, 2007). Across the Taiwan Strait, residents of the island are still debating whether they should consider themselves Chinese, and survey data show that many island residents would consider themselves simply as Taiwanese.[1] Certainly the discussion is inevitably swayed by the interests and rhetoric of political groups and parties, and most recently, as evidenced in the 2012 Taiwan elections, the economic interests of business groups.[2]

Given these facts, the specific aspects of "nationalism" in this study must be restrained by the reality of Chinese societies, as nationalism is historically bounded and spatially delimited. The representation of a nation must be socially constructed. It could be argued that the Chinese conception of national identity, like that of any other nation, is highly subjective. The complex history contains many matters that may be controversial and open to competing interpretations (e.g., whether Tibet is a part of China). Political rhetoric plays an important role in the process of constructing a nation. The official nationalism preached by the CCP calls for special attention. The state-controlled media in China employ a strategy of "reviving" traditional Chinese culture to save the legitimacy of the government. Meanwhile, the other side of official nationalism plays the "national achievement card," trying to promote a positive media representation of the government. The following will elaborate on the meanings of the two pillars of official nationalism in China.

CULTURAL NATIONALISM IN OFFICIAL DISCOURSE

The recent upsurge of nationalism in mainland China has been described by some as a type of self-serving pragmatism (Zhao, 2005). These heightening nationalistic sentiments are partly attributable to the booming economy in the past three decades, but they could not have gained momentum without influence from the government. Despite the fact that cultural and the political nationalists have often been in confrontation in the history of nationalist movements (Hutchinson, 2003), the coexistence of cultural and state nationalism was made possible by the party's rhetoric of "patriotism."

Specifically, the Cultural Revolution crippled numerous cultural traditions and destroyed countless cultural relics, leaving the whole country in chaos. Although the opening and reform policy carried out in the late 1970s has brought to China unprecedented economic progress, marketing efforts and commercialization have literally claimed the end of orthodox Marxist ideology. Furthermore, the prodemocracy movement of June 1989 alerted the government to the serious "threats" posed by political liberalization and the relaxation on ideological control. Against this background, the CCP then launched many political campaigns and implemented new policies to propagate its nationalism-patriotism discourse across the country.

Intensive patriotic indoctrination immediately followed the crackdown on the prodemocracy movement in 1989, when people began to cast doubt on the legitimacy of the party's governance. In late 1989 and 1990, national leader Jiang Zemin delivered many speeches on the topic of "being patriotic" to the Youth League (*People's Daily*, 1989, July 17), to intellectuals (*People's Daily*, 1990, April 5), and to the People's Liberation Army (*People's Daily*, 1990, May 11). In addition, the party's Department of Propaganda and the State Education Committee, along with other government bodies, launched their programs of "one hundred patriotic books" and "one hundred patriotic films." By developing a chain of equivalences linking the nation, the state, and the CCP, the version of nationalism outlined in these efforts the party highlighted the importance of being loyal to it and the state.

This, nevertheless, does not mean that the Chinese government reverted completely to hard-core propaganda to "brainwash" the people. Accompanying the hard-core ideological persuasion was a "softer" approach to encouraging cultural identification. In 1991, the Central Propaganda Department issued a decree calling for the use of cultural relics for the purpose of patriotism education (*People's Daily*, 1991, September 15). In 1997, 100 "bases for patriotism education" were set up across the country for students, party members, and travelers to visit.[3] Of the first batch of such approved "Red Tourism Sites" across the country, some exhibit and celebrate Chinese history and culture (e.g., the Beijing Natural History Museum, the Great Wall, and so on) and some praise loyal party members and government officials after the founding of new China (e.g., Jiaoyulu Martyr Cemetery); the large majority are historical sites depicting the role of the party in the anti-Japanese War and the Civil War. The second (100 sites), third (66 sites), and fourth (87 sites) batches of patriotism education bases were announced in 2001, 2005, and 2009. Nationwide promotion of "excellent national traditions" quickly became a fad among local government branches. To justify the "wholeness" of a state with more than 50 ethnicities, the party encourages identification with being the children and grandchildren of the Yellow Emperor and the descendants of the Dragon. Confucius reappeared as a handy branding gadget for marketing official nationalism (*People's Daily*, 1995, June 26), as if Confucianism had never been vilified and trashed by Mao and the Party during the Cultural Revolution.

In more recent years, the Internet also became an important platform for propaganda work. Patriotism education went online quickly. In 2006, the government set up a website fully devoted to disseminating news and ideas about "patriotism"—the China Patriotism Education website (Zhongguo aiguozhuyi jiaoyu wang, www.aicn.org). China Network Television, in collaboration with the Propaganda Department, built an interactive web page that introduces the approved patriotism education bases across the country using multimedia technologies (zuguo.cntv.cn).

If we take a detailed look at the official definition of patriotism in China, it is evident that the party's nationalism-patriotism discourse gives high priority to Chinese traditional culture as a persuasive branding device that has the potential to domesticate individuals with diverse ideological inclinations and ethnic backgrounds.

> Pride in the country's outstanding contributions to the civilization of humanity, its broad and profound traditional culture, to acknowledge the basic national conditions, to follow the political line of the Communist Party of China, to recognize the party's achievements, to uphold socialist democracy and abide by the law, not to harm national defense, national security or national unity, and accept the principles of peaceful reunification, and one country two systems. (*Beijing Review*, 1994, cited in Guo, 2004)

The playing of the "cultural card" is a response to the erosion of traditional identities and social morality—through the process of modernization, liberalization, social stratification—and decline in the trust of the regime. A more practical function is to save the legitimacy of the party's authoritative rule. Therefore the party's version of patriotism could be described as state nationalism coated with cultural appeals. Jiang Zemin's theory of "the Three Represents" includes the claim that the vanguard CCP represents the most advanced culture of the Chinese people. "Culture" comes as a convenient discursive resource for political purposes. However, regardless of the intention, the government-initiated campaigns for patriotism did create an amiable climate for popular and cultural nationalistic sentiments to flourish. And this could not have been accomplished without the help of mass communication and the party's logic of news production, which manifest the notion of developmental nationalism and a more direct appeal to the public.

DEVELOPMENTAL NATIONALISM AND THE MEDIA

The success of the authorities' efforts of persuasion depends on individuals' internalizing the dominant belief system, which in turn depends on strategies of ideological indoctrination through the use of media propaganda. In the past two decades, the functions of the Chinese media have undergone a profound structural transition to accommodate the needs of the market as well as the Party (Chan, 1993; Lee, 1994; Zhao, 1998), a phenomenon aptly described as "one servant, two masters" (Li and Shen, 1995; Polumbaum, 1990). Under the new "party-market corporatism" (Lee, He, and Huang, 2007; Pan, 2000), Chinese media still faithfully follow an institutionalized agenda, but strategies of propaganda in China today have changed substantially. The media have reinvented themselves to become the "Party Publicity Inc." (He, 2000; Lee, He, and Huang, 2006), whose functions are to legitimize party domination and consolidate national identity while also serving to make profit. The dramatic transformation of media discourse from blatant ideological dogmatism (e.g., worshiping Mao during the Cultural Revolution) to sugar-coated commercial seduction (e.g., underscoring the country's economic achievement under the leadership of the party) belies the commonality in the ultimate goal of persuasion.

Media articulation of nationalism has two major ingredients: an everyday routine called banal nationalism (Billig, 1995) and an event-triggered ostensible promotion of patriotism. First, "banal nationalism" refers to routine, low-key means of symbolizing the cohesion of a nation. Billig's (1995) study revealed that ordinary words—for instance, "the nation" and "we" used in different sections of newspapers (e.g., home news, sports news, or even the weather forecast)—constantly reproduced a basic worldview for the readers: they are a part of a nation existing within a world of nations. The reproduction of this worldview occurs subtly and without people's conscious attention. But in the long run, the effect of internalizing the idea of being a member of a nation can be immense. In China, other metaphoric phrases such as "motherland China" and "the party, the savior of the nation" in news and popular media also have the same function of reinforcing a basic nation-centered worldview.

Second and more important, the media from time to time report "big events" (e.g., sports, ceremonies, National Congress meetings) and state achievements (e.g., GNP growth, dams, speed trains) and tie them to nationalist sentiment with measured intensity. Emphasis on national achievements constitutes the core of developmental nationalism rhetoric. The most typical manifestation is the tendency to showcase the country's domestic and overseas accomplishments and relate them to perceptions of the "Chinese pride": China's entry into the WTO; successful hosting of the 2008 Olympic Games; the 2010 Shanghai World Expo; the 2011 Guangzhou Asian Olympic Games; launching of manned spaceships; and the quick recovery from the recent global economic downturn. In analyzing media coverage of

Hong Kong's handover to China in 1997, Lee and colleagues (2005) found that the Chinese media strictly followed the rules of party journalism, which rendered the whole event into a national celebration sprinkled with intense patriotic sentiments. All other interpretations of the event, whether explicit or implicit and by journalists at home and abroad, were herded into "hostile news" and thus justifiably excluded from the public eye.

The decision to differentiate between cultural and developmental nationalism has its contextual basis. As alluded to earlier, two of the most prominent rhetorical devices used to propel the party's Chinese patriotism-nationalism discourse are "cultural tradition" and "economic development." Both intended to sustain a sense of "pride," but "cultural nationalism" refers to one's affective evaluation of the shared Chinese cultural legacy, whereas "developmental nationalism" refers to one's psychological commitment to having a thriving nation. The former hinges upon one's ties to the past, whereas the latter speaks to the country's future and modernity. However, the party has to be highly selective in terms of presenting "facts" to drive up the people's pride, in that not every element that crystallized into Chinese culture sounds brilliant and noble. Similarly, not every party policy or national project receives favorable evaluations (e.g., the controversy over the Three Gorges Dam). Therefore, in addition to these two catalysts of rising national identification (i.e., cultural and developmental), the state-controlled media in China provides an important channel for stirring up nationalism.

As is known to many, harsh censorship is usually applied to sensitive political and social topics in the Chinese media (He, 2008; Zhao, 2008). The most widely used strategy of media censorship could be characterized as the "positivity bias frame." Central to this frame is consistent and powerful manipulation of news to strip media discourse of "social anomie," to consecrate exemplars of accepted behavior, and to locate proper scapegoats for social problems. To select and highlight social occurrences and to package news in favor of domination are the essential tasks of party journalism that are closely related to one central concept in political communication research: news framing (e.g., Pan and Kosicki, 1993; Scheufele, 1999; van Dijk, 1988). To frame is to concentrate on a certain part of reality and to increase its salience so that "a particular problem definition, causal interpretation, moral evaluation, and/or treatment recommendation" can be promoted (Entman, 1993, p. 52). In China, a major part of the media's institutional arrangement is to make sure that rampant polarization of wealth, unethical business conduct, and various social ills anchored in structural antecedents are kept hidden. Thus the state can direct grievances and discontent in people's everyday life to "greedy and corrupted individuals" rather than to any possible institutional defects.

Indirectly, manipulated news can present a rosy picture of the country to the whole citizenry, claiming credit for the party and producing a sense of pride in the nation. This contributes much to the growth of nationalism among the public. National achievements, rhetorically presented by the mass media, accentuate the pride associated with being a Chinese. Ordinary citizens, as beneficiaries of these achievements, feel beholden to the party. Without the party-state, ordinary people in China would still suffer the pains of living in a feudal society. Previous studies have found that television plays a role in national integration (Pan and Chan, 2000), and media exposure has a positive effect on the sense of patriotism among mainland Chinese (Fairbrother, 2003).

As a note of caution, however, the above discussion does not entail that the ruling authorities in China dedicate much of their energy to fervently promoting nationalism. First, political force is not the sole cause for the explosion of media content imbued with nationalism: the nature of news and market imperative also play their roles. For one thing, ethnocentrism is a long-lasting journalistic value and the press has a natural inclination to breed a sense of community and unity (Park, 1922). On the other hand, editors of commercial media in China, in the face of cutthroat market competition, find the fanning of nationalism to be both a shortcut and a safe haven for economic gain (Guo, Cheong, and Chen, 2007). Second, the flipside of nationalism, xenophobia, can backfire on both foreign policy and national economy (Gries, 2004). Voiced in different political pitches, pragmatic nationalism is inherently beneficial to solidifying the ruling legitimacy of the party (Guo, Cheong, and Chen, 2007).

US VS. THEM: HOW PEOPLE SEE "THE OTHERS"

Nationalism could not survive without inputs from the "others side." Admittedly, the rising nationalism in China has its external driving forces: the 1999 NATO bombing of the Chinese embassy in Belgrade, Japan's head of state's visit to the Yasukuni Shrine in honor of the war dead (who, to Chinese and Koreans, were war criminals), the Chinese and U.S. military aircraft collision over the South China sea, the most recent renewal of the dispute over the Diaoyu Islands with Japan, and the dispute over the South China Sea with the Philippines in 2012. These events and incidents could be further amplified by the news media, boosting nationalistic sentiments and swaying people's perceptions of foreign nations and states. Therefore, in discussing nationalism, we can also ask a follow-up question: how do Chinese people perceive and evaluate other countries and how does nationalism relate to these perceptions?

The literature on the public's ratings of foreign nations suggests several key determinants: cultural similarity, national interests, and the media. In an early study, two U.S. scholars found that perception of similarity between one's own country and another and perception of national interest explained a considerable amount of the variance in Americans' ratings of 25 countries (Nincic and Russett, 1979). At the individual level, there is no shortage of psychological explanations that lend support to the important roles of similarity and interest in predicting interpersonal attractiveness: shared personal interests lead to likeness while differences in beliefs and values drive out-group rejection (Tajfel, 1982b). In addition to these two factors, Tims and Miller (1986) argued that the media play a significant role in the process of shaping individual's feelings about another nation. Perry (1990) found that news exposure was positively related to greater knowledge about and favorable evaluations of other countries. To the extent that most people do not possess firsthand experience of visiting another nation, perceived cultural commonalities and perceived shared interests easily give way to media representation or even manipulation. When a particular characterization of a nation is repeated for a long time, social stereotypes crystallize and people tend to rely on such typifications to make inferences and decisions (Dunning and Sherman, 1997; Macrae, Milne, and Bodenhausen, 1994).

The Chinese media's representation of foreign countries is more or less tainted by the predetermined missions. Under authoritarian control, the coverage of international events serves not only serves the purpose of transmitting news but also helps to produce an "ideal" international environment for the Chinese audience to decode domestic politics and news in general. The Xinhua News Agency is solely entrusted with covering international news on behalf of the nation's media outlets. The *People's Daily* is reluctant to place international news on the front page for fear of being misread as reflecting China's policy positions; it therefore created the *Global Times* as a subsidiary to carry foreign policy issue discourses. Moreover, there is a popular parody spreading on the Internet that sarcastically summarizes the ethos of the 30-minute-long *Xinwen Lianbo* (the daily news broadcast) of CCTV (China Central Television): "The first 10 minutes, [the news tells us] government officials are very busy; the second 10 minutes, Chinese people are living a good life; the third 10 minutes, foreign countries are in total chaos." Despite its witty exaggeration, the parody does contain a grain of truth. Zhou (2010) has enumerated three international news reporting strategies adopted by the party media in China: (1) self-prioritizing in order to emphasize Chinese leaders' roles in international news coverage; (2) comparing domestic and foreign events in order to highlight the achievements of China and the negative news of foreign countries, and (3) minimizing sensitive news in order to downplay the possible negative political consequences of the contents (e.g., coverage on elections in liberal democracies). By adopting the concept of "linkage politics" (Rosenau, 1969; Lee, 1981), Zhou (2010) argued that these strategies are used for the purpose of maintaining national identification and legitimizing the party's governance.

In other words, international news reporting in China is a highly politicized practice, and international news constitutes the "context" for decoding domestic news. The "domestication" of international news is not a random process (Cohen, Levy, Roeh, and Gurevitch, 1996) but subject to the concerns of national interest and the dominant ideological framework of the host nation (Entman, 1991; Lee and Yang, 1995; Lee, Chan, Pan, and So, 2005). Chang and colleagues (2002) argue that coverage of foreign nations in the Chinese media is influenced by national interest and foreign policy. This echoes the view of Liu Yunshan, head of the Chinese Propaganda Department, that international news must follow the principle of serving national interests and promoting an agreeable international public opinion climate for China's development (Liu, 2006). Compared with domestic news, international news is particularly likely to embrace the "bad news is good news" logic. Analyzing CCTV's *Xinwen Lianbo*, Zhou (2010) found that 27.4 percent of international news contained conflicts, whereas the percentage is only 5.1 percent for domestic news.

It should be noted that the newest developments in international news reporting by the Chinese media would include a "going out" policy pursued by both the government and the media. That is, with its economic growth and integration into the global community, the Chinese government has attempted to exert more international influence by requiring the media organizations to expand their international news coverage. Major national news organizations such as CCTV and the Xinhua News Agency have been expanding the number of bureaus they have around the world (Hong, 2011; Xin, 2011). Today even local media organizations may send a larger number of reporters abroad to cover major foreign events. After the March 2011 Japanese earthquake, for example, media organizations from Guangzhou alone sent more than 40 parachute journalists to Japan (Wang, Lee, and Wang, 2013). Nevertheless, overall the background sketched in the previous paragraphs should remain highly relevant, especially since our survey was conducted in 2006 and 2007. What impact, therefore, do the aforementioned features of international news coverage have on the Chinese audience? Would they lead the Chinese audience to formulate negative impressions of foreign countries? Or would it be the case that, as indicated by the *Xinwen Lianbo* parody, that Chinese people are well aware of the government's propaganda tricks and hence are not affected by the contents? These are some of the important questions that we can try to tackle in the following analysis.

To recapitulate, the foregoing discussions focus on three core concepts: cultural nationalism, developmental nationalism, and evaluations of foreign nations. Notably, beginning with this chapter, our analysis will address the various "dependent variables" of the framework outlined in Chapter 1. Hence, different from the previous two chapters, our interests no longer reside solely in providing a basic portrait of the respondents. Rather, we will put more emphasis on examining the predictors of the core variables. For the sake of clarity, the following three major questions can be stated:

1. What is the intensity of cultural nationalism and developmental nationalism in China? How do such nationalistic sentiments vary across geographical areas?
2. Do different levels of media exposure, foreign travel experience, and transnational social connections relate to intensity of cultural nationalism and developmental nationalism?
3. How do Chinese people evaluate other countries? Which countries are among the most favored by Chinese? How are their evaluations related to their levels of nationalism, media consumption, and personal experiences?

EXAMINING CHINESE PEOPLE'S NATIONALISTIC SENTIMENTS

Intensity of Cultural Nationalism and Developmental Nationalism

In our survey, the respondents were asked to express their levels of agreement, by means of a five-point Likert scale, with three items that pertain to one's perceptions of and feelings toward Chinese culture. The three statements are (1) In today's world, only Chinese culture could resist liberal-democracy as the axis of western values; (2) China's spiritual civilization is superior to that of the West; and (3) China's ethnic group is the best in the world. These three items are taken as indicators of urban Chinese residents' degree of cultural nationalism.

Overall, 38.2 percent of the respondents from our sample agreed or strongly agreed that only Chinese culture could resist western values, whereas 15.2 percent of the respondents disagreed or strongly disagreed. About 48.8 percent thought of China's civilization as superior to that of the West; only 17.6 percent took exception. As many as 67.8 percent of the respondents believed that the Chinese people were of the best quality in the world; only 8.2 percent disagreed. In other words, almost 7 out of 10 respondents endorsed the Chinese people as being of the best quality, 4 out of 10 regarded Chinese culture as the only cultural force that could counteract western culture, and close to half believed that China had a superior civilization.

There are between-cities differences in people's degree of cultural nationalism. When answers to the three statements were combined into an overall index, the mean score was highest among the Beijing residents, followed by residents in Xi'an and then Chengdu and Shanghai. As shown on the right-hand side of Figure 4.1, the between-cities differences are not substantial, but they are statistically significant at $P < .03$ in an ANOVA analysis. The distinction here does not match neatly with the coast-vs.-inland divide. Rather, one plausible interpretation of the between-cities differences is that degree of cultural nationalism existing within a city can be related to the role of the city in a country's history and culture. Xi'an had been the citadel of ancient Chinese civilizations, exuding the nation's mythical glory of historical past dating all the way back to the Tang and Qin dynasties. Beijing has been the imperial capital for a thousand years and still is the seat of political power in contemporary China. The Great Wall and the Imperial Palace in Beijing, as well as Emperor Qin Shihuang's mausoleum in Xi'an, are not only tourist spots but also monuments of China's historical and/or cultural grandeur. Chengdu, in contrast, was not the center of Chinese history, even though the city also has its fair share of cultural and historical heritage, most notably the heritage related to the three-kingdom period in the third century CE. Shanghai's history is short. It became an important seaport in China only since the early Qing Dynasty (around the seventeenth century). In fact, Shanghai did not become officially a "city" until 1927, and its rise to prominence has been tied to its role as a prime bridgehead to the world at large. Therefore Shanghai residents are more open to foreign cultural elements, exhibiting greater pride in modern economic success than in having a strong sense of cultural nationalism derived from the historical past.

The pattern of between-cities differences remains similar when developmental nationalism is concerned. Operationally, developmental nationalism refers to people's rating of the importance of the value of having a strong nation—that is, the value orientation already discussed in Chapter 2. On a five-point Likert scale, our survey respondents scored a mean of 4.72 (1

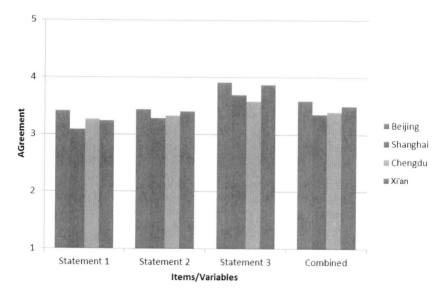

Figure 4.1 The degree of nationalism among urban Chinese.

Notes. Statement 1: In today's world, only Chinese culture could resist liberal-democracy as the axis of Western values; Statement 2: China's spiritual civilization surpasses that of the West; Statement 3: the Chinese is the best ethnic group in the world. Combined: the average of respondents' level of agreement with the three statements. The between-cities differences in each row are all statistically significant at p < .03 in one-way ANOVA analysis.

= very unimportant, 5 = very important). But when the four cities' samples were separated, Beijing residents exhibited the highest level of developmental nationalism (M = 4.80), followed by Xi'an residents (M = 4.72) and then Shanghai and Chengdu (Ms = 4.69 and 4.68 respectively). The differences among the mean scores are statistically significant in a one-way ANOVA analysis (F = 5.71, P < .01). However, the size of the differences in scores is not huge.

It should be noted that the correlations among the three items that constitute cultural nationalism are only moderate in size, with Pearson r ranging from .26 to .34 and the Cronbach's alpha coefficient for the cultural nationalism index at .55. More important, developmental nationalism and cultural nationalism are weakly though significantly, correlated (r = .11, P < .001). One reason for the lack of a strong relationship between the two is the different temporal orientation of the two measures. Whereas the measurement of cultural nationalism indicates whether the Chinese people are proud of what they already have (i.e., their culture and history), the measurement of developmental nationalism refers essentially to what Chinese people want in the future. In sum, the moderately weak correlation between the two suggests that there can be tensions between urban Chinese people's perceptions of China's past and future.

Further, we elaborate the relationship between cultural and developmental nationalism with demographic variables. We suspect that younger and more educated people would be more "future-oriented" and less likely to see China's cultural past as relevant. Indeed, our survey results show such a pattern. The correlation between the two types of nationalistic sentiments is r = .13 (P < .001) among people over 30 years old, but only .07 (P > .10) for people 30 years old or younger. Likewise, cultural and developmental nationalisms have a correlation of .13 (P < .001) for people without university education, but r = -.01 (P > .90) for people with university education. In other words, the younger and more educated urban Chinese were less likely to see cultural and developmental nationalism as linked to each other. They are more capable of differentiating between China's glory in the past and glory in the present and future.

Predicting Cultural Nationalism and Developmental Nationalism

Multiple regression analyses were conducted to examine the predictors of nationalism. The independent variables included the basic demographic factors, three city dummy variables, transnational experiences and connections, and media consumption.

Table 4.1 summarizes the results. All things being equal, female respondents tended to score higher on cultural nationalism than males. Individuals with more education scored lower on cultural nationalism than those with less education. It is possible that, unlike fervent followers of Chinese traditional culture, people with more education were more likely to be exposed to western perspectives; therefore they were less likely than the less educated people to adopt an unconditionally positive view toward Chinese culture. Some of the highly educated people might even have developed certain critical views toward traditional Chinese culture. Age, household income, occupations, and English ability are not significant predictors of cultural nationalism. In other words, there are not many relationships between cultural nationalism and various demographics. At the same time, there is no statistically meaningful relationship between any basic demographics and developmental nationalism. This illustrates that sentiments of developmental nationalism are widespread and diffused throughout the whole society.

Table 4.1 also shows that local media consumption is positively associated with both cultural nationalism and developmental nationalism. Individuals with more exposure to local media content possessed higher levels of cultural and developmental nationalism. Contrary to the expectation, national media consumption does not predict nationalistic sentiments when all other factors are taken into account. Besides, the consumption of foreign media does not have a noticeable influence on the intensity of nationalistic sentiments. Meanwhile, people who had more transnational social connections exhibited a higher level of developmental nationalism. But overall, direct linkage between the communication variables and nationalistic sentiments were not strong.

Based on the findings in Table 4.1, should we conclude that foreign media consumption does not at all relate to urban Chinese people's nationalistic sentiments? Before committing to this conclusion, it would be important to examine certain further possibilities;, for example, although there is no simple linear linkage between foreign media consumption and nationalistic sentiments, there may be some more complex relationships among the factors involved. Specifically, we have illustrated in earlier pages that not all urban Chinese saw cultural nationalism and developmental nationalism as being connected. In fact, historically speaking, the Chinese were "forced" to learn, reluctantly, from the West after the British army had knocked China's door wide open in the mid-nineteenth century. Chinese intellectuals in the late nineteenth century articulated the view that, despite having a superior spiritual culture, China needed to learn from the West in order to become strong in material terms. Again, recognizing one's culture as superior does not entail a recognition of the strength of one's nation in the more material aspects. We have seen that more educated people and younger people were more likely to dissociate cultural nationalism from developmental nationalism. Here, we may add the further possibility that urban Chinese who consumed foreign media to larger extents would also be more likely to dissociate the two types of nationalistic sentiments.

The reason for the latter expectation is that, when people have wider exposure to media and cultural products from around the world, their evaluations of the superiority of Chinese culture as well as their sense of importance of having a "thriving nation" may become the results of more

Table 4.1 Predicting Cultural Nationalism and Developmental Nationalism

	Cultural nationalism	Developmental nationalism
Gender	.06**	.01
Age	-.01	.04
Education	-.13***	-.01
Household income	.04	-.01
English	.02	-.03
Work for state enterprise	.03	.02
Work for foreign companies	-.00	-.03
Shanghai	-.19***	-.12***
Chengdu	-.14***	-.10***
Xi'an	-.04	-.07***
Foreign travel	-.00	-.02
Transnational social connection	-.02	.06*
Local media consumption	.08**	.06*
National media consumption	.02	.01
Foreign media consumption	-.04	-.03
Adjusted R^2	3.8%***	1.5%***

Note: Entries are standardized regression coefficients. * $P < .05$; ** $P < .01$; *** $P < .001$.

complicated considerations and depend on a wider range of information. A person who is a strong developmental nationalist may also tend to presume that China's superior culture can lead the country forward. After all, a person's pride about a country's present can quite "naturally" lead to a sense of pride about the country's past, and vice versa; but when this person consumes a lot of foreign media, she or he may begin to realize that China may have to "learn" many things—about science and technologies, social institutions, and so on—from different countries around the world in order to truly develop itself. The result is that the tie between one's pride about a country's past and one's emphasis on the importance of national development may be weakened.

Further analysis of the present data shows that it is indeed the case. We differentiated the urban Chinese respondents into three groups based on their frequencies of foreign media consumption: (1) those who did not consume foreign media at all (scoring zero in the foreign media consumption index), (2) those who consumed a small amount of foreign media (who consumed one to eight times of different types of foreign media in the week prior to the interview), and (3) those who consumed a large amount of foreign media (who consumed more than eight times of different types of foreign media in the week prior to the survey interview). We examined the correlation between cultural nationalism and developmental nationalism among these three groups of people separately. The result shows that the two forms of nationalism are significantly and positively correlated with each other among those who did not consume foreign media at all ($r = .13$, $P < .001$) and also among those who consumed only a small amount of foreign media ($r = .12$, $P < .001$). In contrast, cultural nationalism and developmental nationalism are not related to each other among people who consumed a larger amount of foreign media ($r = -.17$, $P > .08$).[4]

These additional findings are theoretically important. They show that media consumption can indeed have important implications on people's value orientations, but the relationships are not always simple, linear, and clear-cut. Rather than directly leading people to adopt certain value orientations instead of others, media consumption may affect how different value orientations are articulated with each other.

NATIONALISM AND AFFECT TOWARD FOREIGN COUNTRIES

Having examined the predictors of nationalistic sentiments, we now turn to an analysis of how nationalism and other variables relate to feelings about foreign countries. To determine this, the survey asked the respondents to indicate on a five-point Likert scale (from "very bad" to "very good") their impressions of 16 different countries. Figure 4.2 shows the mean scores for the 16 countries involved. Our respondents rated Singapore and a number of European countries (the United Kimgdom, Italy, Germany, and France) most positively. These countries were followed by Russia and the United States. Urban Chinese people saw most of the developed countries most favorably. In contrast, communist countries were not as well regarded, although the mean scores for North Korea and Cuba were above the midpoint of the scale. Nor were other less developed countries rated highly. Yet Chinese people rated Japan the most negatively, given the history of animosity and persistent tension over the disputed Diaoyu Islands. It should also be noted that people's ratings of Japan and the United States indicated high levels of standard deviation (not shown in the figure), which means that the urban Chinese held more divided opinions about the two countries.

But what factors account for people's ratings of the foreign countries? An exploratory factor analysis showed that the ratings of the 16 countries were clustered into four factors. The United States, the United Kingdom, and Japan constituted one single factor, whereas France, Germany, and Italy formed another. The other two factors comprised the lesser developed countries, but the grouping of countries does not follow obvious conceptual logic: India, North Korea and Russia formed one factor whereas South Africa, Cuba, Afghanistan, Iraq, and Vietnam formed another. For simplicity, we created three groups: (1) Anglo-American countries (plus Japan), (2) continental European countries, and (3) less developed countries. Singapore and the Philippines do not clearly belong to any group in the factor analysis and hence are not included in the subsequent analysis.

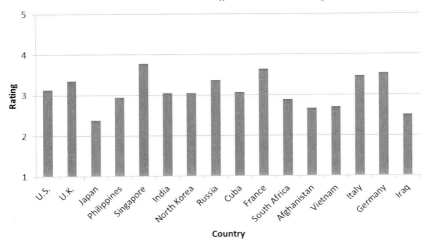

Figure 4.2 Urban Chinese people's affect toward foreign countries.

With the three indices, a series of multiple regression analyses were conducted to examine the predictors of people's evaluations of foreign countries. The independent variables are those in Table 4.1 plus cultural nationalism and developmental nationalism. The results are summarized in Table 4.2.

The findings show that several different factors could explain Chinese people's attitudes toward different groups of countries. Younger people rated the United States, the United Kingdom, and Japan more positively, but age was the only good demographic predictor. City variations exist: Shanghai residents evaluated the group of countries substantially more positively than did Beijing residents, while Xi'an and Chengdu residents rated the Anglo-American group more negatively than did Beijing residents. One possible factor behind the between-cities differences are the historical and contemporary linkages between the cities and the Anglo-American world. Shanghai, in particular, a city with a large population of foreign residents (Americans, Japanese, British, French, Jews, etc.) during the WWII, is overall more friendly toward foreigners.

Foreign travel and transnational social connections do not relate to the dependent variables. Yet there are important relationships between the ratings of the Anglo-American group, media consumption, and nationalism. Given the dominance of Anglo-American media products in international media flow as well as the popularity of Japanese media (e.g., TV drama, manga, music, etc.) in the region, foreign media consumption contributes positively to the ratings of the Anglo-American group. At the same time, both cultural nationalism and developmental nationalism lead negatively to the ratings of the Anglo-American group. This can be seen in the context of the troublesome relationships between Japan and China as well as between the United States and China.

Table 4.2 Predicting Affect toward Foreign Countries

	U.S. / U.K. / Japan	Continental Europe	Lesser Developed
Gender	-.01	-.05*	-.04
Age	-.10***	-.04	-.01
Education	.03	.08**	-.02
Household income	-.04	.00	.03
English	-.05	.02	.01
Work for state enterprise	.00	.01	-.06**
Work for foreign companies	-.01	-.01	-.00
Shanghai	.17***	.08**	-.19***
Chengdu	-.10***	-.14***	-.27***
Xi'an	-.15***	.07*	-.19***
Foreign travel	.03	.03	-.01
Transnational social connection	.03	.03	-.02
Local media consumption	-.02	-.17***	-.05
National media consumption	-.04	.09**	.00
Foreign media consumption	.07**	.01	-.06*
Cultural nationalism	-.05*	-.01	.19***
Developmental nationalism	-.10***	.03	-.01
Adjusted R^2	8.2%***	7.9%***	10.1%***

Note: Entries are standardized regression coefficients. * $P < .05$; ** $P < .01$; *** $P < .001$.

The second column of Table 4.2 shows that males and people with more education tended to rate European countries more positively. Substantial between-cities differences include the following observations: Shanghai and Xi'an residents rated the European countries significantly more positively than Beijing residents, whereas Chengdu residents rated the European countries most negatively. Foreign media consumption did not matter for the ratings of European countries. But interestingly, local and national media consumption related to ratings of European countries in a contradictory manner. High consumption of local media led to lower ratings of the European countries, but high consumption of national media led to higher ratings.

Last, the third column of Table 4.5 shows that most demographic factors are not good predictors of how people rated the less developed countries. The only exception is that workers in state enterprises tended to view these countries more negatively. Again, between-cities differences are substantial, with the residents in Shanghai, Xi'an, and Chengdu all being more negative than Beijing residents on the less developed countries. Foreign media consumption, given its biased representations of the less developed world, contributed to negative ratings of these countries.

Finally, cultural nationalism prompted people to view the less developed countries more positively. This probably reflects a historical articulation of the relationship between China and the developing world during the earlier years of the communist regime. In the 1960s and 1970s, China considered itself a leader of the "Third World." The mixture of cultural superiority vis-à-vis the West and its sense of comradeship with the less developed countries may explain this finding.

SUMMARY AND DISCUSSION

In sum, the data show that mainland Chinese exhibited moderate to high levels of identification with Chinese traditional culture and civilization, and they are avid for seeing their nation make material progress. In comparison with developmental nationalism, measures of cultural nationalism tended to attract relatively neutral answers, suggesting the respondents' ambivalence toward the legacy of Chinese culture. There are important differences between residents from the four cities. Across all three items of cultural nationalism, Beijing residents consistently scored the highest and Shanghai residents the lowest. But in the absence of a random sample at the country level, we chose to refrain from making sweeping arguments about the geographical variation of national sentiments.

Although the rapid and vast economic achievement in China might partly explain why people would feel proud of their nation's civilization, the rise of nationalism owes much to the official promotion of patriotism and, also to severe media censorship. Results from the multiple regression analysis confirm the unique role of media exposure in predicting nationalism. Heavy users of local media were more likely to identify with Chinese traditional culture and to have a stronger desire for a thriving China. Media consumption fosters national pride. Foreigners may see Chinese nationalism as aggressive, anti-imperialist, arrogant, chauvinistic, xenophobic, or even antidemocratic. But the Chinese authorities use nationalism as a means of social and political control.

Surprisingly, national media consumption was not related to either cultural or developmental nationalism. This is inconsistent with the fact that the national media are severely controlled by the Chinese Propaganda Department. Statistically, this discrepancy may be due to the colinearity between local and national media consumption ($r = .57$, $P < .001$). Therefore, in the regression analyses, the predictive power of national media use may have been trumped by local media use. (Nevertheless, the national and local forms of media consumption are at least conceptually distinctive. Hence we will continue to treat them separately in later chapters.)

The findings about the relationship between foreign media use and nationalism are particularly important. On the surface, consumption of foreign media is unrelated to nationalistic sentiments. However, upon further analysis, we find that foreign media consumption does not relate so much to intensity of nationalistic sentiments but to how the two types of nationalistic sentiments are related to each other. Those who consumed foreign media most frequently would dissociate cultural nationalism from developmental nationalism. Thus the findings point to the possible impact of foreign media consumption not on "levels" of nationalism but on the "definition" of nationalism itself—that is, in the present case, whether an emphasis on national development would entail a belief in one's cultural superiority.

It should be noted that the dissociation between cultural and developmental nationalism occurred only when foreign media consumption reached a reasonably high level. And in our data set derived from the 2006/2007 survey, actually only about 5 percent of the respondents in the whole sample were classified as people who used foreign media frequently. However, as foreign media continue to make their ways into the Chinese market, as discussed in Chapter 3, the rearticulation of nationalism triggered by foreign media may become a more widespread phenomenon.

This chapter ends with an analysis of Chinese people's feelings toward foreign countries. Although the previous literature suggests that ratings of foreign nations are largely determined by cultural similarities and national interests, Chinese people's evaluation of foreign nations seems to be influenced primarily by the perceived political and economic strength. Most developing countries were rated less favorably than the developed nations. In terms of the influence of nationalism, urban Chinese residents with high levels of developmental nationalism do not necessarily show negative affect toward foreign countries. Instead, those who identified strongly with the Chinese cultural tradition tended to like the lesser developed countries and to dislike the United States, the United Kingdom, and Japan. Historical and contemporary relations between China and the foreign countries concerned do matter.

Certainly our analysis on feelings toward foreign countries in this chapter is preliminary. As Chinese people gain more and more knowledge about the world at large from various sources, they might develop more complicated and sophisticated images of the world in general and of certain countries in particular. Overall ratings, therefore, do not tell us much about how Chinese people actually see specific foreign countries. In the next chapter, we thus provide a more detailed and sophisticated analysis of how Chinese people see a specific country that is particularly important to China in the contemporary world: the United States of America.

5 Attitudes toward America

A substantial proportion of the phenomena that people usually associate with globalization involves the spreading of American values, institutions, commodities, media products, and ways of life to other parts of the world. For critics of globalization in particular, the symptoms of a "McWorld" (Barber, 1995) include the ubiquitous presence of such things as McDonald's, Nike, Starbucks, Coca-Cola, Hollywood movies, reality TV shows, and more recently Internet applications like YouTube, Google, and Facebook in virtually every corner of the globe. Some people would also include liberal political values and institutions such as democracy, freedom of speech, and the rule of law as exports from the Anglo-American world, even though such people may not agree on whether such values and institutions are truly universal.

Of course this does not mean that globalization and/or cultural imperialism can be reduced to Americanization (Micklethwaite and Wooldridge, 2001; Tomlinson, 1991). Globalization involves a complex web of social, political, and economic relationships in which influences do flow, if unevenly, in multiple and reverse directions (Iwabuchi, 2007; Thussu, 2007). But it is also true that the United States remains the most powerful country in the world today, especially in the post-Cold War era. In a study of public opinion toward globalization and the world at large, people's attitude toward the United States deserves separate treatment.

Chinese people's attitudes toward the United States constitute a significant topic for analysis also because of the importance of the U.S.-China tie to world and regional stability. In a world where, after the end of the Cold War, the United States is allegedly "bound to lead" (Nye, 1990), China would like to think of itself as a nation "bound to rise" (Lee, 2010) in the globalizing process. Today, managing the nation's relationship with the United States is arguably the top priority of China's foreign policy. Yet public opinion within China may affect and constrain how China interacts with the United States. Shih (2003), for instance, warns that popular nationalism, if mismanaged, could lead to confrontation with the United States, which in turn would be detrimental to the interests of both countries.

Toward the end of last chapter, we saw that our survey respondents' overall impression of the United States was slightly positive, having a mean score of 3.14 when overall impression was measured with a five-point Likert scale ranging from 1 = very bad to 5 = very good. Indeed, opinion polls in China in the late 1990s and early 2000s have shown a steady increase in favorable feelings among the Chinese toward the United States (Huang, 2006; Zhang, 2003). However, such overall favorable feelings may conceal the complexities of people's perceptions of and attitudes toward America, which He (1994) described as China's "most respected enemy." Johnston and Stockmann (2007), for example, showed that Beijing residents were generally favorable toward the American people but unfavorable to the U.S. government. At the height of an anti-United States campaign in 1999, following NATO's bombing of the Chinese embassy in Yugoslavia, young Chinese threw stones at the U.S. embassy in Beijing, only to queue up for American visas afterwards (Gao, 2000). Since then, Chinese students continued to see the United States as one of their most preferable locations for overseas study. According to news reports, there were 157,558 students from China in the United States in year 2010, constituting 22 percent of all international students in the United States in the year.[1] Meanwhile, Chinese immigrants to the United States increased quickly during the 1990s and 2000s.[2] This evidence suggests that many Chinese people do not have a simple and unified idea of the United States.

This chapter, therefore, analyzes Chinese people's attitudes toward America by emphasizing the notions of multidimensionality and ambivalence. We are interested in identifying the dimensional structure of the image of the United States held by urban Chinese and in examining the extent to which Chinese people see the United States as an "ambivalent other"—that is, as a cultural other that one loves and hates at the same time. We also examine the factors related to Chinese people's perceptions of the United States and their degree of ambivalence in that regard.

To provide more background information for the core empirical analysis in this chapter, the following discussion begins with a brief review of the history of the China-U.S. relationship. It also reviews existing studies about how the people in the two countries see each other. The analysis of our survey data is then presented.

A BRIEF HISTORY OF CHINA-U.S. RELATIONS

Over the past decades, the relationships between China and the United States have had "much to do with recurring cycles of amity and enmity" (Shambaugh, 1991). Since its establishment in 1949, the People's Republic of China (PRC) had been taken by the United States as a communist enemy. With the Kuomintang's retreat to Taiwan, the PRC's close ties with the USSR, and its involvement in the Korean War, the tension between China and the United States reached its height during the 1950s and early 1960s.

The development of the U.S.-China relationship took a significant turn in the late 1960s as the relationship between the USSR and China turned sour.

Within the Cold War context, the United States and China—a communist country outside the communist bloc—suddenly shared a common interest in establishing a strategic alliance in order to counteract the threat from the USSR. In 1972, U.S. President Richard Nixon visited China, thus paving the way for diplomatic rapprochement in 1979. President Reagan returned from his visit to China in the mid-1980s declaring that the Chinese were good communists and the Soviets were bad communists. Washington maintained a double standard, refraining from criticizing China for the same human rights abuse for which it attacked the Soviet Union (Harding, 1992, p. 201). According to the Gallup Polls, since the end of the 1960s, the American public has held increasingly favorable images of China. From 1967 to 1989, the percentage of American people feeling favorable toward China rose tremendously from a mere 5 percent to as much as 72 percent (Tian and Nathan, 2001; Yu, 1993). Throughout the 1980s, many Americans were hoping for the emergence of a better, freer, more democratic China.

The Tiananmen crackdown in 1989 shattered such high hopes. Womack (1990, p. 239) observed that Americans complacently viewed the change in China in the 1980s as a victory for capitalism and a loss for communism and then equally complacently interpreted the Tiananmen crackdown as "validating our own totalitarian stereotype of Communism." The percentage of Americans holding a favorable image of China went down sharply to only 39 percent in 1990, and the percentage of people unfavorable toward China rose from 13 percent in 1989 to 47 percent a year later (Tian and Nathan, 2001). However, owing to economic and diplomatic interests, the American government's condemnation and sanction against China after the Tiananmen crackdown did not last long. Both U.S. presidents in the 1990s, George Herbert Walker Bush and Bill Clinton, preferred an engagement policy over a containment policy. Yet the shadow of Tiananmen continued to hang over the relationship between the two countries. During the Clinton era, for example, human rights issues were routinely tied to the annual debate over the renewal of China's Most Favored Nation status in trade. In the American media, Tiananmen became a powerful "news icon" associated with the image of China as a brutal dictatorship (Lee, 2002; Lee, Li, and Lee, 2011). As a result, the images of Tiananmen continued to have a long-lasting impact on American public opinion. Opinion polls conducted by the Henry Luce Foundation Project in 1997 and 1999 found that 69 percent of Americans held unfavorable perceptions of the human rights condition in China.

But human rights were not the only issue that strained the relationship between China and the United States. The rise of the idea of "China threat" in the United States in the 1990s showed the United States's disdain of China's strength. This negative attitude was based not only on the perception that China, as an authoritarian country, would potentially act irresponsibly in international affairs but also on the simple fact that China, with its fast economic growth, might overtake the United States to become the most powerful nation in the world. In other words, calculations according to realist principles were as important as, if not more important than, reasoning according to moral-political principles in generating the China threat perception. By the end of the century, the tension between the two countries rose to another peak. In 1999, in a NATO air strike against Serbia, a U.S. bomber hit the Chinese embassy in Belgrade and killed three Chinese citizens, leading to widespread anti-American protests in China. In 2001, a U.S. spy plane crashed with two Chinese fighter planes over the South China Sea. Despite strong protests from the United States, China refused to release the American military officers until President George W. Bush, then newly elected, expressed "regrets" over the incident.

Whereas the NATO bombing and the spy plane incident signified an increasingly troubled relationship between the two countries, U.S.-China relationship took another u-turn after the September 11 terrorist attack in New York City and Washington, DC. The American government treated China as an important ally in its "war on terror." Without being an enthusiastic supporter of U.S. actions in the Middle East, China was nonetheless willing to cooperate owing to its own problems with "Muslim terrorism" or "Uyghur terrorism" in the Xinjiang province. Meanwhile, China's policy of fully engaging with the processes of economic globalization saw the country joining the WTO formally in 2003. Despite their misgivings about Washington's intentions, elite Chinese media perceived their country as going through a rite of passage to world greatness; in order to avoid sidetracking its developmental aims and to take advantage of the opportunities afforded by the globalizing process, it was felt that China would have to refrain from any direct confrontation with the powerful United States (Lee, 2010). China began to play increasingly active and visible roles in various international organizations. The growing international influence and economic prowess of China meant that cooperation between the two countries became increasingly inevitable and important to both countries and to the world at large.

Nevertheless, the continual rise of China also arguably deepened the perception of the "China threat" to America's status as *the* world superpower. Gries, Crowson and Sandel's (2010) analysis of American perceptions of China during and after the 2008 Beijing Olympics provides a case in point. Their survey found a significant increase in negative attitudes toward China among the American public throughout the month of August 2008. As they stated, "seeing such a 'modern' China may have undermined many Americans' view of America as special in regard to technology and modernity. . . . by staging such a wonderful Games, Chinese organizers may have inadvertently contributed to greater American anxiety and wariness towards China" (Gries, Crowson and Sandel, 2010, p. 130). The rise of China was beginning to challenge the long-held notion of "American exceptionalism."

From the other side, the Chinese public has long treated the United States with both admiration and resentment and with both fear and respect. As in the case of American public opinion toward China, favorable and unfavorable sentiments held by the Chinese toward the United States have varied historically. Having emerged from the shackles of the Cultural Revolution, Chinese people looked up to the United States as a model of development at a time when the United States played the "China card" against the Soviet Union in the 1980s (Harding, 1992). An active liberal Chinese intellectual ferment in the 1980s, symbolized by the famous television documentary *River Elegy*, pointed to western democracy as a solution for China's problems. Chan (2005) described the 1980s as a period of China "chasing glory and the dream" (p. 938). Chen (2003) even argued that the Tiananmen student movement was a direct consequence of pro-Americanism among the Chinese college students of the 1980s, who "were attracted to [the] material prosperity, free way of life and democratic political systems of the West" (p. 7).

Chinese people's positive attitude toward the United State culminated in 1989. But the 1990s witnessed the rise of nationalistic sentiments and a related "nationalist backlash" against the United States (Chan, 2005). The strong anti-American sentiments within the society were best represented by and captured in the huge popularity garnered by books such as *China Can Say No* and *Behind the Demonization of China*. Based on a survey conducted in 2004, Johnston and Stockmann (2007) found that attitude of urban Chinese toward the United States was generally negative.

Of course positive perceptions of certain aspects of America did not completely disappear. Even after the incident over NATO's bombing of the Chinese embassy in Belgrade, university students in Beijing continued to acknowledge the United States as a superpower rather than as an enemy and believed that China should not be so anti-American as to sacrifice its own economic development (Yu and Zhao, 2006; Zhao, 2002). As already indicated in Chapter 4, Chinese people's nationalistic sentiments can be complicated. As an ironic episode, it was openly ridiculed that some Beijing students might throw stones at the U.S. embassy during the protest in the morning but then, in the afternoon, line up in front of it to await visa approval for study in the United States.

It would therefore be more meaningful to describe the Chinese people as holding a multidimensional image of and ambivalent attitude toward the United States. There has not been much research that systematically tackled the multidimensionality and ambivalence in Chinese public opinion about the United States. One exception is Chen (2003), who interviewed Chinese college students and found "two Americas" in their hearts. The first is America as a global hegemon; the other is an "advanced and developed United States that excites admiration and yearning" (p. 15). The students were critical toward the United States's self-appointed "world policeman" role, but they admired the educational and social systems of the United States. Yet Chen's study is limited to college students, and the notion of "two Americas" may still not capture certain additional dimensions of the image of America held by the Chinese people. The following analysis, therefore, should fill an important gap in the literature.

THE MULTIDIMENSIONAL IMAGE OF THE UNITED STATES

There has been a substantial body of literature on the notion of "anti-Americanism" around the world (e.g., Fabrini, 2003; Kizilbash, 1988; Kim, 2002; Kim and Lim, 2007; Langley, 1988; Nolan, 2005; Parker, 1988; Rubenstein and Smith, 1985), but only a few scholars have attempted to identify dimensions of people's attitude toward the United States. Isernia (2007), for instance, found that Europeans were willing to distinguish between the American people and the American government. Using Pew Research Global Attitudes Survey data, Chiozza (2007) came up with eight dimensions of attitude toward America: democracy, customs, popular culture, science, business, war on terror, value clash, and power balance.[3] But on the whole, there is still no widely accepted typology regarding the dimensionality of people's attitudes toward the United States, and it is not certain that the typology developed by Chiozza (2007) is applicable to China. Together with practical concerns for the length of the questionnaire, the following analysis of the multidimensionality of people's attitude toward the United States is more exploratory than an effort at formal hypothesis testing.

In the survey, the respondents were asked to indicate the degree to which they would agree with a set of 19 statements about the United States. The statements were designed to capture features of the American political system, society, and culture as well as America's role in the international community. Some of the statements were phrased positively and some were phrased negatively. For example, "The two-party system in America prevents the corruption of the powerful" is a positive statement about the U.S. political system, whereas "materialistic desires pervade the American society" is a negative statement about the American society. Of the 19 statements, 3 were not included in the analysis because they involved explicit linkages between the United States and China (and hence they are "contaminated" indicators of people's attitude toward the United States). The remaining 16 statements were subjected to an exploratory factor analysis.

Table 5.1 summarizes the statements, their basic descriptive statistics, and the result of the factor analysis. What a factor analysis can do in this context is to see, based on how the items are correlated with one another, whether specific items would cluster together. When such clusters appear, we can argue that the items represent an underlying latent "factor" or concept. In the present case, the factor analysis generates five factors. The first factor is constituted by three statements about U.S. leadership in world politics. Although the statements are phrased positively, the mean scores are all very low—they range from 2.30 to 2.53 on a five-point Likert scale, with 1 = strongly disagree and 5 = strongly agree. The low mean scores thus indicate

Table 5.1 Factor Analysis of Chinese People's Attitude toward the United States

	Mean	S.D.	F1	F2	F3	F4	F5
Only America can lead the world	2.30	1.00	.81				
America is the protector of world peace	2.30	0.97	.81				
No one can prevent America from dominating the world	2.54	0.98	.83				
U.S. policy is concerned only with interests, not principles	3.25	0.88		.76			
The ultimate goal of U.S. foreign policy is to control the entire world	3.47	0.89		.77			
American society discriminates against racial minorities	3.37	0.87		.53			.36
Materialistic desires pervade American society	3.30	0.81		.55			
The two-party system in America prevents the corruption of the powerful	3.30	0.86			.86		
The American media leads to less corruption in the society	3.24	0.88			.86		
The United States is a powerful country because of its good institutions	3.02	0.99			.58		
I long for the American way of life	2.77	0.96				.43	
American society is full of opportunities	3.33	0.79				.76	
American culture is rich	3.32	0.84				.75	
The system of separation of power in the United States is inefficient	2.85	0.82					.58
Freedom of the press in America only serves rich people	3.20	0.90					.63
Human relationships within American society are weak	3.09	0.89					.72
Variance explained			20.5%	14.7%	8.9%	7.5%	6.4%
Eigen-values			3.29	2.35	1.43	1.20	1.03

Note: Entries in the first column are mean scores based on a five-point Likert-scale with 1 = strongly disagree and 5 = strongly agree. The entries in the last five columns are factor loadings in the pattern matrix derived from a principal component analysis with direct oblique rotation. Factor loadings smaller than .30 are not shown.

that our respondents held generally very negative attitude toward ideas such as "only America can lead the world" and "America is the protector of world peace." This is consistent with past studies of Chinese attitudes toward the United States (Chen, 2003; Johnston and Stockmann, 2007).

The second factor consists of four statements. In terms of propositional contents, the four statements are all negative toward the United States. Whereas the first two statements are mainly about the questionable motivations of U.S. foreign policies, the other two statements are about the characteristics of the American society. In other words, the four statements do not share a sharp conceptual focus. Moreover, the statement that "The American society discriminates against racial minorities" actually crossloads on both the second and the fifth factors in the factor analysis (with factor loadings > .30). Interestingly, the fifth factor is also consisted of four negatively phrased statements about the United States. Two of the statements are about the American political system and the other two (including the statement about discrimination against racial minorities) are about U.S. society.

That is, these four statements also do not share a sharp conceptual or topical focus. Furthermore, it is notable that, in terms of mean scores, our respondents tended to agree with all the statements constituting the second and fifth factors with the exception of the statement about the efficiency of the system of separation of powers.

We take these findings as showing that the Chinese public does hold various negative perceptions about the society and political system of the United States. It seems that the Chinese public is willing to acknowledge the validity of many arguments pointing toward "something bad" in or about America, but they do not necessarily distinguish clearly between what is bad about the U.S. polity and what is bad about American society. For conceptual clarity, we combine the second and fifth factor in Table 5.1 into a single dimension of "critical perceptions about the United States."

The third factor is constituted by three positively phrased statements focusing on the political system of the United States. The mean scores for all three statements are at least nominally above the midpoint of the scale. Chinese people tended to agree that having more than one political party and having free and independent media have helped to prevent corruption in America, although fewer people are willing to explain the powerfulness of the United States in terms of its political institutions. In any case, these three statements do form a distinctive dimension of "positive perceptions of U.S. institutions."

Finally, the fourth factor is also constituted by three positively phrased statements about the society and culture of the United States. Our respondents tended to agree with the statement that American society is full of opportunities. Interestingly, despite the stereotypical notion that U.S. culture consists mainly of mass-produced and highly commodified products ranging from Disneyland to McDonald's, our respondents tended to agree with the statement that "American culture is rich." Yet the respondents tended to disagree with the statement "I long for the American way of life." Nevertheless, the fact that the respondents disagreed with this last statement is possibly due to the specific phrasing of the statement: "Long for" is a strong expression hinting at not only a general liking but also an active desire to pursue it. It also implies a willingness to leave behind one's existing way of life. Hence it is actually understandable that people would be less likely to agree with the statement. But on the whole, the urban Chinese seemed to hold certain positive perceptions regarding American society and culture, and such perceptions form the fourth dimension of Chinese people's attitude toward the United States.

In sum, we derive four distinctive dimensions of urban Chinese people's attitude toward the United States from the analysis. Following the results, four indices for the four dimensions were produced by averaging the items belonging to each of the dimensions.[4] Figure 5.1 shows the mean scores of the four dimensions. As already discussed, the respondents were generally negative about the notion of U.S. leadership, but they also held some positive perceptions about the political institutions as well as the society and culture of the United States. At the same time, they tended to agree that there are various undesirable characteristics of the American political system, society, and culture.

One additional thing to note about the four indices is the difference in their standard deviations (not shown in the figure). U.S. leadership has the largest standard deviations, followed by the indices for perceptions of U.S. institutions and U.S. society (0.82). The index for critical perceptions of the United

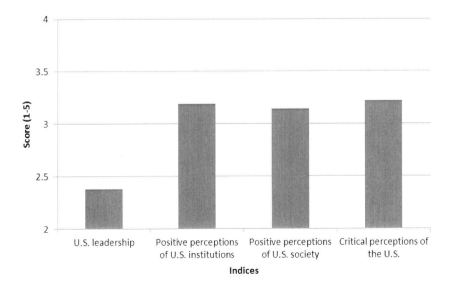

Figure 5.1   The four dimensions of Chinese people's attitude toward the United States.

States has the smallest standard deviation (0.51). These numbers indicate the extent to which the respondents expressed varying answers to the questions involved. For example, although the index of positive perceptions of U.S. institutions and the index of critical perceptions of the United States had basically the same mean score, more people had "extreme scores" on positive perceptions of U.S. institutions than on the critical perceptions index: 11.7 percent of the respondents had a score below 2 or above 4 on the U.S. institutions index, whereas only 5.0 percent scored below 2 or above 4 on the critical perceptions index. In more concrete terms, what these findings suggest is that questions related to U.S. leadership in the world and those related to the desirability of the political institutions of the United States remain relatively likely to generate heated debates among the Chinese populace. Comparatively, the idea that the United States does have some undesirable features is unlikely to generate much disagreement among the urban Chinese.

To understand how the four dimensions may combine to generate people's overall feelings toward the United States, a regression analysis was conducted by using the four indices to explain the respondents' overall favorability ratings of the United States—that is, the rating reported in Chapter 4. All the indices are significantly related to overall ratings in the expectable directions: people who rated the United States more favorably tended to hold relatively more positive views toward U.S. leadership, U.S. institutions, and U.S. society; they also tended to hold critical perceptions toward the United States to lesser extents. The differences in the sizes of the regression coefficients are not substantial, however (the size of the beta ranges from .12 to .20). In other words, none of the four indices has overwhelming importance in explaining the overall favorability rating. It also means that urban Chinese's overall attitude toward the United States is indeed a combination of their perceptions of the various aspects of the country.

PREDICTORS OF ATTITUDES TOWARD THE UNITED STATES

With the dimensions of attitude toward the United States established, we can now examine the factors related to the different dimensions. Three sets of predictors are included in the analysis. The first set of predictors simply includes the basic demographics (age, gender, household income, education), English ability, occupation, and the city in which the respondents resided (turned into three city dummies with Beijing as the reference category, as in the previous chapters).

The second set of predictors includes a number of attitudinal and value orientation measures. Five specific variables are involved. First, we are interested in whether people would be more positive toward at least certain dimensions of the United States if they were more receptive to the idea of moving abroad to further their careers and/or life goals—that is, the variable "adventurism," as discussed in Chapter 2. Second, we examine if people's attitude toward the

United States would relate to whether they see certain western liberal values and some of the more traditional and conservative social values as important. Again, the relevant variables were already discussed in Chapter 2. In addition, the analysis also examines the relationship between nationalistic sentiments and attitude toward the United States. Following the discussion in Chapter 4, we differentiate between developmental nationalism and cultural nationalism. These are included in the analysis as two separate variables.

The third set of predictors was constituted by foreign travel experiences, transnational social connections, and media use. There have not been many studies examining the relationship between media consumption and attitude toward the United States. One exception is Gentzkow and Shapiro's (2004) analysis of public opinion in Muslim countries. They found that the consumption of Middle East news adds to negative perceptions about the United States. But in the case of China, without systematically gathered data on its media contents, it would be difficult to predict whether the consumption of national and local media would relate to more positive or negative attitude toward America. Meanwhile, Carlson and Nelson (2008) examined people's perceptions of the United States in 26 Asian countries and found that individual contacts with the outside world were positively related to the perceived influence of the United States on people's home countries. Their findings are consistent with Norris and Inglehart's (2009) argument about cosmopolitan communications. It is plausible that foreign media consumption and personal experiences with the outside world would relate to more positive attitudes toward the United States.

The first column of Table 5.2 shows the results of the multiple regression analysis regarding the predictors of positive perceptions of U.S. institutions. Among the demographics, females were significantly less positive toward the political institutions of the United States. At the same time, residents in Shanghai and residents in Chengdu held significantly more negative perceptions regarding U.S. institutions as compared with residents in Beijing. It should be noted that, at the bivariate level, residents in Xi'an were more positive toward U.S. institutions as compared with residents of the other three cities ($r = .08$, $P < .001$). But the multivariate relationship shows that there is no difference between residents in Xi'an and residents in Beijing on the dependent variable.

Among the five attitudinal and value orientation variables, two obtain a statistically significant coefficient. Adventurism relates positively to positive perceptions of U.S. institutions. That is, people who were more positive toward the idea of pursuing career and personal development in other countries tended to hold more positive attitude toward the political institutions of the United States. Yet support for democracy and freedom itself does not relate to the dependent variable; it is possible that many Chinese people might not understand democracy and freedom as American-style democracy and liberty. Neither does support for the more conservative values of harmony and stability relate to perceptions of U.S. institutions. Yet nationalistic sentiments do relate to perceptions of the

Table 5.2 Predictors of Different Dimensions of Attitude toward the United States

	U.S. Institutions	U.S. Society	U.S. Leadership	Critical Perceptions
Gender	-.05*	-.04	-.02	-.01
Age	-.02	-.06*	-.00	.00
Education	-.02	.05	-.05	.00
Income	.02	-.01	.01	.02
Ability to speak English	-.05	-.01	-.01	-.06*
Work in state enterprise	-.01	-.02	-.05*	-.04*
Work in foreign companies	.01	.02	.02	.01
Shanghai	-.09**	-.05	-.07*	-.03
Chengdu	-.07*	-.11***	-.19***	.01
Xi'an	.03	-.02	-.17***	.07*
Adventurism	.13***	.14***	.12***	.09***
Traditional values	.03	.02	.00	.09***
Liberal values	.02	.03	.03	-.03
Developmental nationalism	-.05	-.09***	-.16***	-.03
Cultural nationalism	-.06*	-.00	-.07**	.28***
Foreign travel experience	-.02	.03	-.01	.03
Transnational connections	.02	.02	-.03	-.04
Local media consumption	-.05	-.00	-.03	-.09**
National media consumption	-.01	-.07*	-.06*	.04
Foreign media consumption	.03	.02	.10***	-.06*
Adjusted R²	3.4%***	4.3%***	7.1%***	11.9%***

Note: Entries are standardized regression coefficients. * $P < .05$; ** $P < .01$; *** $P < .001$.

United States: when all other variables are controlled, more nationalistic people were significantly more negative toward the political institutions of the United States.

The addition of the foreign experiences/connections and media use variables does not add significantly to the explanatory power of the model. None of the five individual variables can explain the dependent variable in the first column. That is, communication does not explain Chinese people's perceptions of U.S. institutions.

The second column summarizes the results for the predictors of positive perceptions of U.S. society. Younger Chinese were more inclined to have positive images of the U.S. society, which is not a surprising finding given the appeal of western/American popular culture to young Chinese. Chengdu residents were significantly less likely to hold the positive perceptions of the U.S. society as compared with Beijing residents, but there are no meaningful differences between Shanghai and Beijing residents or between Xi'an and Beijing residents.

As with the results in the first column, adventurism and nationalism predicted the dependent variable in the second column. People who regarded seeking development in foreign countries as a good thing were more likely to hold positive perceptions of U.S. society, whereas people who exhibited higher levels of developmental nationalistic sentiments were less likely to hold such perceptions.

Again, the variables of foreign travel experience, transnational social connections, and media use have very limited relationships with the dependent variable. In fact, at the bivariate level, none of the five communication and personal experience variables has a significant relationship with positive perceptions of U.S. society. However, in the full regression model and where individual variables are concerned, people who consumed national media to larger extents were less likely to agree with the statements about the positive features of the American society.

The third column of Table 5.2 summarizes the results of the regression analysis regarding attitude toward U.S. leadership. Among the demographics there is only a weak relationship between working in state enterprises and the dependent variable. That is, workers in state enterprises were less likely to recognize the leadership role of the United States in world affairs. Comparing among the cities, residents in Xi'an, Chengdu, and Shanghai were all more negative toward U.S. leadership in world affairs as compared with Beijing residents. Age, gender, education, and income do not relate to the dependent variable in either the bivariate or multivariate analyses.

The impact of attitudinal and value orientations is consistent with the findings in the first two columns. Adventurism is positively related to attitude toward U.S. leadership, whereas both developmental nationalism and cultural nationalism are related negatively to attitude toward U.S. leadership. That is, people with higher levels of nationalistic sentiments were less likely to recognize the United States as a legitimate and powerful leader in world affairs, yet people who saw moving abroad in a positive light were more likely to recognize U.S. leadership. Support for liberal values again fails to register significant relationships with the dependent variable. Support for traditional values has a negative relationship with attitude toward U.S. leadership at the bivariate level ($r = -.08$, $P < .001$), but the relationship became insignificant in the multivariate analysis, probably because the relationship is explained away by the impact of nationalistic sentiments.

The addition of the personal experience and communication variables add significantly to the predictive power of the regression model reported in the third column. In bivariate analysis, attitude toward U.S. leadership relates negatively to local media consumption ($r = -.05$, $P < .04$). But interestingly, in the full regression model, the other two media consumption variables are significantly related to the dependent variable. People who consumed various foreign media to larger extents were relatively more receptive to the idea of the United States being the leader in world politics. Besides, people who consumed national media to larger extents were more negative toward the idea of the United States being the leader in the world.

Finally, the last column of Table 5.2 presents the results on critical perceptions of the United States. In bivariate analysis, more educated people and people with higher levels of English ability were less likely to hold critical perceptions of the United States (r = -.07 and -.08, P < .01 and < .001 respectively). Shanghai residents were also less likely to uphold the critical perceptions when compared to residents in other cities (r = -.08, P < .001). However, some of these relationships become insignificant in the multivariate analysis. In the full regression model, English ability remains related, though only weakly, to critical perceptions of the United States. Workers in state enterprises were also less likely to entertain critical perceptions of the United States. In addition, Xi'an residents held more critical perceptions toward the United States as compared with Beijing residents.

Attitudinal and value orientations have strong relationships with critical perceptions of the United States. Adventurism again obtains a positive and statistically significant coefficient in the regression analysis. People who were more open to the possibility of seeking development abroad nonetheless held more of the negative perceptions of the United States. Besides, people who put more emphasis on the traditional values of harmony and stability as well as those who had stronger cultural nationalistic sentiments also held more negative perceptions of the United States. The latter relationship is particularly strong. The unstandardized regression coefficient for the variable is 0.23— that is, as a person's score on cultural nationalism increases by 1 point, the person's score on the critical perceptions of the U.S. index would increase by 0.23 points. The increase is quite substantial for a five-point scaled variable.

Regarding the personal experience and communication variables, at the bivariate level, foreign social connections have a significant negative relationship with critical perceptions (r = -.05, P < .03). That is, people with more social connections in foreign countries tended to hold fewer critical perceptions of the United States. This relationship does not survive statistical control, however. Instead, what remains statistically significant in the multivariate analysis is the impact of foreign media consumption and local media consumption. People who consumed local media to larger extents and those who consumed foreign media to larger extents both tended to hold fewer negative perceptions about the United States.

In sum, Table 5.2 shows that the various dimensions of people's attitudes toward the United States can be explained by somewhat different factors. Some variables may have relatively "consistent" relationships with the various dimensions. Cultural nationalism, for example, is negatively related to the notion of U.S. leadership, negatively related to positive perceptions of U.S. institutions, and positively related to critical perceptions of the United States. In other words, cultural nationalism is consistently related to a more negative attitude toward the United States. The impact of adventurism, in contrast, is more complicated. Although it relates positively to positive perceptions of U.S. institutions, U.S. society, and U.S. leadership, it also relates positively to critical perceptions. In other words, people with higher levels of adventurism seem to be both more positive and more negative toward the United States. What this suggests is a relationship between adventurism and attitudinal ambivalence, a problem to be addressed in the next section.

But before we go on to tackle the problem of ambivalence, it will be useful to end this section by examining the predictors of overall attitude toward the United States. To argue that people's attitude toward the United States is multidimensional and ambivalent does not mean that we cannot meaningfully analyze people's overall attitude toward the country. Here, instead of employing the overall favorability rating examined in the previous chapter, we created an overall attitude variable based on the four dimensions examined in this chapter by using the average of the three "positive dimensions" (U.S. leadership, U.S. institution, and U.S. society) and subtracting the critical perceptions index.[5] Multiple regression analysis was then conducted, with the regression model in Table 5.2 used to explain overall attitude.

Table 5.3 summarizes the results. There are limited relationships between the demographic variables and overall attitude toward the United States. At the bivariate level, young people, better educated people, and people who

Table 5.3 Predicting Overall Attitude toward the United States

	Overall Attitude toward the United States
Gender	-.04
Age	-.03
Education	-.01
Income	-.01
Ability to speak English	.02
Work in state enterprise	.00
Work in foreign companies	.01
Shanghai	-.06
Chengdu	-.14***
Xi'an	-.12***
Adventurism	.07**
Traditional values	-.05*
Liberal values	.05*
Developmental nationalism	-.09***
Cultural nationalism	-.26***
Foreign travel experience	-.02
Transnational connections	.03
Local media consumption	.04
National media consumption	-.08**
Foreign media consumption	.10***
Adjusted R^2	9.8%***

Note: Entries are standardized regression coefficients. * $P < .05$; ** $P < .01$; *** $P < .001$.

had better English ability were more positive toward the United States (r = -.07, .07 and, .08 respectively, all significant at $P < .01$). But these variables do not relate to overall attitude when other variables are controlled. However, there are significant differences in attitudes among residents of different cities. Residents of Chengdu and Xi'an held more negative overall attitudes toward the United States as compared with Beijing residents.

All five value and attitudinal orientation variables are related to overall attitude toward the United States. As already noted, nationalistic sentiments, especially the "cultural" variant, are related to more negative attitudes toward the United States. Despite its seemingly contradictory relationship with the various dimensions of people's attitudes toward the United States, adventurism does have a positive relationship with overall attitude. More interestingly, although support for the liberal values of democracy and freedom does not explain any of the four specific dimensions of attitude toward the United States in Table 5.2, it does have a positive though only very weak relationship with overall attitude toward the United States. In contrast, support for the traditional values of harmony and stability contributes negatively to overall attitude toward the United States.

Last, foreign media consumption relates positively to overall attitude toward the United States. National media consumption relates negatively to overall attitude. This pattern of findings echoes that found by Gentzkow and Shapiro (2004) in the case of Muslim countries, as people who consumed the media from their own country and/or region tended to hold more negative attitudes toward America. Yet consumption of foreign media (which is likely to be constituted mainly by American media) did contribute to more positive views of America.

AMBIVALENCE TOWARD THE UNITED STATES

Attitudinal ambivalence is the other conceptual focus of this chapter. In psychology, the concept can be defined as "the co-existence of both positive and negative dispositions toward an attitude object" (Ajzen, 2001). The underlying idea is that the invoking of thoughts and attitudes of positive valence does not necessarily suppress the invoking of negative thoughts and attitudes. Psychologists also differentiate between objective and subjective ambivalence. The former refers to the coexistence of negative and positive thoughts about the same object, whereas the latter refers to the subjective feeling of conflicts toward an attitude object (e.g., deMarree et al., 2011; Lee and Chan, 2009). Our survey does not contain items asking the respondents about their subjective feelings of conflicts regarding the United States, but the range of items analyzed in the previous sections allows us to examine Chinese people's objective ambivalence toward the United States.

In fact, the previous section has already hinted at some evidence regarding Chinese people's ambivalence toward the United States. As Table 5.1

Table 5.4 Correlations among the Four Dimensions of Attitude toward the United States

	U.S. Society	U.S. Leadership	Critical Perceptions
U.S. institution	.30***	.35***	.12***
U.S. society		.35***	.08***
U.S. leadership			.12***

Note: Entries are Pearson correlation coefficients. Ns range from 1993 to 1997. *** $P < .001$.

shows, our respondents generally agreed with the positive statements about the political institutions of the United States. Yet they also tended to agree with a number of statements that are negative toward the United States. To further illustrate the phenomenon of attitudinal ambivalence, Table 5.4 shows the correlations among the four dimensions of people's attitudes toward the United States. It is not surprising that the three positive perceptions of the United States are positively correlated. That is, people who viewed the United States's political institutions favorably tended to also hold more positive perceptions of and attitudes toward U.S. leadership and U.S. society. But more important to the notion of ambivalence, people who were more positive toward U.S. institutions, U.S. society, and U.S. leadership in world affairs were, at the same time, also more likely to hold a range of critical perceptions about the United States. These findings show that, among the urban Chinese, having more positive perceptions about the United States by no means implies having fewer negative perceptions about the country.

Psychologists have developed a number of measures of attitudinal ambivalence (e.g., Kaplan, 1972; Priester and Petty, 1996). The present analysis adopts the relatively simple formula of Thompson and colleagues (1995):

Ambivalence = (P + N) / 2 -| P—N |
where P = positive thoughts and N = negative thoughts

This formula, put into words, treats ambivalence as intensity (the total strength or amount of positive and negative thoughts, i.e., P + N) minus polarity (the absolute difference between the strength or amount of positive and negative thoughts, i.e., | P—N |).

Applying the formula to the present data requires us to define and calculate the strength or amount of positive and negative thoughts regarding the United States held by our respondents. For this purpose, we counted the number of critical statements—that is, the seven statements constituting the "critical perceptions toward the United States" index—with which a respondent has expressed agreement (i.e., the respondent scored 4 or 5 on the statement). This counting procedure thus gives rise to a variable ranging from 0 to 7, representing a continuum from having the smallest amount of negative attitudes to having the largest amount of negative attitudes about the United States.[6] Similarly, the amount of positive thoughts was calculated by counting the number of positive statements with which the respondents had expressed agreement: (1) the three positive perceptions of "U.S. society;" (2) the three positive perceptions of "U.S. institutions;" and (3) the statement that "America is the protector of world peace." The other two statements belonging to the attitude toward "U.S. leadership" index were not included in the calculation partly in order to keep the total number of positive statements at 7 and thus equal to the number of negative statements in the calculation. Besides, the two excluded statements— "only America can lead the world" and "no one can prevent America from dominating the world"—are arguably less clearly "positive" attitudes. For example, people may adopt the idea that no one can prevent American domination only as a judgment about the reality, when they may actually resent the reality of American domination.

With the counts generated, we are now in a better position to see the proportion of our respondents holding both positive and negative thoughts about the United States. Cross-tabulating the counts of negative thoughts and positive thoughts shows that as many as 1,493 of the 2,000 survey respondents held at least one positive attitude *and* at least one negative attitude regarding the United States at the same time. In other words, close to 75 percent of the respondents were objectively ambivalent if not necessarily strongly so. They could be positive about aspects of the United States and negative on other aspects. In contrast, only 25 percent (380 respondents) held solely negative or solely positive attitudes regarding the United States (the remaining respondents held no positive and no negative attitudes regarding the United States). Furthermore, the cross-tabulation also shows that 995 respondents (i.e., close to 50 percent of the sample) held at least two negative attitudes simultaneously with at least two positive attitudes. The number of respondents with at least three positive *and* three negative attitudes regarding the United States also amounts to 551, or 27.6 percent of the whole sample.[7]

Admittedly these figures are not easy to interpret because of the lack of reference points. Cross-national or longitudinal comparisons, for example, would allow us to say whether the degree of ambivalence existing in the current sample is higher or lower than that existing in other samples. But the degree of ambivalence toward the United States among the Chinese urban population does seem substantial.

Then what explains ambivalence at the individual level? There are three major theoretical approaches to explaining ambivalence in the psychological literature (Lee and Chan, 2009). First, ambivalence is considered by some psychologists as the result of value conflicts (e.g., Alvarez and Brehm, 1995; Citrin and Luks, 2005; Craig et al., 2005). When two values come into conflict on a certain issue—for example, on the conflict between the right to life and personal choice over the issue of abortion—a person is likely to become ambivalent if she or he takes both values seriously. Second, ambivalence can be related to communication behavior. Being ambivalent can directly result from holding conflicting thoughts and attitudes that are communicated to a person by the media or through interpersonal channels (Holbert and Hansen, 2006; Price, Nir, and Capella, 2005). Third, ambivalence can also be related to how people process the information communicated to them. Rudolph and Popp (2007), for example, found that people with a strong need for cognition and people of high motivation tend to have more ambivalent attitudes. The reason is that these people are more likely to process information systematically. They are willing to seriously consider competing arguments and thoughts instead of processing information selectively in order to reinforce their own existing views.

We conducted another set of multiple regression analyses to examine the predictors of Chinese people's ambivalence toward the United States. The regression model is based on the ones employed in Tables 5.2 and 5.3. To examine if value conflict could generate ambivalence toward the United States, an interaction term between support for liberal values and support for traditional values was included in the model. That is, we are interested in whether Chinese people would be particularly ambivalent toward the United States if they regarded both liberal values *and* traditional values as important. Besides, another interaction term between national media consumption and foreign media consumption was also created. Here, we are interested in whether Chinese people are particularly ambivalent toward the United States if they consume both national and foreign media frequently. Nevertheless, our analytical interests are not restricted to these interaction variables. The other independent variables may also have important relationships with ambivalence, and the theoretical arguments regarding the causes of ambivalence discussed above may help us to interpret such relationships when they appear.

The first column of Table 5.5 summarizes the results of the regression analysis. A number of factors do relate to ambivalence. Residents of Shanghai and residents of Chengdu were less ambivalent as compared with residents of Beijing. Among the value and attitudinal orientations, adventurism relates positively and moderately strongly with ambivalence. Interestingly, the influences of the two indicators of nationalistic sentiments are in opposite directions. People with higher levels of developmental nationalistic sentiments were less ambivalent toward the United States, but people with higher levels of cultural nationalistic sentiments were more ambivalent.

Among the media use and foreign connections variables, only local media consumption relates significantly and negatively to ambivalence. Last, there is indeed an interaction effect between support for liberal values and support for traditional values on ambivalence toward the United States, but the direction of the effect is contrary to expectation. Instead of generating ambivalence, the combination of liberal and traditional values tends to alleviate ambivalence toward the United States.

Table 5.5 Predictors of Ambivalence and its Components

	Ambivalence	Intensity	Polarity
Gender	-.06**	-.07**	-.01
Age	-.03	-.01	.04
Education	-.00	.00	.01
Income	-.00	.03	.07**
Ability to speak English	-.04	-.01	.05
Work in state enterprise	-.05*	-.03	.04
Work in foreign companies	.02	.02	-.01
Shanghai	-.22***	-.22***	.00
Chengdu	-.09**	-.05	.08**
Xian	-.04	.02	.12***
Adventurism	.17***	.18***	.02
Traditional values	.04	.01	.02
Liberal values	.01	.06*	.04
Developmental nationalism	-.05*	-.04	.02
Cultural nationalism	.14***	.15***	.01
Foreign travel experience	.01	.01	.01
Transnational connections	.00	.01	.02
Local media consumption	-.08**	-.14***	-.11***
National media consumption	-.01	.02	.06*
Foreign media consumption	.01	-.03	-.08**
Liberal vs. traditional values	-.06**	-.05*	.02
National vs. foreign media	.02	.04*	.05*
Adjusted R²	12.5%***	15.7%***	2.5%***

Note: Entries are standardized regression coefficients. N = 1,999.* P < .05; ** P < .01; ***
P < .001.

For more precise interpretations of these findings, we also conducted regression analyses on the two components of Thompson et al.'s (1995) measure of ambivalence—intensity and polarity—separately. "Intensity," conceptually, refers to the total strength of feelings that a person has toward an object. In the present analysis, intensity is represented by the total number of thoughts (positive + negative) about the United States held by an individual. "Polarity" refers to how one-sided people's attitudes toward an object are (that is, either one-sidedly positive or one-sidedly negative). Operationally, it is the absolute value of the difference in number of positive attitudes and number of negative attitudes. To reiterate, our ambivalence measure is calculated in terms of intensity minus polarity. That is, being ambivalent toward an object actually means having *intense and less polarized* feelings toward the object. Therefore a factor may actually lead to ambivalence toward an object by leading to more intense feelings toward the object, less polarized feelings toward the object, or both.

The second and third columns of Table 5.5 summarize the results of the analysis. The regression model is more successful in accounting for the intensity than for the polarity of people's thoughts about the United States. In fact, looking across all three columns in Table 5.5, we can see that most of the factors that explain attitudinal ambivalence in the first column are also predictive of intensity. Both adventurism and cultural nationalism, for example, relate positively and moderately strongly to intensity, but neither relates significantly to polarity. The overall result is therefore a positive relationship between these two factors and attitudinal ambivalence. The same applies to the Shanghai residency variable, the interaction effect between support for liberal values and support for traditional values, and, to a lesser extent, the developmental nationalism variable.

Local media consumption relates negatively to both intensity and polarity. That is, people who consumed local media tended to have fewer thoughts about the United States (i.e., they agreed with fewer statements regarding the United States). This contributes to the negative relationship between local media consumption and ambivalence in the first column. Interestingly, people who consumed local media to larger extents also tended to have less polarized thoughts about the United States. Yet this impact was more than cancelled out by local media consumption's impact on intensity.

The Chengdu residency variable constitutes the exception to the general pattern in that intensity matters more than polarity in linking an independent variable with overall level of ambivalence. Whereas Chengdu residents were less ambivalent toward the United States as compared with Beijing residents, the relationship appears because Chengdu residents held more polarized attitudes toward the United States.

It is also noteworthy that the interaction between national media consumption and foreign media consumption does have a significant and positive coefficient in the case of intensity. People who consumed both national and foreign media to larger extents did hold a larger number of thoughts about the United States—that is, they tended to agree with a larger number of statements about the United States in the questionnaire. Yet the interaction term also has a slightly positive, though statistically insignificant, relationship with polarity. That is, consuming both national and foreign media also led people to entertain more one-sidedly positive or negative thoughts about the United States, thus undermining attitudinal ambivalence.

More theoretically speaking, some of the findings in Table 5.5 point to the significance of Chinese people's information sources and information processing strategies in generating ambivalence toward the United States. The negative effect of local media consumption on ambivalence, for instance, can be explained in terms of the lesser amount of information about foreign countries in local media. Frequent consumers of local media are therefore less likely to acquire and/or develop a large number of attitudes and thoughts, whether positive or negative, toward foreign countries including the United States. Besides, the effect of adventurism on

LIVERPOOL JOHN MOORES UNIVERSITY
LEARNING SERVICES

ambivalence can be understood as the result of people processing information about foreign countries more objectively and systematically when they have the desire to move abroad to seek career and personal development. Instead of dismissing part of the information they are exposed to in order to maintain a one-sided image of the United States, these people are more likely to seriously weigh the pros and cons of moving abroad. They have a heightened awareness of the United States's strengths and weaknesses. In the process they are more likely to develop a higher degree of objective ambivalence toward the United States.

The impact of cultural nationalism can also be explained in terms of people's motivation to process information about a foreign country. As shown in Table 5.5, cultural nationalism leads to higher levels of ambivalence mainly by encouraging people to entertain a larger number of thoughts/attitudes about the United States. That is, cultural nationalists tended to agree with a larger number of both positive and negative statements about the United States. One way to explain this is to argue that cultural nationalists are more concerned with the United States as a powerful "cultural other," but they did not simply dismiss the U.S. culture and society. Rather, the cultural nationalists also seem to be able to appreciate the positive sides of the United States. Whereas these people took pride in Chinese culture, they also seemed to be willing to learn from foreign countries in order to maintain China's superiority.

AMERICA AS THE "AMBIVALENT OTHER"

The analysis in this chapter has systematically examined the attitudes of urban Chinese toward the United States by focusing on the problems of multidimensionality and ambivalence. Our factor analysis of people's agreement with 16 statements resulted in four conceptually and empirically distinctive dimensions of attitude toward America. Three of the dimensions are constituted by statements phrased positively, in terms of people's attitude toward U.S. leadership in world affairs, positive perceptions of American political institutions, and positive perceptions of American society and culture respectively. The fourth dimension is constituted by a number of statements phrased negatively, encompassing critical perceptions of the political system, the society, the culture, and the international role of the United States.

In other words, our respondents seemed to be differentiating more in thinking about the positive and desirable characteristics of the United States. For urban Chinese people, recognizing the quality of the political institutions of America does not entail accepting the legitimacy of its "world police" role. Putting these findings into context, it seems that the urban Chinese people we surveyed were carefully identifying the aspects of the American polity and society that China can indeed learn from or aspire to, yet they did not clearly distinguish between the undesirable features of the United States. There was only a general and vague perception that the American polity and society do have various problematic features.

As stated at the beginning sections of this chapter, our analysis of the dimensional structure of people's attitude toward the United States is exploratory. Methodologically speaking, how many and what dimensions could be identified from our data would be fundamentally dependent on the items that were included in the survey in the first place. Therefore we do not claim that we have identified the best or most valid dimensional structure of Chinese people's attitude toward the United States. However, its face validity is assuring: the four dimensions identified covered both positive and negative perceptions while also highlighting the United States's role in world affairs as well as the country's political system and societal culture. Our four-dimensional conception is less simplistic than a mere people-vs.-government distinction on the one hand (Isernia, 2007) but less complex than the eight-dimension conception proposed by Chiozza (2007) on the other. We believe that our four-dimensional conception should be useful for researchers studying public opinion toward America not only in China but also in other countries around the world.

Within this chapter, distinguishing the four dimensions allows us to discern the complexities in Chinese people's attitudes toward America. Some of our findings are consistent with the extant literature (Chen, 2003; Johnston and Stockmann, 2007). Our respondents were very negative toward the notion of U.S. leadership in world politics and generally agreed that there are various problems in American society. But at the same time, Chinese people held positive perceptions toward the political institutions of the United States, and they also tended to agree that America is a land of opportunities. Therefore, if there was any kind of anti-Americanism within the Chinese society, it was largely restricted to matters of international politics. This type of anti-Americanism may be particularly "visible," since its expression was often tied to major news events, such as Chinese people's "counterprotests" against western countries' criticism of China on the Tibetan crisis in 2008. But our findings show that Chinese people also held positive perceptions of American people, even though these positive perceptions may be more diffuse and less "newsworthy."

In terms of the factors that explain Chinese people's attitude toward the United States, the differences between the predictors of the four dimensions are relatively minor. Instead, more conceptually and socially meaningful results were obtained when we combined the dimensions to form an overall attitude index. Most important, overall attitude toward the United States is best explained by a couple of attitudinal orientations. First, there is indeed a substantially negative relationship between nationalistic sentiments and attitude toward the United States. Nationalists—both the "developmental" type and the "cultural" type—were more critical not only toward the notion of U.S. leadership in world politics but also toward other aspects of

American society and less positive toward American political institutions. This supports Shih's (2003) warning that nationalistic sentiments within the society present a potential problem for the U.S.-China relationship. This finding is also consistent with that provided by a more recent study by Shen (2011).

Nevertheless, there are also other social forces which can counteract the rise of anti-Americanism. Specifically, adventurism is positively related to attitude toward the United States. Within the Chinese context, many young people, especially university students, tend to be psychologically mobile and harbor the hope of studying and even working and living abroad. Many of them list the United States among their first choices of places to go to if they were to leave their home country. This serves as an important factor weakening negativism toward the United States within the Chinese society. As the geographical mobility of Chinese people is likely to continue to increase, the United States is likely to continue to serve as a "desired object" for many Chinese.

Media consumption also relates significantly to overall attitude toward the United States. There is a weak but negative relationship between national media consumption and overall attitude toward America. This may suggest that the representation of the United States in mainstream national media in China tends to be negative. But this may also be the result of the fact that people who consumed national media to larger extents were more likely to interpret U.S.-related information in specific manners. At the same time, foreign media consumption related positively to overall attitude toward the United States. Similar to national media consumption, this latter relationship can be the result of generally more positive images and representations of the United States in foreign media (most of which are American media) and/or the result of foreign media consumers' tendency to interpret information and images in ways that are favorable to the United States.

This chapter has also provided a systematic and formal analysis of Chinese people's ambivalence toward America. Focusing on objective ambivalence—that is, the mere coexistence of positive and negative thoughts—we found that about three fourths of urban Chinese can be classified as being at least minimally ambivalent toward the United States (i.e., holding at least one negative thought and one positive thought about America). Even if we set the criterion for ambivalence at having at least two positive and two negative attitudes at the same time, about half of the respondents would still qualify as being ambivalent. Putting it somewhat differently, there are very few Chinese people holding purely negative or purely positive views toward the United States. We contend that America constitute an "ambivalent other" for many urban Chinese, a mirror through which many people perceive themselves and their own country.

Our analysis shows that ambivalence is related to a couple of value and attitudinal orientations, namely cultural nationalism and adventurism, which have probably motivated Chinese people to process U.S.-related information systematically. In contrast, we do not find evidence regarding value conflicts as a source of ambivalence. Admittedly, the analysis of ambivalence in this chapter has a couple of limitations. First, it does not deal with subjective ambivalence. Theoretically, people may be capable of articulating and integrating the competing attitudes into an overall view, or they may rationalize the opposite views at a higher level of abstraction. Second, the lack of evidence about value conflicts as a cause of ambivalence may simply be due to the lack of variables representing the exact value orientations that can lead to ambivalence. Further research can try to rectify these limitations.

Last, this chapter has not tackled the question of the implications of people's perceptions of the United States. It should be noted that one cannot simplistically deduce people's social and political attitudes toward domestic matters based on their attitude toward a foreign country. For instance, whereas our analysis shows that many urban Chinese people tended to agree that the two-party system in the United States can prevent corruption, it does not entail that they would actively call for the ending of one-party dictatorship in China. People may regard it as too politically unrealistic, or they may actually think that the two-party system is good in theory but unsuitable for China. There is also the more fundamental question of how Chinese people actually understand two-party politics. In other words, a desirable two-party system may constitute only a vague idea for Chinese people, with few concrete political implications.

For another example, throughout this chapter we did not find very substantial influence of people's preference for democracy and freedom on their attitude toward the United States. Notably, most survey respondents expressed support for the values of freedom and democracy. But it is unclear what their conceptions of liberty and democracy were. Today, urban Chinese people are not unfamiliar with American-style democracy and elections. In particular, Barack Obama's U.S. election victory in 2008 was widely covered in the Chinese media. The story of the first African American winning the presidency did inspire quite a few, and Chinese people may indeed perceive democratic elections as a good thing. Yet it is also possible that they value American democracy only as an ideal, while finding some of its concrete electoral institutions and behaviors abhorrent. In any case, the linkages between perceptions of the West and attitude toward domestic social, economic, and political reforms can be complicated and require clarification through systematic analysis.

6 Awareness and Conceptions of Globalization

When the general population is brought into the equation, globalization as a concept and a phenomenon involves at least two aspects. That is, two interrelated questions can be raised: Have people ever heard of globalization? If yes, what do they think of it? These two apparently simple questions touch on the important issue of whether people are aware of the phenomenon of globalization or, more precisely, whether they are aware of the discursive resources that they might use to make sense of a range of phenomena that are happening in the world. This issue involves what Mills (2000) called the sociological imagination, or the quality of mind, through which the local evidence of consciousness of globalization (Hobsbawm, 1994) could be ascertained. If people are aware of the term "globalization," they are more likely to actually observe and discern the social and cultural phenomena that point to the ways in which different parts of the world are becoming more interconnected. Even if they do not understand the complexity of the phenomenon or experience or the full forces of globalization, their conception of globalization, no matter how vague, at least demonstrates a realization of the world they live in or an appreciation for the location of their place vis-à-vis other places.

The word "globalization" has entered into common usage in different languages, and there is a plethora of essays, articles, and books discussing the role people play in the processes of globalization. However, a perusal of the literature shows that little research asks people directly about their awareness of the phenomenon and their understanding of its meanings. Answers to these questions have profound theoretical and practical implications for the structure and processes of globalization. Theoretically, personal knowledge (Polanyi, 1958) may help to shape people's perception of the world, which in turn may lead them to think of the world differently and thus to do things differently. Practically, the extant knowledge, however imprecise and fleeting, may serve as a signpost or road map directing people where to go or what to expect in times of global flux. To paraphrase Mills (2000, p. 151), such knowledge is a statement of at least "from where" and "to where."

This chapter tackles globalization from two main aspects: Are the Chinese people aware of the phenomenon? If yes, how do they conceive of it? From a cognitive perspective, the first part discusses whether the Chinese people have any knowledge of globalization and how that might affect their under-standing. The task is to provide a general profile of the factors that separate the people who have heard of globalization from those who have not. The assumption is that there are individual attributes and external sources that lead to variations in contacts with the reality. From a cultural perspective, the second part addresses what globalization might mean to the Chinese people in terms of their actual usage of words. The qualitative analysis should shed light on their conceptual response to an abstract global phenomenon. Ideas, of course, do not exist in a social vacuum, even at the personal level. If media research on agenda setting or framing is any guide, it is important to explore how the Chinese people's conception of globalization might be affected by channels of interpersonal and mass communication. The analysis, in other words, is an attempt to locate the potential factors that help explain how and why the Chinese people came to view globalization in the way they did.

CHINESE AWARENESS OF GLOBALIZATION: A PROFILE

There is little theoretical guidance in the literature regarding whether peo-ple in countries around the world are aware of the phenomenon of global-ization and what factors might contribute to their awareness. Although the American journal *Foreign Policy* has, over the past years, created a global-ization index to compare how countries might be globalized, not much is known at the individual level. The lack of such knowledge leaves much to be desired in the debates over the consequences of globalization, especially when the people who stand to be largely affected one way or the other by the process have remained unexplored in social inquiries. This is particularly true with regard to people in the developing and underdeveloped world, such as those in China, who have been considered to be most vulnerable to the onslaught of globalization. This chapter should provide a baseline as to how the presence of globalization might be felt in urban China.

In the survey, a simple, open-ended question was first asked of the respon-dents: Have you ever heard of globalization (*quan qiu hua*)? Respondents had a choice of yes, probably, or no as an answer. Those who answered maybe (10.7 percent) were counted as yes in the analysis even though there was a sense of uncertainty. Their inclusion was based on a conservative consider-ation so that the number of those who answered no was not unduly inflated. The results show that in the four cities, nearly 6 in 10 of the respondents (55.8 percent) indicated that they were not aware of globalization. Only 4 in 10 (44.2 percent) were aware of it. Although China has been increasingly integrated into the world's economic system, 40 percent of its urban popula-tion still had no knowledge of the term "globalization." From the sociology of knowledge perspective, in most cases what people have not heard of sim-ply does not exist. For a concept to register in the public's mind, it must at least have a real possibility of existing for people to experience it.

Table 6.1 Urban Chinese People's Awareness of Globalization

| | Awareness of Globalization | | | |
	Yes	No	N	χ^2
Age				109.69***
30 or below	60.5	39.5	542	
31 to 50	43.8	56.2	881	
51 or above	29.4	70.6	575	
Gender				28.63***
Male	50.0	50.0	1,014	
Female	38.1	61.9	984	
Education				301.50***
< Junior high school	20.3	79.7	596	
High school	43.3	56.7	813	
Post-secondary	64.2	35.8	358	
University	77.6	22.4	232	
Household income				37.50***
< RMB 1,000	29.1	70.9	141	
RMB 1,001–5,000	43.3	56.7	1,627	
RMB 5,001–10,000	59.0	41.0	210	
RMB 10,001 or above	73.3	26.7	15	
English proficiency				219.24***
Don't know at all	27.5	72.5	925	
Little	52.3	47.7	598	
So-so	64.4	35.6	379	
Fluent or native	74.2	25.8	97	
Work at state enterprise				0.68
Yes	45.8	54.2	467	
No	43.7	56.3	1,532	
Work at foreign companies				27.12***
Yes	72.5	27.5	80	
No	43.0	57.0	1,919	
City				66.75***
Beijing	55.6	44.4	500	
Shanghai	40.7	59.3	499	
Chengdu	31.4	68.6	500	
Xi'an	49.0	51.0	500	
Foreign travel				13.83***
Yes	62.8	37.2	94	
No	43.3	56.7	1,905	
Transnational connections				2.99
Yes	51.0	49.0	145	
No	43.6	56.4	1,852	

Continued

Table 6.1 Continued

| | Awareness of Globalization | | | |
	Yes	No	N	χ^2
Read newspapers				58.35***
Yes	48.0	52.0	1,663	
No	25.3	74.7	336	
Read books				144.84***
Yes	64.7	35.3	597	
No	35.4	64.6	1,402	
Listen to radio				16.15***
Yes	49.9	50.1	745	
No	40.7	59.3	1,235	
Watch TV				2.53
Yes	44.0	56.0	1,927	
No	59.3	40.7	27	
Watch movies				43.22***
Yes	55.9	44.1	556	
No	39.6	60.4	1,443	
Visit websites				234.16***
Yes	66.0	34.0	753	
No	30.9	69.1	1,245	
Media use indices				
Local	4.04	3.88	1,999	3.36**
National	3.56	3.13	1,999	8.86***
Foreign	1.62	1.36	1,999	4.17***

Note: Respondents were asked the question: Have you heard of globalization? There were three choices: yes, probably, or no. Although the answer "probably" did not indicate affirmation, it leaned toward yes in some way and was thus included in the "yes" category. Except the media use indices, the entries for all other variables are row percentages. #For media use indices, the entries are mean scores and the values in the last column are t-values derived from independent-samples t-tests. * $P < .05$; ** $P < .01$; *** $P < .001$.

The fact that most urban Chinese have not heard of globalization raises an interesting question: What distinguishes the "awares" from the "unawares"? Table 6.1 presents key descriptive statistics to show the differences between the two groups of people in terms of their demographic characteristics (age, gender, education, monthly household income, city), employers, English ability, foreign travel experience, transnational social connections, and media use. Table 6.1 paints the general picture of those Chinese who were aware of globalization as being younger, male, better educated, from a higher-income household, more proficient in English, and living in Beijing. They were more likely to have had some experience of foreign travel and they were also more likely to be hired by foreign companies or joint ventures. Transnational social connections, however, seem unimportant to awareness of globalization.

Chinese who were aware of globalization were more likely to read newspapers, magazines, and books, listen to the radio, watch movies, and visit websites. Watching TV had no statistically significant impact on Chinese people's awareness of globalization because almost everyone in the sample (98.6 percent) had watched TV in the week prior to the interview. Differentiating among local, national, and foreign media, people who were aware of globalization were not only more likely to have consumed foreign media but were also more likely to have consumed national and local media.

The overall sketch of the urban Chinese with an awareness of globalization probably reflects the emerging middle class in China, which has enjoyed the fruits of economic prosperity and social progress the most and thus has better access to information through both mass media and interpersonal channels.

Although the overall pattern might have practical implications (e.g., who benefits from globalization) in contemporary China and deserves to be further investigated, theoretically more significant is the conception of globalization that is conjured up in the minds of people. The remainder of the chapter explicates the relationship between their conception and experience. Specifically, how do the Chinese people address this subject matter? Do they approach it by conceiving new problems brought about by the notion of globalization that are related to their everyday lives? In essence, as far as the external reality is concerned, their definitions of the concept by the words they used should be a useful indication of the interplay between the macro (globalization) and the micro (individuals) in the Chinese society.

In academic and journalistic communities, globalization, both as an object of research and a subject of discourse, has in most cases been theoretically conceptualized and empirically tested—albeit in a limited fashion—as a multidimensional phenomenon. In fact, our next chapter will also revert to such a more "conventional approach" in examining people's perceptions of the impact of globalization. But in addition to the technological, economic, social, and political dimensions, cultural globalization has increasingly attracted intellectual and scholarly attention in the field of cultural studies and mass communication research. The essence of the problem of cultural globalization resides in how globalization has altered the ways in which people come to think of their lives and worlds and what it may mean in everyday terms. Against that backdrop, this chapter seeks to determine the parameters within which ordinary Chinese citizens construct the meanings of globalization and the extent to which such constructions might be affected by the mass media, which tend to vary in their ability to shape how people think and talk about the reality.

For the most part, people's lived reality and their experience with the reality through its representation in the mass media generate different forms of consciousness. In a broader context, are average citizens in countries around the world indeed, as Robertson argued (1992, p. 26, emphasis added), like experts and professionals, "increasingly constrained to think in terms . . . . . . of *the world as a whole*?" By invoking the world as one unit at the highest level of abstraction, this question tackles the essence of globalization as a phenomenon that has dominated contemporary thinking about the postmodern world since the mid-1990s, if not earlier. For one thing, if the notion of the world as a single place is to have any compelling explanatory power in the globalization debate, it must be examined not only in terms of what scholars, researchers, or theorists may conceive in abstract terms but also by what ordinary citizens, in this chapter the urban Chinese, may come to think of it in their everyday life.

GLOBALIZATION, DETERRITORIALIZATION, AND THE WORLD AS A SINGLE PLACE

In the context of globalization, to argue that the world has become a single place does not necessarily prioritize one particular conceptual domain, thus elevating it to a master concept; nor does it reduce the complex phenomenon to one simple, geographical dimension or the lack of it. It has been well documented in the literature that one defining attribute of globalization is the disappearance of distance, deterritorialization (Appadurai, 1990; Tomlinson, 1999), or the compression of time-space (Harvey, 1990). According to Robertson (1997), the notion of the world as a united, single community has had a long history. Historically, it is rooted in two interrelated aspects of human development, both concrete and symbolic. First, the concrete or physical structure of the world has become more interconnected and interdependent through technological and other material linkages. Second, for better or worse, people have consciously become more aware of a singular world in which actions from afar have local ramifications and vice versa.

Elaborating on Robertson's view, Holton (1998, p. 33) has argued that the historical emergence of the ideas of humanism, individualism, citizenship, and environmentalism contains within them "ways of seeing the world as a single place occupied by a single humanity, sharing converging conceptions of rights and identities." This line of thought suggests that the nation-centered perspective or nation-specific theory in social science research can no longer adequately accommodate the conditions and direction of global unity (Appadurai, 1990), thus requiring a conceptual and methodological revision to take the world as a whole as the unit of observation and analysis. Wallerstein's (1974) articulation of the world system based on the expansion of capitalism in the 1970s followed much of the same logic that has emerged in later theoretical discussions. This is not simply an intellectual task germane to various academic communities. It also presents an intriguing question to laypeople around the world, raising a few intertwined epistemological issues that are crucial in the global cultural representation. Do the Chinese people think of the world as a single place in their everyday lives? What is their conceptual frame of reference? Is it unrelated to their locality or specifically tied to it?

Whether real or imagined, the world as a single place is presented in various literatures as part of the conceptions and consequences of globalization. To be more accurate, the notion of a single place at the global level is highly abstract, as it does not refer to a particular point of reference or locality. Such a high level of conceptual abstraction means that its indicators will be empirically difficult to locate because it is vague and imprecise (e.g., Hayakawa, 1941). Leaving aside its vagueness, however, if people indicate that there is a single place, at least in an abstract sense, then that place exists as an object in their minds regardless of how they may conceptualize the world. A logical question to be asked immediately is: How do people come to see the world as such? There is no denying that a small number of financially, socially and educationally privileged people would be able to personally experience the world as a single place. For most people everywhere, that experience tends to be vicarious and is largely made possible by the ubiquitous mass media, particularly the Internet and its surrounding digital technologies.

MEDIA COMMUNICATION AND GLOBALIZATION

Since the advent of newspapers as a mass medium in the mid-nineteenth century, both the print and broadcast media have emerged to be more than means of communication, which historically has been viewed as a fundamental function of their existence in contemporary society. With the recent convergence of analogue and digital media in one single platform, the mass and personalized media have provided a variety of frameworks (e.g., online games, virtual living, and podcasting) for the users to see or experience the world in local and remote settings, through largely negotiated or quasi-interactions (Thompson, 1995) between the world out there and the users located in a fixed place. Because people are always situated in a specific context of nation-states, not to mention their particular locales, a shared sense of the world as a single place means that individuals in different parts of the world are able to form a common bond or imagine a mutual community (Anderson, 1991) by the increasing uses of texts and images made feasible by digital technologies of information and communication, such as Facebook, Twitter, and YouTube.

In other words, a psychological interconnectedness among people (e.g., Held and McGrew, 2000) is established by their awareness of the world as timeless and borderless. As Thompson (1995, p. 174) has argued, globalization can be understood or perceived only by individuals "who are situated in specific spatial-temporal locales" as something that is larger than their own locality but which nevertheless encloses that place. If location affects or determines what one may be able to see in the world and how one may perceive in it, then it is difficult to imagine that an understanding of globalization has nothing to do with one's location, both physical and psychological. As people become more globalized psychologically through their awareness of changing world structure and processes, what should we expect them to communicate in terms of their thinking of the reality? What would they express in thinking about the world and its issues? Would they talk about issues (e.g., climate change or global environment) that underline complex connectivity, as Tomlinson (1999) proposed? Against all these questions, where do we find those Chinese people who are aware of globalization?

If globalization has indeed made the world a more intimate place, the psychological interconnection is reasonable for most people only through representational vehicles such as various media of communication by way of textual and visual portrayals of a shrinking world. For example, there are symbolic experiences, in that most major cities around the world—especially such global cities as Shanghai, New York, and Paris—can be observed or visited vicariously via television, movies, and the Internet. Given that the reception of media content among different individuals is not necessarily static but interactive between the text and the context (Liebes and Katz, 1988), their understanding of globalization should follow similar patterns, which are in some respects interactive. If the mass media have presented globalization as either a topic of social change or as a critique of its consequences, whether positive or negative, its presentation and representation are likely to be found in the primary discourse, the overt content of news and opinions (Abrahamson, 2004).

It has been well documented in the literature that mass communication in almost all places is still an endeavor of national focus, devoid of a comparative context. In cases where international communication is part of the media diet, exposure to the content of mass media about distant landscapes of cultures, peoples, or ideas does not really dislocate people from their comfortable or familiar places, no matter how close they are to an external reality. Practices and experiences are always felt actually within localities. Other than the immediate surroundings, individuals cannot just pack up and move across physical borders in an instant. As far as foreign lands are concerned, they will have to travel over long distances. More often than not, people in different parts of the world are connected not by physical affinities but by psychological unity. In the modern world, people are not only rootless but their minds also become homeless (Berger, Berger, and Kellner, 1973). If the world has been felt to be a single place by ordinary citizens in different localities, one of its cultural consequences should be what Tomlinson has called the shift of the "context of meaning construction" (p. 20), which affects, among other things, their sense of "the experience of place and of the self in relation to place."

To think about what globalization is is to engage in the construction of its meanings. With the alteration of context, an abstract conception of the world as a whole means that, in thinking of globalization, people in different parts of the world should go beyond the empirical conditions of localized notions or points of reference. There should be little attachment (i.e., deterritorialization) to a real or particular place. According to Adams (1992), a place is more than physical but can be conceived as "center of meaning" or context. As a result of consciousness of a globalized world, individuals may express views that are devoid of physical attachments in that the ideas do not necessarily invoke places implied by a geographical locality or identified by its name when they think of globalization as a phenomenon. People who are consciously aware of the global are world citizens who inhabit "an abstraction" and may be less attached to the local (Barber, 1995, p. 99). If average citizens, as Robertson asserted earlier (1992, p. 26), "are increasingly constrained to think . . . of the world as a whole," their conceptual frame of reference should converge at a more abstract level. This involves a separation of vocabulary and place in that what comes to their minds tends to be more abstract than specific.

Implied in the notion of "world citizens" is the assertion that locality does not affect how one may come to view the reality, whether local or remote. This runs counter to the theoretical contention proposed by the sociology of knowledge (Mannheim, 1936, p. 265), which argued that "mental structures are inevitably differently formed in different social and historical settings." The local is more concrete, whereas the remote is more abstract or symbolic. A conception of what globalization is or is not certainly is mental and therefore is a matter of perspective, which is delimited by where one finds oneself. As Berger and Luckmann (1966, p. 22) put it, "The reality of everyday life is organized around the 'here' of my body and the 'now' of my present." The "here and now" obviously cannot be detached from one's locality, both physical and social. Therefore the following hypothesis is proposed:

> Hypothesis 1: Localities are likely to affect how people think of globalization. More specifically, people in different localities tend to think of globalization differently.

For those who have heard of the idea of globalization, a mere awareness of the existence of such a phenomenon, if understood properly in any of its dimensions, should probably undermine more or less the traditional view that one's place is detached from other localities. As noted earlier, other than personal experience, the source of such consciousness is likely to come from the media. Whether authoritarian or democratic, a society establishes its media system in ways that allow for the self-monitoring of social activities. To a large extent, the mass media belong to the social institutions that monitor various practices and experiences at the collective level, with serious implications for individuals in their everyday lives. For example, there is a close relationship between "TV as a gathering place" and real places: "the more time people spend watching television, the less time they can spend in public places" (Adams, 1992, p. 118). Moreover, although not necessarily related to the conception of the world as a single place, it has been well documented in the literature of public opinion and communication research that different media tend to have different effects on how people come to acquire knowledge of public affairs. Numerous studies have found that newspapers are associated more with knowledge of public affairs than is television (e.g., Salwen, 1998; Salwen and Driscoll, 1995).

Like individuals who are located in specific settings, media organizations (e.g., CBS News), including multinational corporations (e.g., News Corporation), are physically situated in particular nation-states, although their footprint or reach may extend far beyond national boundaries. The fact that a media company is always tied to a specific place means that its particularity sets it apart from other media outlets. For example, China Central Television (CCTV) is clearly not CNN. The word "China" denotes something particular, and CCTV is bound by what is Chinese, not American. The same can be said of Atlanta-based CNN. Although China today is more open than it had been, most Chinese people still do not often travel abroad or encounter cultures that are different from their own, as we have already discussed in earlier chapters. The proportion of urban Chinese who had extensive transnational social connections is also small. Therefore, for the most part, Chinese citizens are likely to obtain knowledge about the world from the domestically oriented media whose content is intended for local consumption. Besides, there are certainly "traveling cultures" that come to them through the media of mass communication, such as U.S. movies, TV programming, music, and other popular cultural forms.

In terms of form and content, not all media are created equal; they are not capable of presenting reality in a similar fashion or the world with comparable quality. If the relationship between usages of media type and public affairs knowledge (e.g., Ridout, Grosse, and Appleton, 2008; Semetko, Brzinski, Weaver, and Willnat, 1992) in international communication is any indication, it is reasonable to expect that the discourse of globalization in the media would follow their structural limitations and representational logic by focusing on the global dimension(s) most easily accessible to each medium. For example, TV requires the most empirical materials as ingredients (e.g., visual imperative) of its news reports (Fenton, 2005), whereas newspapers and magazines are well positioned to tackle more complex issues in more contextualized manners. TV is often devoid of context; hence it is less capable of conveying abstract thinking and reporting stories with historical causes (Fenton, 2005). Such functional differentiation may lead to differential consequences among different types of media.

Whereas the previous chapters have analyzed mainly the differences among local, national, and foreign media consumption, the distinction between media types is at least equally important, if not more important, for the purpose of the following analysis. Specifically, for people who rely on the print and broadcast media respectively for news, information, and entertainment, their usage may create an uneven awareness of the world as a single place because not all media are capable of presenting the reality in a more abstract manner. According to Adams (1992, p. 125), "television is less abstract than other communication media" because "it is accessible to those on the peripheries of the linguistic system," such as those who are limited in their mastery of a particular language. This should be particularly true if the abstract notion of globalization is found to be different among people in different localities. As Tomlinson (1999, p. 24) convincingly put it, "People do not produce meanings within some entirely separate interpretative channel which, as it were, runs parallel with other social practices but leaves them untouched." The same can be said of media communication: It is a form of social practice that does not leave people's construction of meanings untouched. It is therefore proposed that:

> Hypothesis 2: People's conceptions of globalization are likely to vary depending on their uses of print and electronic media.

The "measure" of Chinese people's conception of globalization was based on an open-ended question: "When talking about globalization, what would come to your mind?" A total of 883 respondents provided answers to this question. They were used in the following analysis to ascertain how globalization might be conceived by the Chinese people. The first responses were coded into one of the four categories: "local," "global," "mixed," and "unclear or ambiguous." The coding of these categories was conservative in that they were designed to be sensitive to the classification of local vs. global. The local was defined as responses that implied receptiveness to and understanding of issues in a context specifically related to one's own locality. An answer was coded as "local" when the name of a *Chinese* place was explicitly mentioned, such as Beijing and Shanghai in particular or China in general. The answer was also coded as local if, while no local place was explicitly mentioned, the point of reference was nonetheless clearly identified (e.g., the use of "I" or "the Chinese") or could be inferred as local by the topic/issue mentioned. For instance, the following issues were considered local: typhoons, weather, exports, a rise of the gasoline price, a price drop in automobiles, convenience in lives, improvement of living standards, employment, and etc.

The global was defined as responses that implied receptiveness to and understanding of issues in a context *not* specifically related to one's own locality, that is, when nonlocal or non-Chinese places were explicitly mentioned, such as the United States or Europe. Similar to the coding of answers as local, an answer would be considered as global if, when no particular place was explicitly mentioned, a nonlocal point of reference was clearly implied (e.g., foreign, overseas, and so on) or could be inferred by the topic/issue mentioned. Some global topics included the internet, global warming, environmental protection, free trade, free flow of people, e-commerce, McDonalds, severe acute respiratory syndrome (SARS), and so on.

A third category of coding was the "glocal," a combination of the global and the local. This includes those responses that implied receptiveness to and understanding of issues in a context related to both the local and the global. When more than one place was identified or the points of reference were multiple, they were coded as "mixed." For instance, responses focusing on a treaty between China and America, foreign enterprises entering the Chinese market, or China becoming westernized were considered as exhibiting glocal conceptions of globalization. Lastly, when the topic or issue did not clearly imply either a local or a global place, or when the response was ambiguous or difficult to determine (e.g., mass media or keen competition), it was coded as "unclear." Because they did not directly address the questions raised above, in the analysis, the mixed and unclear categories were excluded.

To test the reliability of the coding scheme for the open-ended responses, two coders were trained and independently coded a small sample (10 percent) of the responses. With a kappa value of .82, the intercoder reliability was considered to be satisfactory. One of the two coders then coded the entire responses.

ANALYSIS AND RESULTS

Overall, the data show that the majority of respondents tended to think in abstract terms in talking about globalization. More than 70 percent of the responses were classified as global (74.4 percent), whereas 18.6 percent were classified as local. The remaining responses were either mixed (glocal, 2.3 percent) or unclear/ambiguous (4.7 percent).

Table 6.2 compares the conceptions of globalization between the local and the global against the same set of independent variables reported in Table 6.1. Unlike the question of awareness, most of the factors no longer account for the differences between the local and the global conceptions of globalization. This is not necessarily unexpected, given that the analysis now focuses on those who had heard of globalization. But education continues to have significant relationships with the dependent variable. People with less education tended to conceive of globalization more in local terms than those who were better educated. But the percentages suggest that the relationship is not linear. People became particularly more likely to talk about globalization in global terms once they had some university education. It seems that university education in particular, rather than educational level in general, has contributed to a capability of talking about globalization in more abstract, "delocalized" manner.

Besides education, newspaper and magazine reading, as well as book reading, also relate to conceptions of globalization. But for these two variables, it is those people who have consumed such media who tended to talk about globalization in more local terms. One possible interpretation is that the use of such informational media would give people a sense of what "globalization" actually means to what is happening around their own societies. As a result, people become more likely to talk about globalization not as an abstract and faraway phenomenon but as something with concrete and nearby consequences and/or implications.

Table 6.2 Conceptions of Globalization

	Local	Global	N	χ^2
		Conception of Globalization		
Age				3.58
30 or below	18.5%	81.5%	308	
31 to 50	18.8%	81.2%	340	
51 or above	25.3%	74.3%	162	
Gender				1.21
Male	18.7%	81.3%	461	
Female	21.8%	78.2%	349	
Education				8.10*
< Junior high school	23.7%	76.3%	114	
High school	21.7%	78.3%	318	
Post-secondary	21.6%	78.4%	208	
University	12.4%	87.6%	170	
Household income				3.82
< RMB 1,000	16.7%	83.3%	42	
RMB 1,001–5,000	21.5%	78.5%	647	
RMB 5,001–10,000	14.5%	85.5%	110	
RMB 10,001 or above	10.0%	90.0%	10	
English proficiency				1.88
Don't know at all	22.6%	77.4%	234	
Little	19.7%	80.3%	284	
So-so	18.8%	81.2%	224	
Fluent or native	16.2%	83.8%	68	
Work at state enterprise				3.10
Yes	24.4%	75.6%	197	
No	18.6%	81.4%	613	
Work at foreign companies				0.74
Yes	15.4%	84.6%	52	
No	20.3%	79.7%	758	
City				15.11**
Beijing	27.5%	72.5%	251	
Shanghai	15.5%	84.5%	181	
Chengdu	13.4%	86.6%	149	
Xi'an	19.9%	80.1%	231	
Foreign travel				1.60
Yes	27.1%	72.9%	48	
No	19.6%	80.4%	762	
Transnational connections				0.22
Yes	17.9%	82.1%	163	
No	20.3%	79.7%	648	

Continued

Table 6.2 Continued

	Conception of Globalization			
	Local	Global	N	χ^2
Read newspapers				6.53*
Yes	21.1%	78.9%	733	
No	9.0%	91.0%	78	
Read books				3.54*
Yes	23.1%	76.9%	355	
No	17.8%	82.2%	456	
Listen to radio				2.06
Yes	22.3%	77.7%	345	
No	18.2%	81.8%	466	
Watch TV				1.70
Yes	20.3%	79.7%	795	
No	6.7%	93.3%	15	
Watch movies				1.22
Yes	22.2%	77.8%	279	
No	18.9%	81.1%	533	
Visit websites				2.01
Yes	21.8%	78.2%	455	
No	17.7%	82.3%	355	
Media use indices				
Local	4.11	4.01	810	1.12
National	3.55	3.57	810	0.21
Foreign	1.62	1.64	810	0.18

Note: Respondents were asked the open-ended question: When you think of globalization, what comes to your mind? Their responses were coded into four categories: local, global, glocal (a combination of the global and the local), and unclear/ambiguous. The last two categories were excluded in the analysis. # For media use indices, the entries are mean scores and the values in the last column are t-values derived from independent-samples t-tests. * P < .05; ** P < .01..

The same line of thinking may also explain the counterintuitive relationship between foreign travel experience and conception of globalization. Table 6.2 shows that the two are not significantly correlated. But percentagewise, people who had at least some travel experience were more likely to talk about globalization in local terms. We conducted a further analysis by looking separately at the relationship between travel and conception of globalization among people who had or did not have university education. The findings show that, among university graduates, people who had or did not have foreign travel experience were equally likely to talk about globalization in global terms. But among people who did not have university education, those who had at least some foreign travel experience were indeed significantly more likely to have talked about globalization in *local* terms (39.3 percent vs. 21.4 percent, χ^2 = 4.98, P < .03). Travel, presumably, should have provided people with firsthand experience and knowledge of the world at large. Yet such experience and knowledge are constituted by concrete observations of things happening in reality. And people can also develop concrete ideas of how things in other parts of the world differ from those in their own localities. Hence people may acquire the ability to talk about globalization in local terms as a result of having traveled.

Beijing residents were more likely to talk about globalization in local terms, whereas the residents in the other three cities were more or less equally likely to talk about globalization in global terms. The between-cities differences are highly statistically significant. The findings tend to support hypothesis 1. Localities do matter in considering how people think and talk about globalization.

To further determine what distinguishes those Chinese people who conceived of globalization in global terms from those who used local references, we conducted a discriminant analysis to separate the two groups. This statistical technique allows the researchers "to study the differences between two or more groups of objects with respect to several variables simultaneously" (Klecka, 1980, p. 7). The emphasis of the analysis is on the interpretations of how well the indicators discriminated the group differences between the local and the global conceptions, not necessarily on classification of the respondents into the two groups. A stepwise method was used to select the single best discriminating variable to enter into the equation. Nevertheless, because most of the demographics were unrelated to conceptions of globalization, as shown in Table 6.2, they were excluded in the discriminant analysis. Rather, we retain the city dummies and a dichotomized university education variable (i.e., comparing only people with and without university education) while also examining whether there is any relationship between conception of globalization and a number of value orientations discussed in previous chapters, namely adventurism, cultural nationalism, and developmental nationalism. Also, we included the dichotomized "read newspaper or not" and "watch TV or not" variables in the analysis. Moreover, in order to be consistent with the analysis in other chapters, we also included the indices of foreign traveling experience, transnational social connections, and the three types of media consumption—local, national, and foreign—into the analysis.

Table 6.3 reports the results of the analysis. Putting aside the technical details, the findings show that the set of variables was indeed able to separate people who provided a "global" conception of globalization from those who provided a "local" conception of globalization.[1] Nevertheless, the stepwise discriminant method shows that the three value orientation variables, travel experience and transnational social connections, local, national, and foreign media consumption, television watching, and the city dummy for Xi'an did not enter into the analysis, suggesting that they were not useful in discriminating between the two groups. The only factors with any discriminating power are the dichotomized university education variable, the city dummies for Chengdu and Shanghai, and newspaper and magazine reading.

Table 6.3 Discriminant Analysis of Conceptions of Globalization

	Means For "Local"	Means For "Global"	Canonical Func. Coeff. (full)	Canonical Func. Coeff. (stepwise)
University education	0.13	0.23	0.49	0.61
Shanghai	0.17	0.24	0.65	0.50
Chengdu	0.12	0.20	0.70	0.54
Xi'an	0.28	0.29	0.40	
Adventurism	3.56	3.54	0.15	
Cultural nationalism	3.49	3.42	-0.13	
Developmental nationalism	4.75	4.74	0.10	
Foreign travel	1.01	1.01	-0.18	
Transnational connection	1.01	1.02	0.08	
Read newspapers	0.95	0.89	0.31	0.51
Watch televisionn	1.00	0.98	0.14	
Local media consumption	4.11	4.01	-0.35	
National media consumption	3.54	3.57	0.20	
Foreign media consumption	1.62	1.65	-0.06	

Note: For the full function, Wilks' Lambda = 0.96, $P < .01$. With the stepwise procedure, Wilks' Lambda = 0.97, $P < .001$.

Hypothesis 1 proposed that localities are likely to affect how people think of globalization. More specifically, the hypothesis suggested that people in different localities are likely to think of globalization differently. The discriminant analysis indicates that the locality of the Chinese people contributed to how they might conceive of globalization. Coupled with the results in Table 6.2, in which conception of globalization is more or less related to the Chinese people's locality across the four cities: Beijing, Chengdu, Shanghai, and Xi'an (χ^2 = 15.11, df = 4, $P < .01$), the evidence therefore supports hypothesis 1. On the one hand, the dominant pattern is that the urban Chinese in different localities indeed thought of globalization in very much the same way: they tended to describe the phenomenon in more global, abstract terms, detached from the local, concrete place where they might find themselves. On the other hand, the results are not systematic, leaving room for specific settings of a particular locality (i.e., Beijing or Shanghai) to undercut the conceptual claim of the world as one place. To err on the side of caution, the results appear to question the conception of the world as a single place, given that the notion of locality could not be fully ruled out as competing places.

Consistent with Table 6.2, reading newspaper does relate to conceptions of globalization, with newspaper readers being more likely to have local conceptions of globalization. But television watching is unrelated to conception of globalization. Hypothesis 2, which posits that conception of globalization is influenced by the type of media the Chinese people might use, is therefore only partially supported.

CONCEPTIONS OF GLOBALIZATION: THE CHINESE STORY

The preceding statistical analyses provide empirical and local evidence that urban Chinese view globalization differently according to where they live. The data have portrayed a general picture of the Chinese people's conceptions of globalization as either local or global. What should be more revealing is how they actually talk about globalization. This section seeks to capture the discourse by the Chinese respondents through the words and phrases they used to describe what they thought of globalization. The most often used words are the *world* or the *global* in connection to other concepts in areas of transportation, telecommunication and information technologies, the Internet, international relations, financial markets and economic activities, and environmental protection. In the thinking of urban Chinese, the global therefore tends to be associated with such terms as "world peace," "world economy," "world market," "world communication," "world trade," "global warming," "global temperature," "global currency," "global economy," and "global information." These terms often point to the flows of goods, people, services, and other tangible and intangible things across national borders.

For the local conceptions, the departure point is different and specific. The name of China in general or the city where the respondents lived in particular was usually invoked as a point of reference in the responses. Such concepts began with concerns over what globalization might bring to the country, the city itself or to the respondents themselves. Some of the responses pointed toward both positive consequences and negative impacts. The following descriptions are typical examples: globalization would make the Chinese government more transparent, it is conducive to the Chinese economy, it would destroy the Chinese ecological environment, it would allow local companies in the city to be controlled by cross-national corporations, it increases the chance of my being laid off, it means foreign companies coming to China, it would westernize the Chinese lifestyle, or it would enhance the Chinese culture. In such conceptions, globalization appears to the Chinese people that the place in which they live, whether in the national or in the local/metropolitan setting, could not be detached from the larger context. Globalization is something that would have practical ramifications in their lives.

SUMMARY AND DISCUSSION

Within the conceptual framework of the world as a single place, the focus of this chapter centers around what the Chinese people come to think of globalization, regardless of who they are or what they may do. Whereas demographics and media uses tend to be related to the urban Chinese people's awareness of globalization in some way (e.g., literacy and newspaper reading), how they might affect their conception of globalization is a different matter and has yet to be further addressed. For the purpose of the present chapter, age, gender, and household income did not produce any systematic difference in the way people thought of globalization, suggesting that demographics has nothing to do with people's conception of the phenomenon. Although not definitive, it implies that explanatory factors need to be sought beyond demographic variables.

As conceived by global theorists, if globalization is indeed leading to a common perception that the world has become a single place, then people's physical location should have no impact on how they might perceive the global phenomenon. Our finding shows, however, that locality does make a difference in terms of how the urban Chinese respondents perceived globalization. Further analyses of paired comparisons among the four cities (z-tests not reported here) indicate that respondents in Beijing, the capital of China, were mostly responsible for the differences between locality and conception of globalization. Beijing respondents appeared to think of globalization in more concrete terms than did those in the other three cities. When Beijing responses were removed from the comparison, conceptions of globalization among respondents in the remaining three cities show not much difference. The results suggest that factors other than locality, such as Beijing as the political center of China and its tendency to attract global attention both at home and abroad, might be at work with regard to how the Chinese people viewed globalization.

Our findings thus challenge the notion that individuals will necessarily consider the whole world as one single, undifferentiated, and deterritorialized place in the age of globalization. In general, the majority of the Chinese people in the four cities think of globalization in abstract terms. But if we compare global cities such as Beijing and Shanghai, we find that Beijing residents appeared to care more about its local impact when thinking of globalization. This suggests that individuals' lives in the globalized world are still lived and experienced locally (e.g., Lin, Song, and Ball-Rokeach, 2010; Sassen, 2001). In particular, Beijing was more pronounced on the world map after it hosted the 2008 Olympic Games. Even though the survey was conducted in late 2006 and early 2007, the city was already drawn into the process of preparing for that megaevent. The residents might come to realize the physical impact of globalization, such as employment opportunities or improving life conditions, because of the intensified flow of information, people, and capital associated with the event. The place thus became central, and the term globalization became concrete to their everyday lives. Along this line of thinking, it would be for future studies to see whether the 2010 World Expo held in Shanghai had a similar influence on the city's residents.

Despite the possible new developments in the empirical scene, theoretically the findings in the present chapter remind us of the importance of conceptual sensibility. To identify people's conceptual framework as the consequences of globalization, it is theoretically and practically important to probe their awareness of the larger world to which their localities are increasingly linked. At the conceptual level, to think about globalization does not and should not require one to put aside one's rootedness in a locality. People can think of the world as a single place, but this "single place" may still have its internal variations and complexities. In fact, when people talk about globalization not in relation to their own localities, it may not necessarily represent an ability to understand the interconnectedness between different parts of the world; it may actually reflect an inability to understand in more concrete terms how one, as an individual who is always rooted in a locality, really relates to globalization. Moreover, mass media are only one, although an important one, of the many forms and processes whereby people come to experience globalization, especially with respect to remote settings. This chapter does not find, however, that media uses are influential in shaping individuals' conceptions of globalization. Even though McLuhan (1964) and his followers might have believed in the power of electronic media to retribalize the global village, their views do not help average citizens to consider the world as a whole.

In conclusion, this chapter demonstrates the importance of context within which meanings are generated in thinking of the popular conception of globalization. The findings contribute to existing knowledge about globalization, especially with regard to the involvement of individuals in the process. We argue that, whereas globalization remains an abstract term to most Chinese people, the place where they live still matters. It is where they are that provides a point of reference from which they may conceive of the larger picture. Globalization is not something remote; it can be closer to home, either to the country as a whole or to the city in which the urban Chinese people experience their world. Although limited, the local evidence reveals the quality of Chinese minds in that a sizable number of urban people were able to see globalization from different perspectives. Although this chapter has tackled the various elements that might be involved in the awareness and conceptions of globalization in the four Chinese cities, there are still factors that have not been taken into consideration. For one, the relevancy or salience of issues in media uses should be included in the equation. Issues may play an important role in deciding whether individuals consider globalization to be abstract and distant or concrete and close. For another, the changing media landscape made possible by the Internet has made the interplay between communication and deterritorialization even more complex and deserves further, fuller investigations.

7 Attitudes toward Globalization

As the prominent transnational protests often surrounding the meetings of major international organizations such as the WTO and IMF signify, globalization has been a contentious process. Even optimistic proponents of globalization cannot deny its fair share of potential problems. It is debatable whether economic globalization is delivering mainly prosperity or exploitation, whether political globalization is generating peace or terrorism, and whether cultural globalization is offering pleasure or killing off traditions.

More important is the fact that within any single country there are likely to be winners and losers as the country engages with the processes of globalization more broadly. Economic globalization is likely to benefit mainly those who own the economic, social, and cultural capital to perform well in a globalized economy. And as Bauman (1998) puts it, if globalization leads to the increasing mobility of people across the world, some will travel as tourists and some travel as vagabonds.

In this contemporary human condition, how do common people perceive the benefits and pitfalls of globalization? In the previous chapter, we pointed out that some urban Chinese respondents would indeed mention certain positive and negative impacts of "globalization" when they were asked what they think of the term. But the previous chapter focuses mainly on the distinction between local and global conceptions of globalization, and the open-ended question analyzed was put forward to those who had already heard of the term "globalization." This chapter, in contrast, utilizes a set of questions that asked all respondents about their perceptions of the influence of globalization. This analysis was intended to focus on how urban Chinese perceive the impact of globalization.

Although public opinion research on people's views of economic liberalization, a key aspect of globalization in the late twentieth century, has had a rather long history, scholars have just begun, in the past few years, to tackle more systematically and comprehensively the question of public opinion regarding the various dimensions of globalization. This chapter draws upon and also adds onto this growing literature. We will examine how Chinese people's social structural positions, value orientations, and cultural capital influence their attitudes toward globalization.

But as we explain in the following pages, besides social structural positions and value orientations, our analysis emphasizes particularly the potential influence of media consumption. In the context of urban China, examining media influence on attitude toward globalization is especially important because the national media, being state-controlled, are likely to reflect the dominant policy direction of the Chinese state regarding globalization (Lee, 2009; Zhao, 2003). More specifically, since Deng Xiaoping's southern tour in 1992 to reenergize the marketization drive in China, the Chinese government's policy has been one of active engagement with the process of globalization. In view of this, would media consumption lead to more positive views regarding globalization among the urban Chinese population?

This chapter will provide a descriptive overview of Chinese people's attitude toward globalization as well as an examination of the factors influencing such attitudes. It begins with a review of the extant literature on public opinion toward globalization around the world. Then we provide an account of the Chinese official rhetoric and media discourses related to globalization. These conceptual and background discussions lead to the setup of the main research questions and hypotheses. We then present the relevant data analysis. The final section discusses the implications of the findings.

PUBLIC OPINION OF GLOBALIZATION

There is a growing but still limited body of literature examining common citizens' attitude toward globalization in the past 10 years. It would be tricky to summarize the findings because of the various ways in which the key notion of globalization was employed and operationalized in these studies. As already noted above, a body of studies on public opinion regarding international trade policies has been accumulating over the decades (e.g., Hiscox, 2006; Rogowski, 1989). Into the 2000s, a few studies purportedly examining attitudes toward globalization were actually examining people's opinions regarding trade liberalization. Hellwig (2007), for instance, used longitudinal data in France to determine whether the degree of the country's openness to international trade in various years was related to people's confidence in their political leaders. Hainmueller and Hiscox (2006) similarly defined attitudes toward globalization solely in terms of attitude toward trade liberalization. Somewhat differently, Wolfe and Mendelsohn (2005) made a distinction between trade liberalization and economic globalization. They used the term "economic globalization" to refer to the general phenomenon of increasing economic interdependence between different national economies, whereas "trade liberalization" refers to a policy that national governments can adopt in dealing with such economic interdependence. Yet their study retains an economic focus and ignores the political, cultural, and social dimensions of globalization.

Studies that have used alternative or more comprehensive measures of attitude toward globalization include that of Woodward, Skrbis, and Bean (2008), who examined people's perceptions of the impact of globalization on the economy, on personal consumption and choices, and on cultural diversity and human rights. Hsiao, Wan, and Wong (2010) employed a number of questions about people's attitudes toward international organizations to measure support for globalization. As they noted, their measurement assumes that "people who look favorably on supranational agencies should be more supportive of the forces of globalization" (p. 37). Baron and Kemp (2004) measured attitudes toward globalization based on people's beliefs regarding how individuals and nations should act in the global arena. Their index thus focused more on the political aspect of globalization than the cultural, social, and economic aspects, and the beliefs captured are prescriptive rather than descriptive (i.e., what people believe the government and people should do instead of what they believe globalization *is*). Edwards (2006), meanwhile, examined people's attitudes toward both economic and cultural globalization. He used four items to measure such attitudes. The two items concerning cultural globalization are about whether people are positive toward the importation of foreign media and toward international travel.

It is unnecessary to list here all other measures of attitude toward globalization that have been used in past studies (for additional variants, see Alden, Steenkamp and Batra [2006] and Hoffman [2009]). The important point is that attention to the exact operationalization used in the studies can be highly important for us in attempting to make sense of some of the specific findings from the studies. Whereas the above discussion may read like pure methodology, the issue has important conceptual implications. For example, Baron and Kemp's (2004) analysis shows a negative relationship between attitudes toward globalization and attitudes toward business. Yet this relationship probably exists only because their measure of attitude toward globalization is a prescriptive one. Since business corporations are often perceived by ordinary citizens as socially irresponsible, people who believe in the need for individuals and governments to act responsibly in the global society would view business more negatively. In contrast, if attitudes toward globalization are defined in terms of support for economic liberalization, then "attitudes toward globalization" and attitudes toward business are likely to be positively related to each other. For another example, Hsiao and colleagues (2010) found that, in a number of Asian countries, support for globalization is positively related to support for government. But since they measured support for globalization by three questions about support for international organizations and two of the three questions focused on international organizations with national governments as the participating units (such as the UN and WTO), the findings become readily understandable. In contrast, in Hellwig's (2007) study, which used trade openness as an indicator of France's involvement in globalization, a negative relationship between the country's engagement with globalization and public confidence in French political leaders was found.

Nevertheless, the lack of consistent operationalization does not preclude the possibility of drawing useful insights from these studies. A few important findings in the literature are worth highlighting. First, most of the studies cited, regardless of their actual operationalization, found public opinion regarding globalization to be quite positive. For example, Hsiao and colleagues (2010) found that public trust in the WTO, UN, and the World Bank was quite substantial in Australia, the United States, Japan, China, and India. Woodward and associates (2008) also found very positive views regarding the impact of globalization in an Australian study: 83 percent of their respondents believed globalization is good or very good for the Australian economy, 92 percent believed that globalization was good in terms of the respondent's own ability to sample different cultures and 83 percent believed that globalization was good for democracy and human rights abroad.

What factors contribute to public attitudes toward globalization? A number of studies have highlighted the positive relationship between education and attitude toward globalization, especially when the latter was defined in terms of support for trade liberalization (e.g., Hainmueller and Hincox, 2006; Wolfe and Mendelsohn, 2005; Hoffman, 2009). The conventional explanation is that educated people have the skills required to perform well in a globalized economy. Globalization, in other words, tends to benefit better educated people. If so, other measures of the cultural capital pertinent to personal success in a globalized world should also relate positively to attitude toward globalization. Indeed, Hsiao et al. (2010) found a positive relationship between English language proficiency and attitude toward globalization in China, India, and Japan.[1]

Beyond education and cultural capital, other scholars have emphasized the significance of values and norms in shaping people's attitude toward globalization. As Wolfe and Mendelsohn (2005) have argued, people are not just workers or consumers but also members of various kinds of communities ranging from the family to the nation. "As citizens, individuals are concerned not only about the effects of commercial exchanges on their livelihood but also about the effects of new agreements on the ability of the government to pursue valued policy objectives" (pp. 53–54) Their empirical study of the Canadian public found that support for globalization is positively related to attitude toward multinational corporations, internationalism, and attitude toward the welfare state. Support for globalization is also negatively related to support for having closer relationship with the United States and nationalistic sentiments. The importance of values is also supported by Edwards (2006), who found that attitude toward both cultural and economic globalization is positively related to attitude toward modern life, attitude toward consumerism, and attitude toward a market economy. At the same time, people who value traditional ways of life are likely to be more negative toward globalization.

Beyond values and norms, few studies have examined the relationship between attitude toward globalization and people's media consumption and personal connections with the outside world. One exception is our own earlier publication based on which this chapter is derived (Lee et al., 2009). Another exception is the analysis of Hsiao and colleagues (2010), which shows a positive relationship between personal contact with the outside world and attitude toward globalization. This relationship exists in the cases of the United States, Japan, Russia, China, and India. These investigators also found a positive relationship between "digital connectivity" (measured by Internet browsing, use of email, and use of mobile phones) and attitude toward globalization in Russia and India. Yet their study did not examine the possible role of mass media consumption.

Therefore our analysis will offer a unique contribution to the extant literature by examining the influence of media consumption. Nevertheless, how media consumption relates to attitude toward globalization should be dependent on whether the mass media can be expected to be generally proglobalization or antiglobalization given a specific social and political context. Hence we need to turn to a discussion of the Chinese context.

OFFICIAL RHETORIC AND MEDIA DISCOURSES ABOUT GLOBALIZATION IN CHINA

It is widely noted that the term "globalization" entered the official discourses of the Chinese government only in the year 1997 (Lee, 2010). That was also the year of the Asian financial crisis, an event clearly demonstrating the perils facing the developing countries in their engagement with global capitalism. Together with the range of economic and social problems already existing in the early 1990s as a consequence of China's economic reform, let alone the history of suffering from a semicolonial status in the latter half of the nineteenth century, Chinese leaders were certainly aware of the potential challenges and problems that further engagement with global capitalism could bring about. As Nick Knight (2003), a scholar of Chinese politics, has stated, there were debates within the Communist Party about, among other issues, whether China and other developing countries in general are likely to gain or lose in the process of globalization and whether China should hold a positive or negative attitude toward it.

Despite the internal debates, national leaders from Jiang Zemin to Hu Jintao have "in the main been positive, and in some cases extremely enthusiastic" in talking about globalization (Knight, 2003, p. 319). At the same time, a number of interrelated themes and rhetorical means were used to handle the problematic aspects of globalization. For example, Knight (2003) noted that the speeches given by national leaders portrayed globalization as a process that can be brought under control by the state. The belief was that the harm which might be caused by globalization could be reduced, if not eliminated, as long as the state remained in charge. Second, in discussing the potential negative impact of globalization, the leaders focused primarily on the political impact on national sovereignty instead of the impact on issues such as income inequality or cultural autonomy. This not only directed people's attention from some issues to others but also reinforced the notion that the crucial issue is whether the state can remain autonomous and in control. Meanwhile, Deng and Moore (2004) pointed out that the Chinese leaders maintained a distinction between "globalization" and the "international economic system." Problems "associated elsewhere in the world with globalization . . . were attributed to defects in the international economic system rather than to globalization per se" (p. 120).

Moreover, Chinese leaders reconceptualized the relationship between the nation and global capital. As Crane (1999) explained, integration into the world economy "requires a retelling of the national story so that the embrace of capitalist practices . . . will seem consistent with the historical unfolding of the nation" (p. 228). In the Maoist era, global capital was considered the perpetrator of imperialism and the cause of the historical humiliation and sufferings of the Chinese. But into the late 1990s, past victimization was attributed as much to the disastrous Cultural Revolution as to foreign imperialism, whereas the fact of China being underdeveloped became the reason why market reform was needed.

The leaders' rhetoric not only professed a belief that the advantages of engaging with globalization, defined primarily but not exclusively in economic terms, would outweigh the disadvantages and risks but also posited engaging with globalization as the way to realize the century-old dream of a strong, modernized nation (Karl, 2002; Unger, 1996). In this sense, the official rhetoric on globalization was built upon the "state-led pragmatic nationalism" that the Chinese government had promoted since the early 1990s to fill the ideological vacuum left by the decline of communist worldviews (Zhao, 2004). In other words, in China's official discourses, globalization is not the antithesis of nationalism. "Entering the world" and "strengthening the nation" were portrayed as two sides of the same coin.

The official rhetoric was more or less faithfully reported by the national news media. Media reform in China since the 1980s has led to the proliferation of media outlets, a more diverse press structure, the media's increasing reliance on advertising revenues, the emergence of innovative practices and media types ranging from the tabloid press to investigative journalism programs, and state-led conglomeration (Lee, 2003). Yet ideologically the media are still under the heavy-handed control of the state. The media may no longer attempt to be a brainwashing propaganda machine. Today they work more like publicity agents for the state, or what He (2000) and Lee, He, and Huang (2006) have called the "Party Publicity Inc."

The media thus cannot be expected to provide a truly diverse range of viewpoints on important policy matters. For example, Zhao's (2003) detailed examination of how 11 newspapers in China covered the U.S.-China bilateral WTO negotiations in 1999 found that all newspapers fervently supported China's entrance into the WTO. The Chinese media treated WTO membership as "not just about China's right to participate in the making of global trade rules [but also about] China's place, China's face, China's inspirations, and China's identity in the world" (p. 37). The media portrayed WTO membership as beneficial to "common people," with the latter term referring mainly to investors and consumers. The voices of business leaders and selected experts were employed to give authority and credibility to the messages, whereas the voices of the farmers and laborers, who were the likely losers, were systematically excluded.

Lee (2010) made a similar observation in his study of the *Global Times*, China's official English-language newspaper. Analyzing the discourses of foreign policy advisors and interpreters published from 2000 to 2005, Lee found that most writers were supportive of China's active participation in the international division of labor as a way for the country to climb up the economic ladder, and most narratives "were mindful of the opportunities and challenges but came to conclude that gains would be greater than costs." Moreover, the *Global Times* directly repeated the official emphasis on China's peaceful rise in the world order. Lee argued that the Chinese media treated globalization as reducible to economic and geopolitical opportunities for China to rise as a great power. At the same time, Beijing-defined national interest was emphasized, whereas "local" perspectives were suppressed. China saw itself as getting everything ready for its deserved rise to the status of a world power, but the United States presented a stumbling block. Even so, it was argued that China should not confront the United States unnecessarily for fear of undermining its own development agendas. This media discourse sets the stage for how urban Chinese would perceive the United States (see Chapter 5).

Zhao (2003) and Lee (2010) thus provided two case studies highlighting the similarities between China's official rhetoric and media discourses on issues related to globalization. Whereas more content-based studies are probably needed, the fact remains that given what we know about the state-media relationship in China, we have reason to believe that the findings from the two studies are representative of media discourses on globalization in at least the national media in China (which also tend to be most tightly controlled by the state). They are the background against which we set up hypotheses regarding the relationship between media consumption and Chinese people's attitudes toward globalization.

RESEARCH QUESTIONS AND HYPOTHESES

To recapitulate, past studies have shown that people's attitudes toward globalization are shaped by variables such as education, which represent the skills and cultural capital that people have, as well as by social and political values and norms. Adding to these two types of factors, we are also interested in exploring the impact of transnational social experiences and media consumption. Nevertheless, we contend that the relationships between the various "independent variables" and attitude toward globalization must be understood within the context of the Chinese government's "promotion" of China's global integration.

The analysis of this chapter will be relatively more elaborate as it addresses the ultimate dependent variable as indicated in Figure 1.1 of Chapter 1. Hence it should be useful to first explicate and state the major research questions and hypotheses here. This would clarify the logic underlying the flow of the subsequent analysis.

First, we can set up a few hypotheses and questions at the descriptive level regarding the extent to which Chinese people are positive or negative toward globalization. It should be noted that, although past studies typically measured people's overall attitude toward globalization, our survey examined people's perception of both the positive and negative impact of globalization separately. That is, as in the emphasis on Chinese people's ambivalence toward America in Chapter 5, we also allow the possibility that people may be ambivalent toward globalization—that is, they may recognize that globalization does have both positive and negative impacts. Nevertheless, based on the discussions in the previous sections, our first two hypotheses posit that urban Chinese people are more positive than negative toward globalization.

> Hypothesis 1a: Urban Chinese people tend to agree that globalization has various positive influences on China and on themselves.

> Hypothesis 1b: Urban Chinese people tend to disagree that globalization has various negative influences on China and on themselves.

Like some past studies, our measurements attempt to capture various dimensions of globalization. As will be shown later, our measurements incorporate people's perceptions of the economic, political, cultural, and environmental impact of globalization. Although people's attitudes toward political globalization, cultural globalization, and economic globalization are likely to be positively related to each other, having separate measures for people's perceptions about these various aspects of globalization would allow us to empirically ascertain whether and to what extent urban Chinese would draw distinctions among the desirability of these various dimensions of globalization. Here, we do not have specific theoretical or contextual reasons to make specific predictions. Hence we state a research question:

> Research question 1: What are the urban Chinese people's attitudes toward the different dimensions of globalization? Do they see certain aspects of globalization as more desirable than others?

Moreover, our measurements also distinguish the potential impacts of globalization on the national, city, and individual levels. What is good for the country as a whole may or may not be good for a specific city within the country, and what is good for one's own city is is not necessarily good for an individual located within the city. Again, although it is very likely that perceptions of the impact of globalization at different levels would be strongly and positively correlated with each other, analytically they can remain distinct. An interesting question, therefore, is whether people perceive the influence of globalization on themselves to be more positive or negative than the influence of globalization on their city and country. Hence we pose the following research question:

Research question 2: Do urban Chinese differentiate the impact of globalization on the personal, city, and national levels? Do they perceive the impacts of globalization at the personal level to be more positive or negative than the impact of globalization at the city and national levels?

After positing these hypotheses and research questions, we can now turn to the predictors of people's attitudes toward globalization. The predictors of attitudes toward globalization in our analysis can be summarized in four groups. The first group of factors is related to the skills and knowledge that allow people to perform well in the globalized economy. Possessing such capital should be positively related to attitudes toward globalization. More specifically, following past studies (e.g., Hainmueller and Hiscox, 2006; Hsiao et al., 2010), we posit education and foreign language abilities to relate positively to attitudes toward globalization.

Hypothesis 2a: Better educated people hold more positive views toward globalization.

Hypothesis 2b: People with better foreign language abilities hold more positive views toward globalization.

Second, following the suggestion by scholars such as Wolfe and Mendelsohn (2005) and Edwards (2006), we also examine the impact of values and norms on people's attitude toward globalization. Based on past research findings and on the availability of relevant measurement in the existing data, we focus on the possible influence of three value orientations: isolationism, adventurism, and nationalism. "Isolationism" refers to a preference for a country to mind its own affairs and not be involved in other countries or international matters. Historically, the foreign policies of different countries have been marked by different degrees of isolationism at different times. At the individual level, different people may hold isolationist beliefs to varying extents. Obviously increasing global interdependence renders isolationist policies and thinking more and more obsolete and unrealistic. People having a strong isolationist orientation, therefore, can be expected to view globalization more negatively.

Adventurism has already been examined in previous chapters. Just to recapitulate, adventurism is pertinent to whether people are willing to take up the challenges, opportunities, and risks offered by the processes of globalization. In the contemporary world, more and more people have the chance to study and/or work abroad. Migration has also become more common. Yet not everyone is willing to move to a foreign country. Some may still see leaving one's own hometown as a sad happening. Others may simply prefer the comfort of living in the society with which they are most familiar. In any case, contrary to isolationism, adventurism implies openness to the outside world. We believe that people who have a more adventurous orientation will tend to view globalization more positively.

Nationalism, meanwhile, should also relate to attitude toward globalization. But here contextual considerations become extremely important. Theoretically, since more and more issues and problems—ranging from the implementation of copyright law to global warming—today require cooperation among countries to resolve, globalization may be considered as implying a decline in national sovereignty (Habermas, 1999; Held, 1995). People and governments may also see cultural globalization as a mask for cultural imperialism (Tomlinson, 1991)—that is, the local traditions and indigenous cultures may be under threat when more and more people's media diets are dominated by foreign materials. Following these considerations, we may posit a negative relationship between nationalistic sentiments and attitudes toward globalization. However, as the previous section discussed, the Chinese government has been promoting the compatibility of globalization and national development. To the extent that Chinese people's understanding of globalization is shaped by official ideologies, the relationship between nationalistic sentiments and attitude toward globalization should be positive rather than negative. We contend that, when compared with abstract theoretical considerations of the supposed relationship between the nation and globalization, contextual considerations are in the end likely to be more powerful in explaining social reality. Therefore, we hypothesize a *positive* relationship between nationalistic sentiments and attitude toward globalization (For simplicity, we presume that the relationship should be applicable to both cultural nationalism and developmental nationalism.)

Summarizing the above paragraphs, the three hypotheses concerning the impact of values and norms on attitude toward globalization are:

Hypothesis 3a: People with isolationist beliefs are more negative toward globalization.

Hypothesis 3b: People with higher levels of adventurism hold more positive views toward globalization.

Hypothesis 3c: People with stronger nationalistic sentiments hold more positive views toward globalization.

The third set of variables predicting attitude toward globalization is constituted by people's experiences and connections with the outside world. People who have foreign travel experiences and transnational social connections are likely to appreciate global interconnectedness. As noted earlier, Hsiao and associates (2010) have found a positive relationship between people's social connections in foreign countries and their attitude toward international organizations. Hence we also hypothesize a positive connection between the two. Specifically, we posit the following hypotheses:

Hypothesis 4a: People who have more experiences traveling abroad hold more positive attitudes toward globalization.

Hypothesis 4b: People who have more transnational social connections hold more positive attitudes toward globalization.

Finally, media use variables constitute the last set of factors expected to shape people's attitudes toward globalization. As discussed in the previous section, the Chinese national media have largely toed the party line and promulgate the view that engaging with globalization is beneficial to China's national development. Since the media in China have remained under state control, they are unlikely to provide a diverse range of viewpoints on the matter. As a result, the views presented in the mainstream media are likely to be one-sided, reflecting and supporting the official standpoint. This means that the condition of "monopoly," a condition for the presence of strong media effects (Lazarsfeld and Merton, 1964; Simonson and Weimann, 2003), does apply in the present case. Besides, positing global engagement as a means of realizing the national dream of modernization should also resonate with Chinese people's rising nationalistic sentiments. The dominant message, in other words, harmonizes with people's preexisting beliefs. It means that the condition of canalization, another condition for the presence of strong media effects (Lazarsfeld and Merton, 1964; Simonson and Weimann, 2003), also applies. Therefore we have strong reasons to expect consumption of national media to relate positively to attitudes toward globalization.

Meanwhile, we also expect consumption of foreign media to lead to more positive views toward globalization. The reason behind the relationship, however, may not have anything to do with the presence or absence of a dominant message in foreign media contents. Rather, consumption of foreign media itself is a manifestation of cultural globalization. It should be reasonable to expect people who frequently engage in a practice furthered by a social trend or process to view that trend or process more positively, hence the expectation about the positive relationship between foreign media use and attitudes toward globalization.

Summarizing the above two paragraphs, our last two hypotheses are:

Hypothesis 5a: Chinese people who consume national media more frequently hold more positive views toward globalization.

Hypothesis 5b: Chinese people who consume foreign media more frequently hold more positive views toward globalization.

CHINESE CITIZENS' ATTITUDES TOWARD GLOBALIZATION

We can now start to analyze the survey data. For this chapter, the most important information comes from the 32 items in the questionnaire that asked the respondents whether they regarded "globalization" as having different types of impact on the Chinese society and on themselves. Nevertheless, we could not assume that all respondents were able to understand the term "globalization" (*quan qiu hua*). In fact, Chapter 6 has already shown that not all respondents had heard of the term, and individuals may understand the term differently. To reduce the impact of the individuals' idiosyncratic understanding of the term on the findings, we prefaced the set of items by stating:

In recent years we often heard of discussions about "globalization." Some people think that the world market is overcoming national boundaries. There are more and more cultural exchanges between nations. Countries around the world are increasingly interdependent on political, environmental, and safety issues. But there are also people who disagree with such views. I am going to read out a number of views; please tell me if you "strongly agree," "agree," "are neutral," "disagree," or "strongly disagree" with these views.

This preface highlights the phenomenon of increasing global interconnectedness, largely following the general sociological definitions of globalization proffered by Giddens (1991) and Robertson (1992). The definition should be uncontroversial and easy for the respondents to grasp. The preface also highlights the fact that globalization has numerous dimensions. As typical in the survey questionnaire design, the preface stresses the existence of people who disagree so as to minimize acquiescence effects in survey response.

The 32 specific items were then read out one by one. As already pointed out earlier, the items were designed with three distinctions in mind: (1) the distinction between positive and negative impact; (2) the distinction between political, economic, cultural, and environmental impacts; and (3) the distinction between impacts at the national, city, and individual levels. For example, the statement that "globalization will enhance the transparency of the Chinese government" refers to a positive political impact at the national level, whereas "globalization will lead this city to lose its own cultural tradition" refers to a negative cultural impact at the city level. "Globalization can help increase my income" refers to a positive economic impact at the individual level, and "Globalization brings more environmental pollution to the city" refers to a negative environmental impact at the city level, and so on.

Owing to the large number of items involved (see the appendix for the full list of 32 items), we did not discuss the findings of the items one by one. Rather, we created indices for the following analysis.[2] We combined the 32 items into eight indices representing the perceived positive and negative impact of globalization on politics, economics, culture, and the environment. We then created another set of indices by recombining the 32 items according to whether they referred to a positive or negative impact of globalization at the national, city, and individual levels. Finally, we created an overall positive impact of globalization index by combining all items about the positive impact of globalization; an index of overall negative impact of globalization was constructed likewise.[3]

Figure 7.1 shows the mean scores of the various indices. Consistent with hypothesis 1a, our respondents were indeed quite positive toward globalization. They perceived globalization as having various positive impacts— political, economic, cultural, and—on China and on themselves. All the mean scores of the positive impact indices shown in Figure 7.1 are significantly above the midpoint of the five-point scale in one-sample *t*-tests. Also consistent with hypothesis 1b, our respondents were not particularly likely to acknowledge the negative impact that globalization might inflict on China and on themselves. All the mean scores of the perceived negative impact indices are statistically significantly below the midpoint of the scale in one-sample *t*-tests, although in this case the differences between

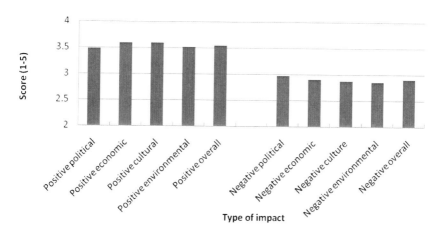

Figure 7.1 Urban Chinese people's perceptions of the impact of globalization.

the mean scores and the midpoint are very small. In other words, there is also not a very strong tendency among urban Chinese to dismiss the negative impact of globalization. Yet comparatively, it remains the case that the respondents were substantially more likely to recognize the positive rather than the negative influence of globalization.

Figure 7.1 also offers insights into the first research question of this chapter. There are only limited differences between the mean scores of the five positive impact indices and the five negative impact indices. This suggests that, again, the respondents did not make sharp distinctions between political, economic, cultural, and environmental impacts. But in paired-samples *t*-tests, the differences between many pairs of mean scores are indeed meaningful in statistical terms. Comparatively speaking, Chinese people were most likely to acknowledge the positive cultural and economic impact of globalization and least likely to acknowledge the positive political impact of globalization. Looking at the perceived negative impact indices, we can also see that Chinese people were relatively more likely to acknowledge the negative political impact of globalization but more likely to dismiss globalization's negative cultural, environmental, and economic impacts.

These findings are meaningful in relation to the characteristics of official discourses regarding globalization. As discussed, the Chinese state has mainly been promoting the economic benefits of globalization while also defending national sovereignty, especially in facing criticisms from western democratic governments on the issues of democracy and human rights. Therefore Figure 7.1 again demonstrates that public opinion toward globalization is consistent with the official view—that is, economic globalization is to be embraced but political globalization is relatively less desirable.

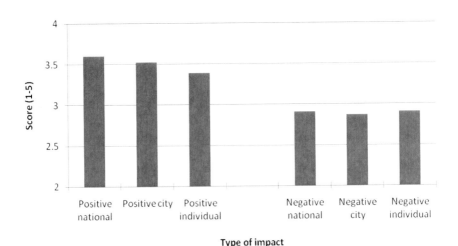

Figure 7.2 The perceived impact of globalization at different levels.

Then what about the perceived impact of globalization at different levels? Figure 7.2 shows the mean scores of the relevant indices. Whereas the mean scores of the three perceived negative impact indices do not differ substantially, there are clearer and more substantial differences between the mean scores of the three perceived positive impact indices. Chinese people were less likely to acknowledge the positive impact of globalization on themselves (i.e., at the individual level), but they were substantially more likely to acknowledge the positive impact of globalization on the nation.

Such a difference is not difficult to understand, however. As a distinctive line of research in public opinion studies has argued and shown, people do not have direct access to information about national political and economic conditions. People are therefore particularly reliant on the media to form evaluations of national conditions (Lippmann, 1922; Mutz, 1998). In contrast, people do not have to rely on any other source of information to tell them how they are doing in their everyday lives. Putting it more concretely, people may need to rely on the media to tell them whether an economic crisis is generating a huge unemployment problem throughout the country, but they need only listen to their bosses to know whether they can keep their jobs. In the present context, the official view about the benefits China can reap by engaging more comprehensively with the processes of globalization is something people learn from the media, and they may not have much alternative information to challenge these claims. Nevertheless, they do know whether they are indeed seeing improvements in their personal well-being through the years of market reform. Given the unequal distribution of wealth and the increasing rich-poor gap, they may indeed feel that they are not the beneficiaries even if China as a whole does profit from globalization.

Along this line of argument, it is also worth pointing out that the indices on the perceived impact of globalization at the city and individual levels

Table 7.1 Perceived Impact of Globalization by Four Cities

	Beijing	Shanghai	Chengdu	Xi'an
Positive impact				
National**	3.55	3.59	3.56	3.70
City**	3.44	3.52	3.49	3.66
Individual	3.39	3.37	3.36	3.42
Overall**	3.48	3.52	3.49	3.62
Negative impact				
National**	2.97	2.87	2.91	2.88
City**	2.96	2.84	2.84	2.84
Individual**	3.04	2.84	2.85	2.91
Overall**	2.99	2.86	2.88	2.88

Note: Entries are mean scores on the indices. Variables marked by ** have statistically significant differences among the four cities' mean scores in a one-way ANOVA analysis.

register larger standard deviations.[4] This means that the urban Chinese hold more divergent views about the impact of globalization on their own cities and on themselves, and they hold relatively more homogeneous views on the impact of globalization on China as a whole. Again, this is understandable, as people's perceptions of the impact of globalization on themselves and on their own cities should be shaped to a larger extent by their personal observations and experiences, such that people positioned differently in society are likely to come up with varying perceptions.

Because our survey was conducted in four Chinese cities, it will also be useful to look at whether residents from different cities viewed globalization differently. Table 7.1 shows the findings regarding the overall impact indices and the indices of impact at different levels. Interestingly, although we might have expected the more modernized coastal cities of Shanghai and Beijing to be the main beneficiaries of China's engagement with globalization, and hence their residents should be more positive toward globalization, the findings in Table 7.1 show that people from Xi'an were most likely to recognize the positive impact of globalization on the nation, on their own city, and on themselves. At the same time, the perceived negative impact of globalization is more likely to be acknowledged by people in Beijing. Admittedly we do not have a ready explanation for the fact that the respondents from Xi'an were more likely to acknowledge the positive influence of globalization or why the respondents from Beijing were more likely to see the negative impact of globalization, but these findings at least point to the inadequacy of the coast-inland dichotomy—the between-cities differences do not clearly reflect a distinction between coastal cities on one hand and inland cities on the other.

Before we analyze the predictors of people's attitudes toward globalization, a look at Table 7.2 reports how the indices are correlated with each

Table 7.2 Correlations among the Perceived Impact of Globalization Indices

Perceived impact	2	3	4	5	6	7	8	9	10
1. + political	.51**	.41**	.47**	.75**	.15**	.04	.07**	.14**	.13**
2. + economic	——	.53**	.52**	.79**	.08**	.05	.01	.02	.05
3. + cultural		——	.60**	.81**	-.01	.03	.02	.06*	.03
4. + environmental			——	.83**	.06*	.01	.09**	.16**	.11**
5. + overall				——	.09**	.04	.06*	.12**	.10**
6. - political					——	.51**	.51**	.52**	.79**
7. - economic						——	.51**	.51**	.78**
8. - cultural							——	.50**	.80**
9. - environmental								——	.81**
10. - overall									——

Note: Entries are Pearson correlation coefficients. N = 1,999. * P < .01; ** P < .001

other. We include in the table only the indices by dimensions of globalization into the table. Yet using the indices by levels of impact would not create substantively different results. The findings show that the five positive impact indices included in Table 7.2 are highly correlated among themselves, and so are the five negative impact indices. This, again, suggests that mainland Chinese respondents were not making sharp distinctions among the impact of different dimensions of globalization. More interestingly, Table 7.2 shows that there are some positive correlations between the negative and positive impact indices. For example, the correlation between perceived overall positive impact and perceived overall negative impact of globalization is .10 ($P < .01$). This means that people who considered globalization to have a positive impact on China also tended, albeit only slightly, to believe that globalization would have a negative impact on China.

The correlation is not strong, but the important point here is that recognizing globalization as having positive impact on China does not entail dismissing globalization as having negative impact on China. As we have already discussed in Chapter 5, public opinion research in the past decade has paid more and more attention to the notion of ambivalence (Lee and Chan, 2009; McGraw, Hasecke and Conger, 2003; Martinez, Craig, and Kane, 2005)—that is, "the co-existence of positive and negative dispositions toward an attitude object" (Ajzen, 2001, p. 39) in people's minds. Researchers now realize that having positive thoughts toward an object ("the United States" in Chapter 5 and "globalization" in this chapter) does not necessarily suppress negative thoughts in people's minds. In the present context, if positive thoughts about globalization (perceived positive impact of globalization) suppressed negative thoughts about globalization (perceived negative impact of globalization), or vice versa, then perceived positive and perceived negative impact of globalization should be negatively related to each other. Yet Table 7.2 shows that the two are not negatively related to each other; instead, they are even significantly positively (though admittedly only weakly) correlated. Therefore we can take the findings of Table 7.2 as a sign of urban Chinese people's ambivalence toward globalization. More precisely, if we focus on the overall positive and negative impact indices and split the sample into groups using the midpoints of the two indices, we can see that 37.9 percent of the respondents scored above 3 on both indices. In other words, more than one-third of the respondents believed that globalization, overall, has both positive and negative impact on China and on themselves.[5]

PREDICTORS OF ATTITUDES TOWARD GLOBALIZATION

The next step of our analysis is to examine the predictors of people's attitudes toward globalization. We have set up a number of hypotheses regarding the potential impact of personal background and cultural capital, values and norms, foreign social experiences and connections, and media use. We conducted a multiple regression analysis to test the various hypotheses at the same time. The independent variables included demographics, people's values and norms, nationalistic sentiments, foreign experiences and connections, as well as media consumption. The measurements of the variables were already discussed in earlier chapters. The only exception is isolationism, which was not included in earlier chapters' analysis. Isolationism was measured by people's agreement, on a five-point Likert scale, with the statement that "China should pay more attention to take care of internal problems; it is unnecessary to intervene in international affairs." Chinese urban residents actually held a rather isolationist worldview, as 45.5 percent of the respondents actually agreed or strongly agreed with the statement; only 29.6 percent disagreed or strongly disagreed.

Regarding the dependent variables, we conducted analyses using all the indices shown in Figures 7.1 and 7.2. Yet for simplicity, Table 7.3 summarizes only the findings regarding the overall positive and negative impact indices as well as the indices about the impact of globalization at the national, city, and individual levels. Findings regarding the predictors of perceived impact of different dimensions of globalization are mentioned when relevant.

All demographics but education have only limited relationship with perceived positive impact of globalization. Young people were more likely to see globalization as having a positive impact at the individual level, perhaps because young people are more likely to come into contact with foreign culture and media as part of cultural globalization. Interestingly, workers at foreign companies or joint ventures were more likely to see globalization as having positive impact at the individual level. This finding does make intuitive sense, as being employed by a foreign company by itself can already be considered as a "benefit" of globalization for the individual concerned. However, being employed by a foreign company does not make an individual more likely to recognize the positive impact of globalization at the city and the national levels.

All three city dummy variables are significantly related to all the dependent variables shown in Table 7.3. People from Xi'an, Chengdu, and Shanghai compared with those from Beijing were more likely to regard globalization as having a positive impact on the nation, on its cities, and on themselves.

Supporting hypothesis 2a, education relates positive to perceived overall positive impact of globalization. Education also relates to the perceived positive impact of globalization at all three levels: nation, city, and individual. Yet hypothesis 2b is not supported. At the bivariate level, there is a significant positive correlation between English ability and perceived overall positive impact of globalization. But the size of the correlation is minimal ($r = .05$, $P < .05$). Moreover, the relationship disappears once education and other demographics are controlled. In

Table 7.3 Predictors of Perceived Positive Impact of Globalization

	Perceived Positive Impact of Globalization			
	National	City	Individual	Overall
Gender	-.05*	-.03	-.04	-.05
Age	-.01	-.00	-.11***	-.04
Education	.10**	.07*	.07*	.10**
Household income	.02	.01	.02	.02
Ability to speak English	-.00	-.02	-.05	-.02
Work in state enterprise	-.01	-.02	.01	-.00
Work in foreign country	.03	.02	.07**	.04
Shanghai	.13***	.14***	.06*	.13***
Chengdu	.13***	.14***	.09**	.20***
Xi'an	-.03	-.05*	-.02	-.04
Isolationism	-.03	-.05*	-.02	-.04
Adventurism	.14***	.12***	.17***	.17***
Developmental nationalism	.12***	.10***	.09***	.12***
Cultural nationalism	.15***	.12***	.11***	.15***
Travel experience	-.00	.02	-.01	-.00
Transnational connections	.03	.02	.07**	.04
Local media	-.14***	-.13***	-.06*	-.13***
National media	-.09**	.08*	.01	.08**
Foreign media	-.07**	-.04	-.04	-.06*
Adjusted R²	9.9%***	7.7%***	7.8%***	11.0%***

Note: Entries are standardized regression coefficients. Missing values replaced by means. N = 1,999. *** $P < .001$; ** $P < .01$; * $P < .05$.

China, English ability is obviously a marker of educational level, but English ability itself does not have an effect on people's perceptions of the positive impact of globalization.

How should we make sense of the findings regarding hypotheses 2a and 2b? As discussed earlier in this chapter, education can represent the amount and range of knowledge and skills that people have. But if cultural capital really matters, one would expect English ability to be particularly relevant to people's performance in the globalized world and hence to exert an influence on their attitudes. The fact that English ability does not have a significant impact in Table 7.3 suggests that the impact of education should also be understood differently. According to Hainmueller and Hiscox (2006), education may represent understanding of liberal economics and/or certain cosmopolitan values and beliefs that people tend to acquire through education. Here, the distinction between perceived impact of globalization on economics, politics, culture, and environment becomes pertinent. When the perceived positive impacts of globalization on these different dimensions were used as the dependent variables, we saw that education relates significantly only with the perceived positive impact of globalization on politics, culture, and environment. There is no relationship between education and the perceived positive economic impact of globalization. This suggests that the impact of education is probably due mainly to the cultural values and beliefs imparted through the educational process.

In fact, this interpretation fits well with the finding of Table 7.3 that two cultural values and norms have relatively strong relationships with the dependent variables. Consistent with hypothesis 3b, people who were more willing to move abroad to develop their careers or pursue their life goals were more positive toward globalization. More importantly, supporting hypothesis 3c, people who exhibited stronger nationalistic sentiments tended to perceive globalization in a more positive light. This suggests that public opinion in urban China did take up the official view that globalization and national development, rather than being antithetical, are actually compatible.

Nevertheless, hypothesis 3a does not receive support. Although the coefficients of the isolationism variable are indeed negative in sign, the sizes of the coefficients are minimal. And the coefficients fail to reach the conventional level of statistical significance in three of the four columns in Table 7.3.

Hypotheses 4a and 4b also do not receive support. Foreign travel experiences and transnational social connections do not have significant relationships with the dependent variables except in the case of the significant relationship between transnational social connections and perceived positive impact of globalization at the individual level. Yet, similar to the case of working for foreign companies, it is indeed reasonable for transnational social connections to relate to perceived impact of globalization at the individual level only, because transnational social connections are constituted by people's communication and contacts in their own immediate lifeworlds. If such connections are going to affect people's perceptions of the world at large, the impact should begin with perceptions of what larger processes such as globalization are doing to individuals instead of to whole cities or even countries.

This line of thinking becomes even more interesting and meaningful when we compare the influence of transnational connections or working for foreign companies vis-à-vis the influence of media consumption. The media variables do have important relationships with the dependent variables in Table 7.3. Indeed, Hypothesis 5a is supported: people who consumed national media more frequently held more positive perceptions about the potential positive impact of globalization. But here, national media use has a significant relationship with perceived positive impact of globalization only at the national and city levels, not the individual level. As we have already pointed out in the previous section, the official rhetoric may be able to persuade urban Chinese about the presumed benefits of engaging in globalization for the nation as a whole, but individuals' judgments about whether globalization is good for them are likely to be primarily based on personal experiences and situations. Hence it is more difficult for media to influence people's perceptions of the impact of globalization at the individual level.

In fact, this argument is also supported by the findings in Table 7.3 regarding the impact of local media consumption. We did not set up hypotheses regarding the impact of local media use. Interestingly, Table 7.3 shows that people who consumed local media more frequently were less likely to see globalization as having positive impacts. This suggests that local media, under relatively looser control by the state, may have been carrying discourses and messages that are "alternative" to the official view. On the other hand, local media may simply contain fewer contents related to the outside world. Hence frequent consumers of local media may have weaker perceptions of the reality of globalization; as a result, they would also recognize the positive impact of globalization to lesser extents. In any case, the important point here is that the negative impact of local media consumption is also significant only in regard to the perceived impact of globalization at the national and city levels. There is no relationship between local media consumption and the perceived positive impact of globalization at the individual level.

Similarly, foreign media consumption is unrelated to the perceived positive impact of globalization at the individual level. A significant relationship exists between foreign media consumption and the perceived positive impact of globalization at the national level, but the relationship is negative and therefore contrary to the prediction of hypothesis 5b. We will return to this finding later.

Then, would the findings be the same for the perceived negative impact of globalization? Table 7.4 summarizes the findings of the regression analyses. Several findings are consistent with those in Table 7.3. First, the city dummies have some significant relationships with the dependent variables, although the amount and strength of the relationships are smaller and weaker than those in Table 7.3. The general directions of the relationships are consistent with the findings of Table 7.3, as Beijing residents were relatively more likely to acknowledge the negative impact of globalization when compared to residents of the other three cities. Second, there is no relationship between foreign travel experiences and transnational social connections with the perceived negative impact of globalization.

Third, developmental nationalism has a significant and negative relationship with perceived negative impact of globalization. In other words, people who valued national development more strongly were less likely to regard globalization as having a negative impact on China and on the respondents themselves. Combined with the findings of Table 7.3, Chinese people with higher levels of developmental nationalistic sentiments were consistently more positive toward globalization.

However, the findings regarding cultural nationalism are intriguing. Table 7.4 shows that cultural nationalism is positively related to the dependent variables. Urban Chinese with higher levels of cultural nationalistic senti-ments were more likely to acknowledge the negative impact of globaliza-tion, whereas Table 7.3 shows that the same people were also more likely to acknowledge the positive impact of globalization. These findings point to the complexities of the relationship between nationalism and globalization. We will return to this point in the concluding part of this chapter.

Fourth, national media use also relates to perceived overall nega-tive impact of globalization negatively and significantly—that is, people who consumed national media more frequently were more likely to have adopted the official view that globalization has little negative impact on China. Therefore national media consumption is also consistently related to a more positive view toward globalization.

More interestingly, Table 7.4 also shows a number of findings that are quite different from those in Table 7.3. Table 7.4 gives support for hypoth-esis 5b, as foreign media consumption is significantly and negatively related to perceived negative impact of globalization. But when combined with the

Table 7.4 Predictors of Perceived Negative Impact of Globalization

	Perceived Negative Impact of Globalization			
	National	City	Individual	Overall
Gender	-.03	-.05*	-.01	-.03
Age	-.07**	-.11***	-.08**	-.10***
Education	.02	.05	-.01	.00
Household income	.03	.04	.01	.04
Ability to speak English	-.10***	-.10**	-.10**	-.12***
Work in state enterprise	-.06**	-.01	-.03	-.04*
Work in foreign country	-.02	-.02	-.00	-.02
Shanghai	-.05	-.04	.09**	-.07*
Chengdu	-.03	-.04	-.10***	-.06*
Xi'an	-.01	-.03	-.04	-.03
Isolationism	.19***	.11***	.19***	.19***
Adventurism	.09***	.10***	.10***	.11***
Developmental nationalism	-.12***	-.11***	-.07**	-.12***
Cultural nationalism	.18***	.16***	.15***	.19***
Travel experience	.01	.01	-.01	.00
Transnational connections	-.01	.01	-.03	-.01
Local media	-.03	-.03	-.03	-.04
National media	-.04	-.09*	-.06*	-.07*
Foreign media	-.06*	-.07**	-.07**	-.08**
Adjusted R²	11.3%***	8.6%***	11.6%***	13.7%***

Note: Entries are standardized regression coefficients. Missing values replaced by means. N = 1,999. *** $P < .001$; ** $P < .01$; * $P < .05$.

findings in Table 7.3, the impact of foreign media consumption is rather counterintuitive: People who consume foreign media frequently are less likely to recognize both the positive and the negative impact of globalization, which suggests that these people tend to recognize the reality of globalization to lesser extents.

Among the demographic variables, age has a consistently negative relationship with perceived negative impact of globalization—that is, younger people were more likely to perceive globalization as having some negative impact on China and on themselves. In contrast, whereas educated people were shown to be more likely to acknowledge the positive impact of globalization, Table 7.4 shows that better educated people were not less likely to acknowledge the potential negative impact of globalization.

Meanwhile, Table 7.4 shows that people with better English abilities were less likely to acknowledge the potential negative impact of globalization. It seems that people with the language skills that would allow them to navigate the globalized world more easily were less afraid of the potential problems that globalization might bring about. Combining the findings about the impact of education and English ability in the two tables, we see the importance of separating the positive and negative impacts of globalization. Factors that drive people to acknowledge the positive impact of globalization may not be the same as the factors that drive people to acknowledge the negative impact of globalization.

The same also applies to the influence of isolationism and adventurism on perceived negative impact of globalization. Consistent with hypothesis 3a, isolationism has a positive relationship with perceived negative impact—that is, people who preferred China to take care only of itself were more likely to see globalization as having negative influence on China and on themselves. Here, obviously the causal direction can go both ways—people who see globalization as bringing about many problems are likely to prefer to see China take care only of itself. This finding is, in the end, not very difficult to understand, as it is simply suggesting that isolationism is a product of perceived external threat. Meanwhile, adventurism has a significant and positive relationship with the perceived negative impact of globalization. Taking the findings of Tables 7.3 and 7.4 together, we see that people who regard moving to another place to seek development as a good thing were more likely to acknowledge both the positive *and* negative impact of globalization. It suggests that the more adventurous people were more likely to acknowledge the reality of globalization.

On the whole, the two tables show that cultural values and norms are relatively more successful in predicting people's attitude toward globalization. This is in line with the arguments by Wolfe and Mendelsohn (2005) and others. Admittedly, the predictive power of the regression model is not substantial. The adjusted R^2 value ranges from 7.4 percent to at most 13.7 percent. Yet it is understandable given the nonsignificance of some of the hypothesized factors. Nevertheless, for the purpose of the present chapter and the book, the findings presented here have already allowed us to draw a number of important conclusions about Chinese people's attitudes toward globalization.

SUMMARY AND DISCUSSION

We started this chapter by discussing past studies on people's attitude toward globalization in different countries. Compared with studies in the literature, our measure of people's attitudes toward globalization is arguably more comprehensive, although the measure is by no means perfect. We differentiated among (1) the impacts of globalization on four dimensions; (2) impacts at the national, city, and individual levels; and more importantly (3) the positive and negative impacts of globalization.

The distinction between positive and negative impacts is particularly important, as scholars and political leaders widely recognize that globalization brings about both opportunities and challenges. Chinese political leaders, in their attempt to justify the policy direction of active engagement with globalization, might have the tendency to downplay the potentially negative consequences of globalization, but they are definitely not blind to those potential negative consequences. Common people, by the same token, are also likely to understand that globalization is neither a utopia nor a sheer nightmare.

Our findings, indeed, suggest that people are ambivalent about globalization. About one third of our respondents believed that globalization has some overall positive impact on China *and* that globalization has some overall negative impact on China. Besides, at the individual level, Chinese people who acknowledged the positive impact of globalization to a larger extent also acknowledged the negative impact of globalization. We contend that the positive relationship between the perceived positive and negative impacts of globalization shows that individuals vary in the extent to which they recognize globalization as a social reality in the contemporary world. When they see globalization as a reality, they tend to acknowledge both the positive and the negative impacts of globalization.

Moreover, it is useful to differentiate between the perceived negative and positive impacts of globalization because they are not predicted by exactly the same set of factors. There are, certainly, factors that explain perceived positive and negative impact of globalization in a "consistent manner": for instance, people in Beijing were more likely to acknowledge the negative impact of globalization and less likely to acknowledge the positive impact of globalization, making them the most negative toward globalization among the four cities. Yet many other factors explained only one of the two types of impact: Education relates positively only to the perceived positive impact of globalization; English language ability relates significantly only to the perceived negative impact of globalization.

One plausible way to make sense of these findings is to see the factors relating to the perceived negative impact of globalization as leading people to become more or less "defensive" against global integration, whereas the factors relating to perceived positive impact as driving people to more proactively embrace processes of globalization. People might feel less defensive if they had acquired certain cultural capital (English language) to perform well in the globalized world. And they might embrace globalization if they had acquired certain values and norms through education. Admittedly we need further analysis to test this hunch.

Another major conclusion we can draw from our analysis is the general correspondence between official ideologies and public opinion in China regarding globalization. A number of key findings are pertinent here. First, urban Chinese people, at least at the time of our survey, remained more likely to acknowledge the positive rather than the negative impact of globalization, although it should be noted that having generally positive public opinion toward globalization is a phenomenon that exists in many other countries too (e.g., Edwards, 2006; Woodward, Skrbis and Bean, 2008). Second, where perceptions about the impact of the different dimensions of globalization are concerned, the Chinese urban public tended to perceive the economic impact of globalization most positively and the political impact of globalization less positively. This is also in line with the Chinese government's emphasis on economic instead of political globalization. Third and even more tellingly, developmental nationalistic sentiments were positively related to attitude toward globalization. This is in line with the Chinese government's emphasis on national development by actively engaging with the world at large.

Why is the Chinese state seemingly successful in persuading the public to accept its own "worldview"? Part of the reason, of course, resides in the fact that the Chinese government maintains tight control of the mass media. National media discourses surrounding globalization have been toeing the party line rather closely (Lee, 2010; Zhao, 2003). Our analysis shows that there is indeed a positive relationship between national media consumption and attitude toward globalization. This does not mean that the Chinese government would necessarily be successful in their attempts to persuade the public to accept their views on every single issue. But as explained in the conceptual discussion section and also in Chapter 4, nationalism itself has also been on the rise since the 1990s (Zhao, 2004). Therefore media and official discourses on the unity of national development and globalization harmonize with many Chinese people's predispositions. This is one of the conditions which render the official and media discourses persuasive. In fact, in our earlier analysis, in which we included fewer variables in the explanatory model but moved a step further to examine the interaction effect between nationalistic sentiments and national media consumption, we found the effects of national media consumption on attitudes toward globalization to be stronger among people who had strong nationalistic sentiments (Lee et al., 2009).

Nevertheless, the relationship between cultural nationalism and attitudes toward globalization complicates the picture. Urban Chinese with higher levels of cultural nationalism were more likely to acknowledge both the positive and the negative impact of globalization. This means that, after all, we cannot posit a simplistic and unvarying positive connection between nationalistic sentiments and positive views toward globalization in Chinese public opinion. More specifically, one way to understand the results regarding the impact of cultural nationalism is to focus on the different "temporal orientation" of developmental and cultural nationalism as measured in our survey. As Chapter 4 has pointed out, developmental nationalism concerns with the future, whereas cultural nationalism is concerned with the past. For people who want China to *become* a strong nation, engaging with globalization does seem to be an important way to achieve the goal. But for people who believe that China is already great, with an invaluable cultural tradition, there may indeed be reasons to feel concerned about whether globalization may damage what China already has. Cultural nationalists do not necessarily treat globalization as a bad thing; they also tend to think that globalization will have various positive impacts on China. They are just also concerned with the potential negative impact of globalization.

Another important finding from our analysis is the lack of relationship between media consumption and perceived impact of globalization at the individual level. Indeed, at the descriptive level, Chinese urban residents were also less positive toward globalization when the questionnaire items were phrased in terms of the impact of globalization on the respondents themselves. These findings show the limits of the power of state ideologies (even under the condition of the ideologies being consistent with the value orientations of the public). Individuals may have to rely on media images and discourses to form perceptions and judgments regarding the national social and economic conditions; hence their judgments about the impact of globalization at the national (and city) level are more susceptible to the influence of media. But they also have their own unique life trajectories and everyday living environment, and their varying personal experiences would inform them about whether globalization is actually good or bad in terms of their own lives.

Last, this chapter also produces the counterintuitive finding that consumption of foreign media seems to relate to lower levels of perceived impact of globalization regardless of whether the impact is positive or negative. One plausible explanation is that the impact of foreign media consumption on attitude toward globalization can be multifaceted. For instance, foreign media consumption may lead people to view globalization more positively by way of greater familiarity with the outside world, greater willingness to move abroad, and so on. Indeed, in the present dataset, foreign media consumption is positively related to English language ability and adventurism, and both of these two variables are related to a more positive view toward globalization. However, foreign media consumption may also generate a sense of differences; that is, by consuming foreign media, people may see that their own country and culture are significantly and substantially different from other countries and cultures. In other words, the contents of foreign media may contribute to a sense of the *un*reality of the global village. Notably, in the multiple regression analysis, some of the factors that may mediate the positive influence of foreign media use on attitude toward globalization (e.g., English language ability, global adventurism) have already been controlled. As a result, the "main effect" of the foreign media use variable in the regression may tend to represent mainly its influence on the perception of the *un*reality of the global village.

This account of the effect of foreign media consumption on attitude toward globalization is, of course, speculative and must be examined in future research. But what we can see here is the potential complexity of the relationship between media and people's perceptions of globalization.

8   Conclusion

This book attempts to provide a systematic analysis of urban Chinese public opinion toward the world at large and the process of globalization at a specific historical juncture—that is, the time when China is arguably "on the rise" and is increasingly engaging with world affairs. In broad terms, our analysis and the structuring of the chapters were guided by the framework presented in Chapter 1, although the study is not restricted to testing the theory of cosmopolitan communications. Based on the premise that people form images of the world through media representation and communication activities, we examined Chinese people's personal experiences and social connections with the outside world as well as their media consumption behavior. We then examined whether and how personal experiences and media communications relate systematically to people's value orientations, especially their nationalistic sentiments. We then further examined how communications and value orientations relate to people's attitudes toward specific foreign countries, especially the United States; their awareness and conceptions of globalization; and finally their perceptions of the impact of globalization.

Instead of summarizing the findings from each chapter separately, we can review some of the major results from our research under four general headings: (1) Chinese people's personal experiences and connections with the outside world, (2) the impact of media communications, (3) the value orientations of the urban Chinese, and (4) the significance of cities as contexts. We will discuss the social and research implications of the findings. Throughout the discussion, we will highlight the findings that we believe would have more general theoretical implications. We then end this concluding chapter by briefly discussing our view on the future of public opinion toward globalization in China.

PERSONAL EXPERIENCES AND CONNECTIONS

Our analysis shows that, by the time the survey was conducted, only a small proportion of urban Chinese had had extensive experiences of traveling abroad or many transnational social connections. As expected, people located differently within the social structure tended to have different amounts of personal experiences and connections with the outside world. Both travel experience and transnational social connections are explained by education and household income. But probably largely because of the small percentages of people with any travel experience or transnational social connections, these two variables do not have strong explanatory power throughout the analysis. Foreign travel experience, for example, relates significantly to interests in foreign affairs even after a number of demographics and other factors are controlled, but it does not explain how people rate the importance of traditional or liberal values. Nor does foreign travel explain nationalistic sentiments, attitudes toward foreign countries, and perceptions of the impact of globalization. Technically speaking, when the amount of variance existing in a variable is small, it becomes more difficult for the variable to explain other things. Therefore in the future, as more and more Chinese people gain such foreign travel experience, we cannot dismiss the *potential* importance of foreign travel and/or transnational social connections on Chinese people's perceptions of the world. What we have found in our study is that, by the latter half of the 2000s, urban Chinese people's personal experiences and transnational connections with the outside world were still so limited that they did not exert a consistent and discernible influence on public opinion toward globalization. Furthermore, we must also take into consideration that although the number of Chinese people with foreign travel experience and/or transnational social ties is small in percentage, it is big in absolute terms if we account for the overall size of the Chinese population. For example, only about 3 percent of our respondents reported having traveled anywhere outside of China. However, if this percentage were to be applied to the entire Chinese urban population, the total number of Chinese with such an experience would be equal to more than half of the entire population of the United Kingdom.

In Chapter 1, we discussed Norris and Inglehart's (2009) view on the importance of "firewalls" in considering the impact of cosmopolitan communications on people's attitudes and behavior. For Norris and Inglehart, the impact of cosmopolitan communications may be limited by firewalls erected at both the societal and individual levels. In focusing on media communications, they pointed to policies of foreign media control as the most important example of societal-level firewalls. In China, however, what we see is that one of the most important societal firewalls established by the Chinese state may actually be those policies controlling the flow of people.

It can also be noted that, throughout our chapters, we have included working in foreign companies or joint ventures as one of the demographic controls. Yet this variable rarely has any significant relationship with different sorts of "dependent variables." The arrival of foreign capital and multinational corporations is a partial result of globalization. But our study shows that, similar to foreign travel experiences, only a very small percentage of urban Chinese were working for such companies at the time of the survey. The small variance in the variable may partly explain the lack of its explanatory power. Of course it is also possible that whether a company is part of a foreign corporation does not have many substantial implications on how the company is run within China. Qualitative studies of the actual working environments and intercultural communication patterns within multinational corporations in China would help to clarify the issues here. In any case, despite the lack of significant results regarding the impact of personal experiences with the outside world and transnational connections, our study should nonetheless have provided a baseline against which future studies can be compared.

THE IMPACT OF MEDIA COMMUNICATIONS

In contrast to personal experiences and transnational connections, we have questioned the utility of the societal-level firewalls established by the Chinese government regarding the flow of foreign media into China. Although the Chinese government did have rules limiting the inflow of foreign movies, TV programs, and other popular cultural products, today the more sophisticated urban Chinese can gain access to such foreign media in a variety of legal and illegal ways. Our analysis shows that, although the urban Chinese still consumed local and national media more frequently, they also consumed overseas media regularly. Interestingly, education is not important in explaining Chinese people's foreign media consumption. Although more educated urban residents did consume foreign media more frequently, they consumed national and local media more frequently as well. The social demographic factor that is most pertinent to foreign media consumption is age; foreign media consumption was more widespread among the younger generations.

Our findings reveal that the impact of media communications on attitudes toward foreign countries and perceptions of globalization is mixed. As we have already argued in an earlier publication (Lee et al., 2011), foreign media in China have not been a major force in fostering the growth of liberal-democratic value orientations or the development of specific attitudes toward foreign countries among the Chinese populace. At most, foreign media use has had a *worldview reinforcement function* for its consumers: whereas people's political value orientations shape their attitudes toward foreign countries, foreign media use strengthens such relationships between people's value orientations and attitudes toward foreign countries. Throughout this book, we saw that foreign media consumption does not relate to attitudinal and value orientation variables in a straightforward manner.

On the other hand, there are indeed some, though usually not very strong, relationships between foreign media consumption and some of the attitudinal variables we have examined. Foreign media consumption is positively related to a more positive attitude toward the United States, and it is also related to weaker perceptions of both the positive and negative impacts of globalization. Moreover, our analysis also pointed to the possibility that foreign media consumption may lead not so much to the adoption or abandonment of value orientations but instead to how people conceive the relationships between various value orientations. In Chapter 4, we saw that cultural nationalism and developmental nationalism tended to relate to each other positively for most urban Chinese residents, but the two types of nationalistic sentiments were negatively related to each other among people who consumed foreign media very frequently. This finding arguably opens up a series of research questions regarding the possible impact of foreign media consumption that scholars can attempt to tackle in the future, not only within the Chinese context but also in other countries.

Nonetheless, the generally weak relationship between foreign media consumption and various attitudinal variables suggests the likely importance of individual level firewalls in preventing media messages from affecting all people in the same way. Such findings should not be taken to suggest that the presence of foreign media in China does not matter. What is absent is an across-the-board, direct, strong relationship between consuming foreign media and a more "westernized" or "global" outlook. Despite the lack of such a connection, it remains plausible that foreign media in China are providing cultural and symbolic resources that individual Chinese citizens may take up to develop different viewpoints.

The findings regarding the impact of foreign media consumption can be considered as consistent with some of the phenomena we have discussed in the introductory chapter. After decades of "reform and opening-up," foreign media and cultural products are no longer new to urban Chinese. Chinese people's reactions to foreign media and cultural products have understandably become more differentiated. As the story of the Imperial Palace's Starbucks illustrated, Chinese people were responding in specific ways to specific foreign cultural products as cultural products located in the larger global cultural field.

More broadly speaking, we have to concede that one limitation of the present study may reside in the general and undifferentiated notion of "foreign media" itself. There are at least three major problems with the notion of foreign media in the contemporary world. First, the Chinese authorities make a rigid distinction between media entertainment and media information that comes from abroad. State control on the inflow of types of entertainment and lifestyle content is increasingly relaxed, but "hard" foreign media information is still being tightly policed. This speaks to the need to differentiate the two genres. Second, with the increase in international collaboration in cultural production and more intense flow of images, people, and capital across national borders, can the national and the foreign still be very clearly demarcated? How should Chinese people in particular understand the "national status" of a movie produced by Ang Lee, a Taiwanese film director who made his name in Hollywood? Or a movie featuring Chinese stars Gong Li or Zhang Ziyi, as in the case of *Memoirs of a Geisha*? Before the unfortunate forced retirement of basketball star Yao Ming, was watching a televised game of the Houston Rockets, the NBA team for whom Yao played, an act of consuming foreign culture for a Chinese individual if she or he was watching the game mainly in order to support Yao? And what about the most recent rise of Chinese-American basketball sensation Jeremy Lin who was born and raised in California in a Taiwanese family?

Third, in the tradition of research inspired by the theory of cultural imperialism, foreign media are often assumed to be containers of "foreign/ western values and norms." However, the interpenetration of national cultures has rendered the correspondence between national media and national culture increasingly problematic. Take Hollywood, for example. Critics have argued that Hollywood has ceased to function as a producer of "national cinema" for the American people because of the commercial drive to make movies that can sell worldwide, which has led to the hollowing out of cultural content in American movies (Wasser, 1995). Today, many Hollywood blockbusters may offer little more than spectacular collages of special effects. As Liebes and Katz (1988) argue, the cross-cultural interpretation of foreign media products is a joint interaction between the culture of the producers and the culture of the consumers. We definitely do not intend to argue that western media products no longer contain cultural values and norms, but we see it as undeniable that the distinctive "American" flavor that was carried by most Hollywood productions over the past century is becoming more and more diluted.

To a large extent, this critique regarding the foreign media is also applicable to the local and national media. Although our survey questionnaire was constructed based on the presumption that local and national media may have different foci in their programming and content, the empirical distinction may not be so clear-cut. In China's television sector today, for instance, almost all provincial television stations operate their own satellite channels, which are broadcast to other provinces within China. This implies that, for many Chinese, although local media may more clearly refer to their own city's or province's media, "national media" is actually a mix of truly national media channels (such as CCTV) and a whole list of "local media" from other provinces and cities.

However, this does not mean that meaningful findings do not emerge. For example, where attitude toward the United States is concerned, national media consumption is negatively related to overall evaluation of the United States. This finding is understandable given the often troubled relationship between China and the United States, especially in view of the fact that China's national media discourse tends to paint the United States as blocking China's rise to the world stage (Lee, 2002). The finding is also consistent with other researchers' claims that China's national television news often presents other countries in a negative light vis-a-vis China itself (Zhou, 2010). In comparison, local media consumption does not relate to overall like or dislike of the United States. What it relates to is a degree of ambivalence toward the United States, with people consuming more local media being less ambivalent. This finding is again plausible because local media may simply provide less information and fewer images about foreign countries. As a result, avid consumers of local media may simply not have much basis to form either positive or negative views of America.

Moreover, Chapter 7 shows that national media consumption does relate to more positive views toward globalization. This is consistent with our hypothesis. The finding suggests that ideologies promoted by the state remain capable of influencing public attitudes through the state-controlled media in China. Although contemporary Chinese media no longer constitute a propaganda machine in the Maoist sense, the range of viewpoints available in the domestic media in China remains limited as regards matters of state policies and politics. On the question of globalization in particular, the Chinese media have largely toed the party line and promoted the view that engaging in the processes of economic globalization is good for the country as a whole (Lee, 2010; Zhao, 2003). And our survey findings suggest that users of national media are indeed taking up the message.

Certainly, as we argued in Chapter 7, we do not presume that such "propaganda effects" exist across all issues in contemporary China. Empirically, we see that national media consumption was related mainly to perceptions of positive effects of globalization on the country and the city but not on individuals themselves. This is another finding that has important general theoretical implications. As the community of nation and/or city is "imagined" (Anderson, 1991), media communications and official rhetoric are relatively more powerful in shaping such imaginations. But when it comes to people's judgment about their own individual lives, media communication is likely to become *relatively* less important. In contrast, information available to them through direct observation and/or interpersonal communication may be more powerful in shaping what people think about the impact of globalization at the individual level as opposed to what they think about the impact of globalization at the national or city level. For instance, urban Chinese who were working for foreign companies or joint ventures did not seem to differ from other urban Chinese on many value orientations or attitudes toward foreign countries, but they were indeed more likely to regard globalization as having positive impact on Chinese people at the individual level.

NATIONALISM AND OTHER VALUE ORIENTATIONS

The impact of national media consumption on perceptions of globalization must also be understood in relation to the pervasive sense of nationalism in the Chinese context. If the official rhetoric was convincing to the Chinese public, it is because that rhetoric harmonizes with the Chinese people's desire for national development. Economic development through globalization has been a central tenet of the state's policy to reclaim its ruling legitimacy from the brink of collapse after the Tiananmen crackdown in 1989. Economic prosperity and nationalism are the new sources of legitimacy for the post-1989 regime. Economic success feeds and sustains itself; now there is no turning back. As Chapter 4 shows, by the mid-2000s, Chinese people had developed high levels of developmental nationalistic sentiments and also moderately high levels of cultural nationalistic sentiments. And Chapter 7 shows that both developmental nationalism and cultural nationalism are important predictors of people's attitudes toward globalization.

However, the relationship between nationalism and attitude toward globalization is not as straightforward as one might expect. Although developmental nationalism did consistently relate positively to perceptions of globalization, a pattern consistent with the state's rhetoric on the matter, cultural nationalists exhibited higher levels of ambivalence toward globalization: they were more likely to agree with both the positive and negative impacts of globalization. As we discussed in Chapter 7, we believe that these findings can be understood in terms of the "temporal orientation" of the measures for developmental nationalism and cultural nationalism. The former is future-oriented, and Chinese people who want the country to become stronger do tend to believe that engaging in globalization is a way of achieving that goal. Cultural nationalism, in contrast, is more past-oriented, and people who believe that China has had its own great cultural achievements may have a more complicated attitude toward globalization. They may still believe that globalization can bring further benefits to China, including its cultural revival, but they are also wary of the potential threats posed by globalization to China's historical, social, and cultural traditions.

More broadly speaking, although this study confirms that nationalistic sentiments can have an important impact on Chinese people's attitudes toward foreign countries and the processes of globalization, the findings also point to the complexities of the notion of nationalism and the importance of specifying its constituent dimensions. This study has examined the distinction between cultural and developmental nationalism, but there are other forms or dimensions of nationalistic sentiments that may deserve analysis in future studies. One example is what we may label "defensive nationalism," or the tendency for some people to take a defensive stance against any criticism of China, especially when such criticisms are proffered by foreign visitors or media. Defensive nationalists are not necessarily xenophobic; they react negatively when they perceive China to have been treated with a double standard or criticized unfairly. We are not arguing that many Chinese are defensive nationalists, but individuals may have higher or lower levels of defensiveness when they are facing critiques of their own nation, and the degree of defensive nationalistic sentiment may yet relate in its own ways to attitude toward foreign countries and the processes of globalization.

Another value orientation that has important implications for the ways in which the urban Chinese see the world is what we have labeled adventurism. As Chapter 2 pointed out, although material and policy constraints have limited the personal experiences that urban Chinese can have with the world at large, many Chinese nonetheless agree that seeking development in another place is a good thing. Willingness to move to other countries did not relate to demographic factors very strongly. Except for a positive relationship between household income and adventurism, people of different age groups, genders, and educational levels did not vary in their willingness to relocate. In reality, many Chinese students do prefer to go abroad to study as long as they have the ability and opportunity regardless of whether they plan to go back to China after graduation. The number of outgoing students has only been increasing since the time the present survey was conducted. In other words, a generally positive view toward globalization is accompanied by a general wish to go abroad. Today the urban Chinese are psychologically mobile, although not all of them are physically so.

Nevertheless, like cultural nationalism, adventurism does not simply relate to a more positive attitude toward the outside world. Rather, Chapters 5 and 7 have consistently shown that adventurism is related to more ambivalent attitudes toward the world. More adventurous people held more positive *and* negative views regarding the United States, and they also held more positive *and* negative views regarding globalization. We contend that, although more adventurous people were more interested in foreign affairs, they also tended to process information about foreign countries in a more unbiased and systematic manner. Their willingness to move abroad means that they would like to know more about the "reality" of foreign countries, both their good and bad sides. This argument about the relationship between willingness to move abroad and systematic processing of information about the world at large constitutes a general theoretical proposition that can be examined in various contexts.

Regardless of whether the psychological argument is correct, we can be certain that, in the era of globalization, more and more people are facing the decision of whether to leave their home country to develop their careers and pursue their life goals. At the individual level, people's willingness to relocate to other countries would shape their views toward the outside world. At the collective level, it would also be interesting for future studies to track changes in Chinese people's adventurism. In traditional Chinese culture, leaving one's hometown—*lixiang beijing*—has been seen in a very negative light. But globalization may be bringing about changes in the perceptions of the urban Chinese regarding such moves.

One value orientation variable that deserves discussion despite its lack of relationship with attitudes toward globalization is Chinese people's support for liberal democratic values. In Chapter 5, we saw liberal democratic values have a weak though significant relationship with attitudes toward the United States only where overall liking or disliking is concerned. In

Chapter 7, we saw that liberal democratic values do not relate to attitude toward globalization at all. Chapter 3 also shows that there is no relationship between foreign media consumption and support for liberal values. In fact, Chapter 2 has shown that even basic demographic factors such as education and age do not relate to support for liberal values. These weak or null findings raise the question of how urban Chinese people understand the notions of democracy and liberty. On the one hand, Chinese people are likely to recognize the desirability of such values. But, on the other hand, it is not implausible that many Chinese would prefer a kind of democracy based on consultation rather than open competition for political power; neither is it implausible that many Chinese would emphasize limits on freedom as much as, if not more than, freedom itself. As a result, a general recognition of the labels of "democracy" and "freedom" may not tell us much about what Chinese people really think about the relationship between governmental power and individual citizenship.

CITIES AS CONTEXTS

An underlying premise of our study is that people's communication behavior and their attitudes toward globalization must be understood within specific national contexts. This premise, however, turns out to be only partially correct. On the one hand, some of this study's key findings are indeed more or less specific in terms of the Chinese contexts. The relationships between nationalism, national media consumption, and attitude toward globalization are the most obvious example. But, on the other hand, throughout this book the "city variables" have consistently shown relationships with the various dependent variables. As some globalization theorists would argue, the declining significance of national boundaries in the process of globalization does not entail complete deterritorialization. Rather, globalization also leads to reterritorialization, and cities may have more significance as a context for understanding the dynamics of globalization (Sassen, 1991).

In designing the survey study, we chose Beijing, Shanghai, Xi'an, and Chengdu as our four sites because we wanted to study two coastal metropolises and two inland cities. But throughout this book we have seen that the majority of the between-cities differences do not map clearly onto the coast-inland divide. In Chapter 2, we saw that residents of Beijing and Shanghai were relatively more interested in foreign affairs than residents of Chengdu and Xi'an. But the between-cities differences indicate other patterns when other variables are concerned. When it comes to nationalism, for example, we see that residents of Beijing were the most nationalistic and residents of Shanghai the least nationalistic. These findings are understandable, however, when we look into the more specific positions of the two cities in the sociopolitical and spatial configuration of the nation, both historically and contemporarily. Beijing residents also differed from the other three cities' residents in their particularly high likelihood to talk about globalization in local terms. When it comes to the perceived influence of globalization, Beijing residents were also particularly negative, whereas the residents of the other three cities did not vary substantially from one another.

What these findings suggest is not that the coast-inland divide is totally meaningless. Rather, they indicate that the coast-inland divide is just one of the many parameters to be considered in trying to understanding the "context" of a city. Moreover, our survey findings also suggest that we cannot assume that the individuals living in a city would take up the characteristics of the city itself. The findings regarding Chinese people's media use in our study are particularly interesting and deserve further explorations in future studies. Whereas foreign influences should be more prevalent in the coastal cities of Beijing and Shanghai and the residents of these cities also had relatively high levels of interests in foreign affairs, they nonetheless consumed foreign media to lesser extents.

We may label this the paradox of communication in a global city. As we discussed in Chapter 3, these findings can be explained in terms of the strength of local media in the coastal metropolises as well as the probable scenario that the local media in these coastal cities are already providing their audiences with significant amounts of information about the world at large. In other words, the blurring of the national and the foreign that we have just mentioned is likely to be more prominent in coastal metropolises. In any case, it would be meaningful to determine whether the same paradox of communication in a global city would appear in other countries around the world, such as India, Brazil, or even the United States. Additional research in other countries can help us further theorize about the relationship between the degree of "global connectedness" of the city context and the exact ways through which city residents communicate with the world at large.

Admittedly, the significance of cities as contexts would put a question mark onto our survey findings regarding the extent to which they can represent "Chinese public opinion" or even just "urban Chinese public opinion" regarding globalization. One can imagine that the same survey conducted in the southern metropolis of Guangzhou might come up with different findings. Or, as Ong (2006) has argued, China engages with neoliberalism and globalization mainly by creating spaces of exceptions, such as the Special Economic Zones in Shenzhen and Chongqing. Conducting surveys in these spaces of neoliberal exception may produce yet other kinds of findings. Representativeness is one of the limitations of the present study that must be conceded and kept in mind. Of course it remains extremely difficult to conduct truly national representative surveys in China. We believe that our survey has achieved what is practically possible and provided valuable insights into Chinese public opinion regarding globalization in at least four distinctive and important cities in China.

Moreover, it should be noted that despite the significance of the between-cities differences, the differences are mostly only matters of degrees. For instance, whereas Beijing residents were relatively more negative toward globalization as compared with residents of Xi'an, Chengdu, and Shanghai, it remains true that even Beijing residents were, overall, positive toward globalization. The same applies to attitudes toward America, nationalism, and other variables. In other words, when some of the key findings in the present study are framed in more general terms, they remain highly likely to be applicable throughout urban China.

FUTURE PROSPECTS OF PUBLIC OPINION
TOWARD GLOBALIZATION IN CHINA

Because the survey reported in this book was conducted in late 2006 and early 2007, it would be appropriate to end our discussion with some brief comments on more recent developments in China and whether and how these developments might affect public opinion toward globalization in urban contexts. On the whole, we believe that some of the findings reported in this book should remain applicable in Chinese cities today or even in the near future. In fact, more recent media discourses and reportage—along with our observations—have led us to believe that the relationships and landscapes we present here seem to have been strengthened rather than weakened. There are no signs of a decline of nationalistic sentiments, although it is probable that more Chinese in 2013 than 2007 would consider the "rise of China" a reality rather than merely a wish. China did, after all, successfully organize the Olympic Games in 2008 and the World Expo in 2010. Moreover, after the global financial crisis of 2008, the role of China in the world economy has seemingly become even more significant. Much current talk surrounds China's readiness, even edginess, to assert a more active and central role in world affairs, thus departing from its "lie low" policy of the 1990s and much of the 2000s. These developments are likely to influence the way in which people around the world look at China as well as how Chinese people look at their own country. Similarly, there have been no fundamental changes in the relationship between the United States and China, and there are no reasons to believe that Chinese people's attitudes toward the United States have changed substantially. For example, as earlier chapters have already pointed out, the number of Chinese students studying abroad has continued to increase.

Nevertheless, we would argue that there are some reasons for researchers to expect changes in Chinese people's attitudes toward globalization in a few respects. When our survey was conducted in late 2006, China has been a member of the WTO for only about five years. Many of the other policies related to active engagement with globalization have been in place for a relatively short period of time. The early 2000s were therefore a time when the concrete consequences of such policies remained relatively uncertain and unclear. In that situation, as we have seen in the analysis of this book, Chinese people's views toward globalization were largely in line with the view promulgated by the state.

However, over time, it is only natural for people to begin to judge whether globalization has delivered its promise. For China in particular, although the country has continued to enjoy impressive economic growth in recent years, social problems—such as irresponsible business practices, income inequality, and other kinds of injustices—have also become more and more conspicuous and serious. Some of the most prominent and tragic events occurring in China in the past few years have ostensible relationships with globalization. An example is the unfortunate cluster of suicides in 2010 at the factory of Foxconn, the largest assembly plant of electronic products in the world. Between January and November, 2010, a total of 18 Foxconn factory workers attempted suicide; 14 died as a result. Media reports and university researchers investigating the matter denounced the company's ways of treating its workers. But without going into the details of the event, suffice it to say that Foxconn is not a mainland Chinese company but is owned by a Taiwan-based business conglomerate. The company mainly provides electronics manufacturing services, and its most important clients include Apple, Cisco, Nokia, Nintendo, Dell, Intel, Motorola, Sony Ericsson, and so on. Factory workers at Foxconn, in other words, are absorbed into the international division of labor of global capitalism. As some media critics in Hong Kong have pointed out, the Foxconn tragedy cannot be understood merely as a problem of the mismanagement of Foxconn itself but must be seen as a symptom of the global political economy.

Given the general lack of media and academic freedom in China, we do not know how the Chinese public actually understands the tragedy of Foxconn. But as these events accumulate, at least a portion of the Chinese public might become disillusioned with the idea of social and economic development as a result of globalization. Some may find fault with the Chinese authorities for mishandling the prevalence of official corruption, the worsening rich-poor gap, and aspects of the often objectionable common way of life, all of which are thought to have been sharpened by the intervention of global forces. Still, nationalists may be fed up with China's willingness to "cave in" to foreign pressure. Causes of grievances may vary, but they inevitably involve the process and consequences of globalization. In fact, the past few years have also witnessed the rise of "collective action events" in China; as a response, the Chinese government has tightened its grip on freedom of communication. Internet censorship has become more stringent, yet the Chinese netizens have continued to devise ways to escape from official censorship and enjoy the evasive pleasure derived from it. A counterculture is seemingly emerging in the online arena in China (Meng, 2011; Wallis, 2011), although one should also be cautious and not exaggerate the potential power of such a counterculture.

We believe that Chinese public opinion regarding globalization may become more polarized as time goes on. There can be polarization between

LIVERPOOL JOHN MOORES UNIVERSITY
LEARNING SERVICES

the winners and the losers in the processes of globalization; there can also be polarization between, on one hand, the more active citizens/netizens who are exposed to much information and critical viewpoints through the Internet, and, on the other hand, a large part of the urban public who may be content with a relatively stable and materialistically improved life in an improved economy. Whether such polarization exists and what its implications for social and political developments in China are should constitute important issues to consider.

We also believe that, as China's engagement with globalization continues, people's personal experiences with the outside world and the individual-level impact of globalization will naturally accumulate over time. It may be more and more difficult for the Chinese government to persuade the general public regarding the benefits of globalization. By saying that the Chinese government would face increasing difficulties in influencing public opinion, we do not intend to offer a naively optimistic view regarding how engagement with the outside world might change China. The state is likely to have its own ways and strategies for responding to the developing situation, and such state actions may in turn shape public opinion in specific ways. Ultimately, the evolution of public opinion is dynamic and shaped not only by macrolevel forces and developments but also by the ways in which social and political actors act, react, and interact.

Appendix
Questionnaire

The following is the full questionnaire employed by this project. Explanations of the interview procedures are included in square brackets. It should be noted that all questions involve a "don't know" and/or "no answer" option, but they are not listed below for space and clarity concerns.

The questionnaire was translated by the current authors. Specific Chinese words or phrases, if they are essential to understanding the phrasing of the questions, would have their *pinyin* italicized and stated in square brackets. The full original Chinese questions are available from the authors upon request.

[Target respondent identification]
S1   City: 1. Beijing 2. Shanghai 3. Chengdu 4. Xi'an
S2   ID: _____
S3   For the purpose of selecting an interviewee, we want to understand how many family members you have and their birthdates. In your family, who has had the most recent birthday?

_____

S4   Gender: 1. Male 2. Female
S5   Age: _____
S6   Are you working for the following units?
       Marketing corporation/consultant companies—End the interview
       Advertising agency / production companies—End the interview
       Mass media, such as TV, newspapers, magazines—End the interview
       Not any of the above—Continue
S7   How long have you been living in this city?
       Less than 3 years—End the interview
       3 years or above—Continue

[The actual interview begins]
It is generally believed that the world has entered the era of global integration. Our study is aimed at understanding your views toward this issue.

1. Have you ever heard of "globalization" [*quanqiu hu*a] or "global integration" [*quanqiu yiti hua*]?
      1. Yes 2. Seems yes 3. No (jump to Q3)
2. When "globalization" [*quanqiu hu*a] is mentioned, what would you think of?
[interviewer records the answers]

_____

_____

_____

_____

_____

_____

3. First, we want to understand how you use various forms of media [interviewer shows card]

3a. In the past week, have you read any newspapers or magazines?
      1. Yes 2. No (jump to Q3b)_____
  1) Local newspapers/magazines   times
  2) National newspapers/magazines _____ times
  3) HK/Macau/Taiwan newspapers/magazines _____ times
  4) Japanese/Korean newspapers/magazines _____ times
  5) U.S./Canadian newspapers/magazines _____ times
  6) Western European newspapers/magazines _____ times
  7) Middle Eastern newspapers/magazines _____ times

3b. In the past week, have you read any informational books (not including novels, comics, and fictional stories)?
      1. Yes 2. No (jump to Q3c)
  1) Local books _____ times
  2) National books _____ times
  3) HK/Macau/Taiwan books _____ times
  4) Japanese/Korean books _____ times
  5) U.S./Canadian books _____ times
  6) Western European books _____ times
  7) Middle Eastern books _____ times

3c. In the past week, have you listened to any radio broadcasts?
      1. Yes 2. No (jump to Q3d)
  1) Local radio programs _____times
  2) National radio programs _____ times
  3) HK/Macau/Taiwan radio programs _____ times
  4) Japanese/Korean radio programs _____ times
  5) U.S./Canadian radio programs _____ times

6) Western European radio programs _____ times
7) Middle Eastern radio programs _____ times

3d. In the past week, have you watched any television programs?
      1. Yes 2. No (jump to Q3e)
1) Local TV programs _____ times
2) National TV programs _____ times
3) HK/Macau/Taiwan TV programs _____ times
4) Japanese/Korean TV programs _____ times
5) U.S./Canadian TV programs _____ times
6) Western European TV programs _____ times
7) Middle Eastern TV programs _____ times

3e. In the past week, have you watched any movies?
      1. Yes 2. No (jump to Q3f)
1) Local movies _____ times
2) National movies _____ times
3) HK/Macau/Taiwan movie _____ times
4) Japanese/Korean movies _____ times
5) U.S./Canadian movies _____ times
6) Western European movies _____ times
7) Middle Eastern movies _____ times

3f. In the past week, have you ever been on the Internet?
      1. Yes 2. No (jump to Q4)
1) Local websites _____ times
2) National websites _____ times
3) HK/Macau/Taiwan websites _____ times
4) Japanese/Korean websites _____ times
5) U.S./Canadian websites _____ times
6) Western European websites _____ times
7) Middle Eastern website _____ times

4. In the past week, how did you communicate with family members, friends [*shu ren*], and strangers [*mosheng ren*]? [interviewer shows card]
    a) Face-to-face
        1) Family members _____ times
        2) Friends _____times
        3) Strangers _____ times
    b) SMS through mobile phones
        1) Family members _____ times
        2) Friends _____ times
        3) Strangers _____ times
    c) Telephone
        1) Family members _____ times

  2) Friends _____ times
  3) Strangers _____ times
 d) Online (such as email, ICQ, QQ, MSN, Skype, etc.)
  1) Family members _____ times
  2) Friends _____ times
  3) Strangers _____ times

5. We also want to understand how you commonly travel, for vacation or work, within or outside the country. [interviewer shows card; Answering categories listed are: Never, Sometimes, Often, and Very Often]
 a) Vacation
  1) Local
  2) Other places in the country
  3) HK/Macau/Taiwan
  4) Southeast Asia
  5) Japan/Korea
  6) U.S./Canada
  7) Western Europe
  8) Middle East
 b) Work
  1) Local
  2) Other places in the country
  3) HK/Macau/Taiwan
  4) Southeast Asia
  5) Japan/Korea
  6) U.S./Canada
  7) Western Europe
  8) Middle East

6a. Do you have relatives or friends [*qinyou*] in the following places? [interviewer shows card; Answering categories are: No, Some, Many, and Very Many]
  1) Local
  2) Other places in the country
  3) HK/Macau/Taiwan
  4) Southeast Asia
  5) Japan/Korea
  6) U.S./Canada
  7) Western Europe
  8) Middle East

6b. Do you usually keep contact with friends and relatives within and outside the country? [interviewer shows card; Answering categories listed are: Never, Sometimes, Often, and Very Often]
  1) Local

2) Other places in the country
3) HK/Macau/Taiwan
4) Southeast Asia
5) Japan/Korea
6) U.S./Canada
7) Western Europe
8) Middle East

7. We receive information from the media. Regarding the following types of information, would you say you are "very interested," "interested," "neutral," "not interested," or "very not interested? [Interviewer shows card and reads out examples for different types of news information (political, social, economy and finance)]

    a. Politics (such as officials' activities, local and central governments' policies, international affairs)

      1) Local
      2) National
      3) HK/Macau/Taiwan
      4) Japan/Korea
      5) U.S./Canada
      6) Western Europe
      7) Middle East

    b. Society (such as social news, crime news)

      1) Local
      2) National
      3) HK/Macau/Taiwan
      4) Japan/Korea
      5) U.S./Canada
      6) Western Europe
      7) Middle East

    c. Economy and finance (such as job opportunities, stock prices, situations in financial markets)

      1) Local
      2) National
      3) HK/Macau/Taiwan
      4) Japan/Korea
      5) U.S./Canada
      6) Western Europe
      7) Middle East

    d. Popular culture (such as activities of movie stars and singers, consumer information)

      1) Local
      2) National
      3) HK/Macau/Taiwan
      4) Japan/Korea

  5) U.S./Canada
  6) Western Europe
  7) Middle East
 e. Education, science, and culture
  1) Local
  2) National
  3) HK/Macau/Taiwan
  4) Japan/Korea
  5) U.S./Canada
  6) Western Europe
  7) Middle East
 f. Leisure and lifestyle (such as life in other countries)
  1) Local
  2) National
  3) HK/Macau/Taiwan
  4) Japan/Korea
  5) U.S./Canada
  6) Western Europe
  7) Middle East
 g. Sports
  1) Local
  2) National
  3) HK/Macau/Taiwan
  4) Japan/Korea
  5) U.S./Canada
  6) Western Europe
  7) Middle East

8. Following the above, we want to understand your views regarding the mass media. Regarding the following statements, would you say you strongly agree, agree, are neutral, disagree, or strongly disagree with the views. [interviewer shows card]

  1) China's TV and film entertainment are more enjoyable than those from foreign countries.
  2) China's TV and film entertainment are more creative than those from foreign countries.
  3) When reporting international news, Chinese media are more believable than foreign media.
  4) When reporting domestic news, Chinese media are more believable than foreign media.
  5) Chinese media are objective and fair when reporting news about China.
  6) Chinese media are objective and fair when reporting about the U.S.

7) American media are objective and fair when reporting about the U.S.
8) American media are objective and fair when reporting about China.
9) There is now too little international news in the media.
10) The media produce misunderstandings in the international arena.
11) The media produce social chaos.
12) The crime rate in the society would be higher when the media report more about violent events.
13) Generally speaking, Chinese journalists have good professional ethics.
14) Generally speaking, Chinese media are becoming more and more irresponsible.
15) Nowadays the media are filled with trivial stuffs.
16) Nowadays the media encourage people to buy things that they don't need.
17) The media help me understand international affairs.
18) The media help me understand domestic affairs.
19) The media help me understand local (this city) affairs.
20) The media are good references when I consume foreign products.
21) The media are good references when I consume domestic products.
22) The media are good references when I consume local (this city) products.
23) The media help me access foreign entertainment for the purpose of leisure.
24) The media help me access domestic entertainment for the purpose of leisure.
25) The media help me access local (this city) entertainment for the purpose of leisure.
26) If the media play a monitoring role, corruption can be reduced.

9a. Every society has some values and ideals. We see some of them as highly important, while we see some others as less important. Below, I will read out a set of values. For you, would they be very important, important, so-so, unimportant, or very unimportant? [Interview shows card]

1) Harmony
2) Stability
3) Prosperity
4) Democracy
5) Freedom
6) Equality

7) Strong nation

9b. Every individual has some values and ideals. We see some of them as highly important, while we see some others as less important. Below, I will read out a set of values. For you, would they be very important, important, so-so, unimportant, or very unimportant? [Interview shows card]
>   1) Wealth
>   2) Reputation / Status
>   3) Ideal
>   4) Leisure
>   5) Health
>   6) Education / Gentility

10. No matter for what reasons, we would have good impressions about certain countries, while having negative impressions regarding other countries. Below, I will read out a list of country names. Would you say your impressions about these countries are very good, good, not good and not bad, bad, or very bad? [Interviewer shows card]
>   1) The U.S.
>   2) The U.K.
>   3) Japan
>   4) The Philippines
>   5) Singapore
>   6) India
>   7) North Korea
>   8) Russia
>   9) Cuba
>   10) France
>   11) South Africa
>   12) Afghanistan
>   13) Vietnam
>   14) Italy
>   15) Germany
>   16) Iraq
>   17) China

11. In recent years we often heard of discussions about "globalization." Some people think that the world market is overcoming national boundaries. There are more and more cultural exchanges between nations. Countries around the world are increasingly interdependent on political, environmental, and safety issues. But there are also people who disagree with such views. I am going to read out a number of views, please tell me if you strongly agree, agree, are neutral, disagree, or strongly disagree with the views. [interviewer shows card]
>   1) Globalization will enhance human rights in various countries.
>   2) Globalization will only help fulfill the goals of strong countries.

3) Globalization has much benefit for economic development of many countries.

4) Globalization will only make rich countries richer and poor countries poorer.

5) Globalization will enhance cultural exchange among various places.

6) The culture of the whole world is increasingly homogeneous.

7) Globalization will lead to international monitoring of the environmental policies of all countries.

8) Increasing levels of international exchange will make it more and more difficult to control transmission diseases such as SARS and bird flu.

9) Globalization will make the Chinese government more transparent.

10) Globalization will subject Chinese politics to the control of Western countries.

11) Globalization is beneficial to economic development of China.

12) Globalization is not conducive for China to become independent economically.

13) Globalization will improve Chinese culture.

14) Globalization will lead to the loss of the traditional Chinese culture.

15) Globalization will urge the Chinese government on adopting more policies to protect the environment.

16) Globalization will damage the ecological environment of China.

17) Globalization will enhance the productivity of this city.

18) In order to pursue globalization, the municipal government often disregards the views of citizens.

19) Globalization is beneficial to economic development of this city.

20) Globalization will subject the companies in this city to the control of transnational corporations.

21) Globalization will bring a more diverse range of cultures to this city.

22) Globalization will lead to the loss of the unique culture of this city.

23) Globalization will urge the city government to adopt more policies to protect the environment.

24) Globalization brings more environmental pollution to this city.

25) Globalization makes me more active in participating in democratic development.

26) Globalization gets me in touch with various political views so that my political views are now blurred.

27) Globalization can help increase my income.

28) Globalization increases my chance of getting unemployed.

29) Globalization allows me to get in touch with other new and exciting cultures.

30) Globalization will only make young Chinese people even more oriented to the Western world.

31) Globalization makes me pay more attention to environmental protection.

32) Globalization increases the chance for me to contract illness.

12. Some people say that the process of globalization is dominated by the U.S., while others disagree. We would like to understand your views about the U.S. Below, I will read out some statements. Please tell me if you would strongly agree, agree, be neutral, disagree, or strongly disagree with them. [Interview shows card]

1) The two-party system in America prevents the corruption of the powerful.
2) The American media led to lesser corruption in the society
3) The U.S. is a powerful country because of its good institutions
4) The system of separations of power in the U.S. is inefficient
5) Press freedom in America only serves the rich people
6) Only America can lead the world
7) America is the protector of world peace
8) No one can prevent America from dominating the world
9) U.S. policy concerns only with interests, not principles
10) The ultimate goal of U.S. foreign policy is to control the whole world
11) The U.S. wants to suppress the development of China.
12) The U.S. collaborates with Japan to suppress China
13) I long for the American way of life
14) Human relationships within the American society are weak
15) The American society is full of opportunities
16) The American society discriminates against racial minorities
17) Materialistic desires pervade the American society
18) American culture is rich
19) Compared to Chinese culture, American culture is shallow.

13. There are some viewpoints and phenomena that people treat as very important, whereas others see them as unimportant. We would like to know your views. Below, I will read out some statements. Would you say you strongly agree, agree, are neutral, disagree, or strongly disagree with them? [Interviewer shows card]

1) China should pay more attention to take care of internal problems; it is unnecessary to intervene in international affairs.
2) To have so many top students going abroad to study is not good for China.
3) The development of globalization is not advantageous to the future of socialism.
4) It would be more chaotic if the United Nations does not exist.
5) It is good for everyone for Asian countries to form an economic alliance.
6) In today's world, only Chinese culture could resist liberal-democracy as the axis of Western values.
7) Westernization is a good thing.

8) China's spiritual civilization surpasses that of the West.
9) The affairs of other countries are irrelevant to me.
10) I am more interested in what happens in America than what happens in rural villages in China.
11) I am concerned with the Iraqi War.
12) Individual rights are more important than national sovereignty.
13) It is too inefficient to do things according to the law.
14) It is acceptable for some people to be treated unfairly during the process of development.
15) The Chinese is the best ethnic group in the world
16) Public affairs are too complicated for common people to understand.
17) No matter on what matters, we should trust the government.
18) It is not good to have too many different opinions in the society.
19) Even if parents treat their children badly, the children cannot treat their parents badly.
20) Luck is more important than ability.
21) Things cannot be done if relationships [*guanxi*] are not established.
22) It is acceptable to sacrifice the environment a bit for the purpose of economic development.
23) I am not against homosexuality
24) Most people in the society can be trusted.
25) People like me do not have influence on government policies.
26) Leaving one's hometown is not a good thing.
27) To move to another place to seek development is a good thing.

14a. Do you consider yourself as a Shanghai *ren* (Beijing *ren*, Chengdu *ren*, Xi'an *ren*)?
    1. Yes 2. No

14b. Were you born in this city?
    1. Yes (to Q14c) 2. No (to Q14b1)
    14b1. If not, when did you move to this city? _____

14c How long have you been living in this city?

14d. Have you lived abroad?
    1. Yes 2. No

14e. Is there anyone among your closest family members [*zhishi qinshu*] who is a non-Chinese?
    1. Yes 2. No

14f. What is your educational level? [Interviewer shows card]
    1. No formal education

2. Primary school
3. Junior high school
4. High school
5. College
6. University (to Q14f1)

14f1. Where did you go to university? _____ [write down city name]

14g. What is your father's educational level? [Interviewer shows card]
   1. No formal education
   2. Primary school
   3. Junior high school
   4. High school
   5. College
   6. University

14h. What is your mother's educational level? [Interviewer shows card]
   1. No formal education
   2. Primary school
   3. Junior high school
   4. High school
   5. College
   6. University

14i. What is your religion? [Interviewer shows card]
   1. No religion
   2. Christian
   3. Catholic
   4. Buddhist
   5. Taoist
   6. Islam
   7. Others. Please indicate: _____

14j. What is the monthly income of your family? [Interview shows card]
   1. 1,000RMB or below
   2. 1,001 to 5,000 RMB
   3. 5,001 to 10,000 RMB
   4. 10,001 to 15,000 RMB
   5. 15,000 to 20,000 RMB
   6. 20,000 or above

14k. Your occupation is: _____

14l Your English level is: [Interview shows card]
   1. Don't know

2. Know a little bit
3. So-so
4. Fluent
5. Reaching the level of natives

14m. In your opinion, your household income five years later would, when compared to current levels: [Interviewer shows card]

1. Increase substantially
2. Increase somewhat
3. Remain the same
4. Decrease somewhat
5. Decrease substantially

Notes

NOTES TO CHAPTER 1

1. The import of foreign movies into China is handled centrally by the government. The number of foreign movies that can be shown in China was restricted to twenty per year in the late 2000s, leading the WTO to rule in 2010 that China had violated free trade laws. In early 2012, the quota was increased to fourteen additional films in I-max and other large formats. According to official statistics, 526 domestic films were produced in China in 2010. See "China to lift its foreign movie quota in 2011?" See *The Shanghaist*, available at: http://shanghaiist.com/2011/02/16/china_finally_upping_its_foreign_mo.php

    Also "Will relaxation of 'great wall' quota set Chinese film-makers free?" *The Guardian*, available at: http://www.guardian.co.uk/film/filmblog/2012/feb/29/great-wall-quota-chinese-film-makers

2. Many of these activities, of course, involve copyright piracy. But interestingly, transnational media corporations have begun to realize that, in the Chinese context, the pirate activities may not be detrimental to their economic interests. For example, for the music industry, suppressing the pirate activities may not boost sales of CDs. In contrast, the availability of pirated copies is instrumental in building the Chinese audience's familiarity with the contents, styles, stars, and brand names of western popular culture. This, in turn, can be crucial to the ability of media corporations and stars to profit from performances (Fung, 2009).

3. The maximum and minimum response rates were calculated by following the formulas of the American Association of Public Opinion Research.

NOTES TO CHAPTER 2

1. http://chinacontact.org/information/approved-destination-status-ads-policy
2. http://www.majiroxnews.com/2011/10/19/chinese-tourists-coming-back-to-japan/
3. http://blogs.wsj.com/chinarealtime/2011/12/27/korea-to-chinese-tourists-thanks/
4. "Students go overseas in record numbers," *China Daily*, April 18, 2011. Available at: http://usa.chinadaily.com.cn/china/2011–04/18/content_12342187.htm
5. The remaining occupational categories include government officials, professionals, students, retired people, etc.

6. In one sense, people can be giving socially desirable answers when rating all the values included in Table 2.2. For example, some people might also see recognizing the importance of harmony and stability as socially desirable. But the cases of wealth and reputation are special in that giving the socially desirable answers in the Chinese context may lead people not to recognize the values of harmony and stability.
7. The other values are not included here for different reasons. "Strong nation" will be examined separately in Chapter 4. Prosperity is not included because it is split between two factors, and equality is also not included because further analysis suggests that it does not relate substantially to democracy and freedom in one of the four cities.

NOTES TO CHAPTER 3

1. This information is derived from the broadcaster's official website, available at: http://english.cntv.cn/20091207/103449.shtml
2. "China limits foreign-made TV programs," *New York Times*, February 14, 2012. Available at: http://www.nytimes.com/2012/02/15/world/asia/aiming-at-asian-competitors-china-limits-foreign-television.html?_r=3andref=china
3. "White House Gets China To Open Market to U.S. Movies," *The Wrap*, February 17, 2012. Available at: http://www.thewrap.com/movies/article/white-house-gets-china-open-market-us-movies-35517
4. The distinction between "local movies" and "national movies," of course, can be rather problematic. The distinction was included in the questionnaire only because of the need to maintain the symmetry of the matrix question.

NOTES TO CHAPTER 4

1. According to a survey conducted by a university research center at National Zhongshan University in Taiwan in late 2011, when asked to choose between the options of "Taiwanese," "Chinese" or "both," 55.4 percent of Taiwan residents chose Taiwanese, whereas 39.6 percent chose "both." Only 5.0 percent chose "Chinese," with the remaining few offering no valid answer. The survey was part of a collaborative project conducted by Francis L. F. Lee, one of the authors of this book, and Frank Liu, associate professor at the National Zhongshan University.
2. The relationship between China and Taiwan constituted one of the most important issues during the presidential election in Taiwan in January 2012. According to media reports, hundreds of thousands of Taiwan businesspeople working in mainland China flew back to Taiwan to vote for the Kuomingtang, the ruling party, which adopted an "engagement policy" toward China. The present Taiwanese government has adopted the "1992 consensus" as its official policy toward China. This refers to the idea that both sides of the Taiwan Strait must recognize that there is only one China but that the two sides can interpret what "one China" means in their own ways.
3. http://news.xinhuanet.com/ziliao/2009–04/28/content_11272773.htm
4. The coefficient is not statistically significant despite its seemingly larger size, owing to the small number of people who consumed foreign media very frequently.

NOTES TO CHAPTER 5

1. "Chinese students enroll in record numbers at U.S. colleges," *The Washington Post*, November 14, 2011.
2. http://www.migrationinformation.org/USfocus/display.cfm?id=781
3. "Power balance" refers to whether respondents "would welcome the emergence of another power balancing the United States" (Chiozza, 2007, pp. 100–101).
4. Cronbach's alpha = 0.79, 0.69, 0.47 and 0.67 for attitude toward U.S. leadership, positive perceptions of U.S. institutions, positive perceptions of U.S. society, and critical perceptions of the United States respectively. The reliability for the positive perceptions of U.S. society index is less than desirable. But based on the factor analysis and for the sake of a more efficient analysis, it remains useful to combine the three relevant statements into an index.
5. This index, based on a much larger number of items, is arguably more reliable and differentiating than a single-item measure of people's overall feeling toward a country.
6. It should be noted that we did not simply take the average of people's agreement with the statements (i.e., the critical perceptions index itself) to represent negative thoughts, because the averaging procedure would give us a variable ranging from 1 to 5. In that case, those respondents who scored 1 would not simply be "not holding" the negative perceptions; they would adamant that the negative statements were wrong. In other words, a score of 1 on an index based on averaging would have represented more intense, not less intense feelings. The counting procedure, therefore, has an advantage over the averaging procedure here because it does capture, and only capture, the presence or absence of negative thoughts.
7. It is also noteworthy that 326 respondents, or 16.3 percent of the sample, held the same number of positive and negative views regarding the United States (i.e., exactly one positive and one negative thought, exactly two positive and two negative thoughts, etc.).

NOTES TO CHAPTER 6

1. Technically speaking, because only two groups were involved (the local and the global), the discriminant analysis generated one discriminant function. As indicated by the significant Chi-square test ($P < .01$), the two group centroids (group means) were statistically different from each other.

NOTES TO CHAPTER 7

1. This positive relationship does not exist in the case of the United States, Australia, and Russia. Yet the lack of significant relationship is understandable, since English is simply the first language for Americans and Australians. Even in Russia and possibly some other European countries, English can be so common that it does not really constitute a "special skill." Hence its value as a form of cultural capital can be much less meaningful in these countries.
2. It should be noted that, when we put the 32 items into an exploratory factor analysis, they did not result in a clean factor structure completely in line with our conceptual thinking. Yet the findings do correspond to our design of the items to a certain extent. More specifically, 7 factors emerged when the 32 items were put into a factor analysis. The first factor was composed by

9 items regarding the positive impact of globalization at different levels. The second factor was composed by 11 items regarding the negative impact of globalization. The other factors were composed by fewer numbers of items. These findings seem to suggest that the urban Chinese did not differentiate between the various dimensions of globalization very clearly.

3. All indices have good reliability coefficients (Cronbach's alpha > .70 in all cases).

4. The SD for the indices are as follows: positive impact at country level = 0.47, positive impact at city level = 0.58, positive impact at individual level = 0.56, negative impact at country level = 0.53, negative impact at city level = 0.63, negative impact at individual level = 0.64.

5. If we follow the method used in Chapter 5 and count the number of positive and negative considerations that every individual has, we will derive even larger figures for proportions of Chinese people being ambivalent toward globalization—that is, as many as 1,306 respondents, or more than 65 percent—had at least three positive and at least three negative considerations about globalization, whereas 854 respondents—more than 42 percent—had at least five positive and at least five negative considerations about globalization.

References

Abrahamson, M. (2004). *Global cities*. New York: Oxford University Press.

Adams, P. C. (1992). Television as a gathering place. *Annals of the Association of American Geographers*, 82, 117–135.

Ajzen, I. (2001). Nature and operation of attitudes. *Annual Review of Psychology*, 52, 27–58.

Alden, D. L., Steenkamp, J.B.E.M., and Batra, R. (2006). Consumer attitudes toward marketplace globalization: Structure, antecedents and consequences. *International Journal of Research Marketing*, 23(3), 227–239.

Alvarez, R. M., and Brehm, J. (1995). American ambivalence towards abortion policy: Development of a heteroskedastic probit model of competing values. *American Journal of Political Science*, 39(4), 1055–1082.

Anderson, B. (1991). *Imagined communities*. London: Verso.

Antecol, M., and Endersby, J. W. (1999). Newspaper consumption and beliefs about Canada and Quebec. *Political Communication*, 16(1), 95–112.

Apostolopoulos, Y., Leivadi, S., and Yiannakis, A. (1996). *The sociology of tourism: Theoretical and empirical investigations*. London and New York: Routledge.

Appadurai, A. (1990). Disjuncture and difference in the global cultural economy. *Public Culture*, 2, 1–24.

Ballrokeach, S. J., and Defleur, M. L. (1976). Dependency model of mass media effects. *Communication Research*, 3(1), 3–21.

Barber, B. (1995). *Jihad vs. McWorld*. New York: Ballantine.

Baron, J., and Kemp, S. (2004). Support for trade restrictions, attitudes, and understanding of comparative advantage. *Journal of Economic Psychology*, 25(5), 565–580.

Baron, R. M., and Kenny, D. A. (1986). The moderator mediator variable distinction in social psychological research: Conceptual, strategic, and statistical considerations. *Journal of Personality and Social Psychology*, 51(6), 1173–1182.

Bauman, Z. (1998). *Globalization: The human consequences*. New York: Columbia University Press.

Berger, P. L., Berger, B., and Kellner, H. (1973). *The homeless mind: Modernization and consciousness*. New York: Random House.

Berger, P. L., and Luckmann, T. (1936). *The social construction of reality: A treatise in the sociology of knowledge*. New York: Anchor.

Billig, M. (1995). *Banal nationalism*. London: Sage.

Blondel, J., and Marsh, I. (2008). How the public evaluates globalization. In T. Inoguchi and I. Marsh (eds.). *Globalisation, public opinion and the state* (pp. 76–94). London: Routledge.

Boyd-Barrett, J. O. (1977). Media imperialism: Towards an international framework for an analysis of media systems. In J. Curran, M. Gurevitch and J.

Woollacott (eds.), *Mass communication and society* (pp. 116–135). London: Edward Arnold.

Breslin, S. (2000). Decentralisation, globalization and China's partial re-engagement with the global economy. *New Political Economy*, 5(2), 205–226.

Brownell, S. (2008). *Beijing's Games: What the Olympics means to China.* Lanham, MD: Rowman and Littlefield.

Bryant, J., and Oliver, M. B. (eds.) (2008). *Media effects: Advances in theory and research.* 3rd ed. New York: Routledge.

Carey, J. (1998). The Internet and the end of the national communication system: Uncertain predictions of an uncertain future. *Journalism and Mass Communication Quarterly*, 75(1), 28–34.

Carlson, M., and Nelson, T. (2008). Anti-Americanism in Asia? factors shaping international perceptions of American influence. *International Relations of the Asia-Pacific*, 8, 303–324.

Castells, M. (1997). *The power of identity.* Malden, MA: Blackwell.

Castells, M. (2000). *The rise of the network society.* Oxford, UK: Blackwell.

Chaffee, S. H., and Mutz, D. C. (1988). Comparing mediated and interpersonal communication data. In R. P. Hawkins, J. M. Wiemann, and S. Pingree (eds.), *Advancing communication science: Merging mass and interpersonal processes* (pp. 19–43). Newbury Park, CA: Sage.

Chan, J. M. (1993). Commercialization without independence: Media development in China. In J. S. Y. Cheng and M. Brosseau (eds.), *China Review 1993* (pp. 25.1–25.21). Hong Kong: Chinese University Press.

Chan, J. M. (1994). Media internationalization in China: Processes and tensions. *Journal of Communication*, 44(3), 70–88.

Chan, Y. Y. (2005). Reimagining China. Social Research, 72(4), 935–952.

Chanda, K., and Kavoori, A. (2000). Media imperialism revisited: Some findings from the Asian case. *Media, Culture and Society*, 22, 415–432.

Chang, T. K., Wang, J., and Chan, Y. (2002), *China's window on the world: TV news, social knowledge, and international spectacles.* Cresskill, NJ: Hampton Press.

Chen, S. L. (2003). Two Americas: How Chinese college students view the United States. *Chinese Education and Society*, 36(6), 7–31.

Chiozza, G. (2007). Disaggregating anti-Americanism: An analysis of individual attitudes toward the United States. In P. J. Katzenstein and R. O. Keohane (eds.), *Anti-Americanisms in world politics.* Ithaca, NY, and London: Cornell University Press.

Chu, D.S.C. (2012). Fanatical labor and serious leisure in the Internet age: A case of fansubbing in China. In F.L.F. Lee, L. Leung, J. L. Qiu, and D.S.C. Chu (eds.), *Frontiers in new media research* (pp. 259–277). London: Routledge.

Citrin, J., and Luks, S. (2005). Patriotic to the core? American ambivalence about America. In S. C. Craig (ed.), *Ambivalence and the structure of political opinion* (pp. 127–147). Gordonsville, VA: Palgrave MacMillan.

Clausen, L. (2004). Localizing the global: "Domestication" processes in international news production. *Media, Culture and Society*, 26(1), 25–44.

Cohen, A., Levy, M. R., Roeh, I., and Gurevitch, M. (eds.). (1996). *Global newsrooms, local audiences.* London: J. Libbey.

Cohen, E. (1984). The sociology of tourism: Approaches, issues, and findings. *Annual Review of Sociology*, 10, 373–392.

Collins, R. (1981). On the microfoundations of macrosociology. *American Journal of Sociology*, 86(5), 984–1014.

Craig, S. C., Martinez, M. D., Kane, J. G., and Gainous, J. (2005). Core values, value conflict, and citizens' ambivalence about gay rights. *Political Research Quarterly*, 58(1), 5–17.

Crane, G. T. (1999). Imagining the economic nation: Globalization in China. *New Political Economy, 4*(2), 215–232.

Crystal, D. (1997). *English as a global language.* Cambridge, UK, and New York: Cambridge University Press.

Cui, L. and Lee, F. L. F. (2010). Becoming extra-ordinary: Negotiation of media power in the case of *Super Girls' Voice* in China. *Popular Communication, 8*(4), 256–272.

Davis, J. L., and Rusbult, C. E. (2001). Attitude alignment in close relationships. *Journal of Personality and Social Psychology, 81*(1), 65–84.

Davidson, R., Poor, N., and Williams, A. (2009). Stratification and global elite theory: A cross-cultural and longitudinal analysis of public opinion. *International Journal of Public Opinion Research, 21*(2), 165–186.

Della Porta, D. and Tarrow, S. (eds.). (2005). *Transnational protests and global activism.* Lanham, MD: Rowman and Littlefield.

DeMarree, K., Morrison, K. R., Wheeler, S. C., and Petty, R. (2011). Self-ambivalence and resistance of subtle self-change attempts. *Personality and Social Psychology Bulletin, 37*(5), 674–686.

De Vreese, C. H., and Boomgaarden, H. G. (2006). Media effects on public opinion about the enlargement of the European Union. *JCMS—Journal of Common Market Studies, 44*(2), 419–436.

Deng, Y., and Moore, T. G. (2004). China views globalization: Toward a new great-power politics? *Washington Quarterly, 27*(3), 117–136.

Deutsch, M., and Gerard, H. B. (1955). A study of normative and informational social influences upon individual judgment. *Journal of Abnormal and Social Psychology,* 629–636.

Department of Foreign Affairs and Trade (2005). *Unlocking China's Service Sector.* Department of Foreign Affairs and Trade, Canberra, Australia.

Diamond, L. (2010). The meanings of democracy: Introduction. *Journal of Democracy, 21*(4), 102–105.

Disdier, A.-C., Head, K., and Mayer, T. (2010). Exposure to foreign media and changes in cultural traits: Evidence from naming patterns in France. *Journal of International Economics, 80*(2), 226–238.

Drinkwater, S., and Ingram, P. (2009). How different are the British in their willingness to move? Evidence from international social survey data. *Regional Studies, 43*(2), 287–303.

Dunning, D., and Sherman, D. A. (1997). Stereotypes and tacit inference. *Journal of Personality and Social Psychology, 73,* 459–471.

Edwards, M. S. (2006). Public opinion regarding economic and cultural globalization: Evidence from a cross-national survey. *Review of International Political Economy, 13*(4), 587–608.

Entman, R. M. (1991). Framing US coverage of international news. *Journal of Communication, 41*(4), 6–27.

Entman, R. M. (1993). Framing: Toward clarification of a fractured paradigm. *Journal of Communication, 43*(4), 51–58.

Erni, J. (2008). Enchanted: Harry Potter and magical capitalism in urban China. *Chinese Journal of Communication, 1*(2), 138–155.

Fabrini, S. (2003).The domestic sources of European anti-Americanism. *Government and Opposition, 37*(1), 3–14.

Fairbrother, G. P. (2003). The effects of political education and critical thinking on Hong Kong and Mainland Chinese university students' national attitudes. *British Journal of Sociology of Education, 24*(5), 605–620.

Feng, Y., and Frich, K. (2008). The growth of international women's magazines in China and the role of transnational advertising. *Journal of Magazine and New Media Research, 10,* 1–14.

Fenton, T. (2005). *Bad news: The decline of reporting, the business of news and the danger to us all.* New York: ReganBooks.

Fitzgerrald, J. (1996). The nationless state: The search for a nation in modern Chinese nationalism. In Jonathan Unger (ed.), *Chinese Nationalism* (pp. 56–85). New York: M. E. Sharpe.

Foot, R. (2006). Chinese strategies in a U.S.-hegemonic global order: Accommodating and hedging. *International Affairs, 82*(1), 77–84.

Fung, A. (2009). *Global capital, local culture.* New York: Peter Lang.

Gao, M.C.F. (2000). Sino-US love and hate relations. *Journal of Contemporary Asia, 30*(4), 547–561.

Gellner, E. (1983) *Nations and nationalisms.* Ithaca, NY: Cornell University Press.

Gellner, E. (1981). *Muslim society.* New York: Cambridge University Press.

Gentzkow, M. A., and Shapiro, J. M. (2004). Media, education and anti-Americanism in the Muslim world. *Journal of Economic Perspectives, 18*(3), 117–133.

Gerbner, G, Gross, L., Morgan, M., Signorielli, N., and Shanahan, J (2002). Growing up with television: Cultivation processes. In J. Bryant and D. Zillmann (eds.), *Media Effects: Advances in Theory and Research*, 2nd ed. (pp. 43–67). Mahwah, NJ: Erlbaum.

Giddens, A. (1984). *The constitution of society. Outline of the theory of structuration.* Cambridge, UK: Polity.

Giddens, A. (1985). *The nation-state and violence*: vol. 2. *A contemporary critique of historical materialism.* Cambridge, UK: Polity Press.

Giddens, A. (1991). *The consequences of modernity.* Stanford, CA: Stanford University Press.

Giddens, A. (2000). *Runaway world: How globalization is reshaping our lives.* New York: Routledge.

Granovetter, M. S. (1973). The strength of weak ties. *American Journal of Sociology, 78*(6), 1360–1380.

Granzin, K. L., Brazell, J. D., and Painter, J. J. (1997). An examination of influences leading to Americans' endorsement of the policy of free trade. *Journal of Public Policy and Marketing, 16*(1), 93–109.

Gries, P. (2004) *China's new nationalism: Pride, politics, and diplomacy.* Berkeley: University of California Press.

Gries, P. H., Crowson, H. M., and Sandel, T. (2010). The Olympic effect on American attitudes toward China: Beyond personality, ideology, and media exposure. *Journal of Contemporary China, 16*, 213–231.

Guo, Y. (2004). *Cultural nationalism in contemporary China: The search for national identity under reform.* New York: Routledge Curzon.

Guo, Z., Cheong, W. H., and Chen, H. (2007). Nationalism as public imagination: The media's routine contribution to latent and manifest nationalism in China. *The International Communication Gazette, 69*(5), 473–486.

Habermas, J. (1999). *The postnational constellation.* Cambridge, MA: MIT Press.

Hainmueller, J., and Hiscox, M. J. (2006). Learning to love globalization: Education and individual attitudes toward international trade. *International Organization, 60*(2), 469–498.

Hajkowski, T. (2010). *The BBC and national identity in Britain, 1922–53.* Manchester, UK: Manchester University Press.

Harding, H. (1992). *A fragile relationship: the United States and China since 1979.* Washington, DC: Brookings Institution.

Hardy, B. W., and Scheufele, D. A. (2005). Examining differential gains from Internet use: Comparing the moderating role of talk and online interactions. *Journal of Communication, 55*(1), 71–84.

Harvey, D. (1990). *The condition of postmodernity: An inquiry into the origins of cultural change*. Oxford, UK: Blackwell.

Hawkins, R. P., and Pingree, S. (1982). Television's influence on social reality. In D. Pearl, L. Bouthilet, and J. Lazar (eds.), *Television and Behavior* (Vol. 2). Rockville, MD: U.S. Government Printing Office.

Hayakawa, S. I. (1941). *Language in action*. New York: Harcourt, Brace.

He, D. (1994). The most respected enemy: Mao Zedong's perception of the United States. *China Quarterly, 137*, 144–158.

He, Q. (2008). *The fog of censorship: Media rights in China*. (Translated by Paul Frank). New York: Human Rights in China.

He, Z. (2000). Chinese Communist Party press in a tug-of-war: A political economy analysis of the Shenzhen Special Zone Daily. In C. C. Lee (ed.), *Power, Money, and Media* (pp. 121–151). Evanston, IL: Northwestern University Press.

Held, D. (1995). *Democracy and the global order*. Cambridge, UK: Polity.

Held, D., and McGrew, A. (eds.). (2000). *The global transformations reader: An introduction to the globalization debate*. Cambridge, UK: Polity.

Hellwig, T. (2007). Globalization and perceptions of policy maker competence: Evidence from France. *Political Research Quarterly, 60*(1), 146–158.

Hiscox, M. J. (2006). Through a glass and darkly: Attitudes toward international trade and the curious effects of issue framing. *International Organization, 60*(3), 755–780.

Hobsbawm, E. (1994). *The age of extremes: A history of the world, 1914–1991*. New York: Vintage.

Hoffman, M. E. S. (2009). What explains attitudes across U.S. trade policies? *Public Choice, 138*(3–4), 447–460.

Holbert, R. L., and Hansen, G. J. (2006). Fahrenheit 9–11, need for closure and the priming of affective ambivalence: An assessment of intra-affective structures by party identification. *Human Communication Research, 32*, 109–129.

Holton, R. J. (1998). *Globalization and the nation-state*. New York: St. Martin's Press.

Hong, J. H. (2011). From the world's largest propaganda machine to a multipurposed global news agency: Factors in and implications of Xinhua's transformation since 1978. *Political Communication, 28*(3), 377–393

Hoskins, C. and Mirus, R. (1988). Reasons for U.S. dominance of international trade in television programmes. *Media, Culture and Society, 10*(4), 499–515.

Hsiao, H. H. M., Wan, P. S., and Wong, T. K. Y. (2010). Globalization and public attitudes towards the state in the Asia-Pacific Region. *Japanese Journal of Political Science, 11*(1), 21–49.

Hu, G. W. (2005). English language education in China: Policies, progress, and problems. *Language Policy, 4*(1), 5–24.

Huang, W. (2006). *Zhongguorenkanmeiguo: haogantisheng, yilubujian* (Chinese See America: good feelings increase, suspicion runs unabated). Beijing: Horizon Research.

Hutchinson, J. (2003). *The dynamics of cultural nationalism: The Gaelic revival and the creation of the Irish nation state*. London: Allen and Unwin.

Inglehart, R. (1990). *Culture shift in advanced industrial democracies*. Princeton, NJ: Princeton University Press.

Inglehart, R. (2000). Globalization and postmodern values. *Washington Quarterly, 23*(1), 215–228.

Isernia, P. (2007). Anti-Americanism in Europe during the Cold War. In P. J. Katzenstein and R. O. Keohane (eds.), *Anti-Americanisms in world politics* (pp. 155–180). Ithaca, NY: Cornell University Press.

Iwabuchi, K. (2007). Contra-flows or the cultural logic of uneven globalization? Japanese media in the global agora. In D. Thussu (ed.) *Media on the move* (pp. 61–75). London: Routledge.

Johnston, A. I., and Stockmann, D. (2007). Chinese attitudes toward the United States and Americans. In P. J. Katzenstein and R. O. Keohane (eds.), *Anti-Americanisms in World Politics* (pp. 157–195). Ithaca, NY: Cornell University Press.

Kaplan, K. J. (1972). On the ambivalence-indifference problem in attitude theory and measurement: A suggested modification of the semantic differential technique. *Psychological Bulletin, 77*(5), 361–372.

Karl, R. (2002). *Staging the world: Chinese nationalism at the turn of the twentieth century.* Durham, NC: Duke University Press.

Katz, E., and Lazarsfeld, P. F. (1955). *Personal influence; the part played by people in the flow of mass communications.* Glencoe, IL: Free Press.

Katz, E., and Wedell, G. E. (1977). *Broadcasting in the third world: Promise and performance.* Cambridge, MA: Harvard University Press.

Keating, B., and Kriz, A. (2008). Outbound tourism from China: Literature review and research agenda. *Journal of Hospitality and Tourism Managements, 15*(1), 32–41.

Kern, H. L., and Hainmueller, J. (2009). Opium for the masses: How foreign media can stabilize authoritarian regimes. *Political Analysis, 17*(4), 377–399.

Kim, S. H. (2002). Anti-Americanism in South Korea. *The Washington Quarterly, 26*(1), 109–122.

Kim, S. H., and Lim, W. H. (2007). How to deal with South Korea. *The Washington Quarterly, 30*(2), 71–82.

Kim, Y. (2007). The rising East Asia "Wave": Korean media go global. In D. Thussu (ed.), *Media on the move: Global flow and contra-flow* (pp. 135–152). New York: Routledge.

Kizilbash, H. H. (1988). Anti-Americanism in Pakistan. *Annals of the American Academy of Political and Social Science, 497,* 58–67.

Klecka, W. R. (1980). *Discriminant analysis.* Newbury Park, CA: Sage.

Knight, N. (2003). Imagining globalization: The world and nation in Chinese Communist Party ideology. *Journal of Contemporary Asia, 33*(3), 318–337.

Knight, N. (2006). Reflecting on the paradox of globalisation: China's search for cultural identity and coherence. *China: An International Journal, 4*(1), 1–31.

Kocher, M. A., and Minushkin, S. (2007). Anti-Americanism and economic globalization, free trade, open markets and public opinion in Mexico. *Politica y Gobierno, 14*(1), 77–115.

Lane, R. E. (1962). *Political ideology: why the American common man believes what he does.* New York: Free Press.

Lang, G. E., and Lang, K. (1981). Watergate: An exploration of the agenda building process. In G. C. Wilhoit and H. deBock (eds.), *Mass Communication Review Yearbook 2* (pp. 447–468). Beverly Hills, CA: Sage.

Langley, L. (1988). Anti-America in Central America. *Annals of the American Academy of Political and Social Science, 497,* 77–88.

Lazarsfeld, P. F., Berelson, B., and Gaudet, H. (1944). *The people's choice: How the voter makes up his mind in a presidential campaign.* New York: Duell.

Lazarsfeld, P. F., and Merton, R. (1964). Mass communication, popular taste, and organized social action. In L. Bryson (ed.), *The communication of ideas* (pp. 95–118). New York: Cooper Square.

Lee, C. C. (1980). *Media imperialism reconsidered.* Beverly Hills, CA: Sage.

Lee, C. C. (1981). The United States as seen through the *People's Daily. Journal of Communication, 31*(4), 92–101.

Lee, C. C. (1994). Ambiguities and contradictions: Issues in China's changing political communication. In C. C. Lee (ed.), *China's media, media's China* (pp. 3–20), Boulder, CO: Westview Press.

Lee, C. C., and Yang, J. (1995). National interest and foreign news. *Gazette, 56,* 1–18.

Lee, C. C. (2002), Established pluralism: U.S. elite media discourse about China policy. *Journalism Studies*, 3(3), 383–397.

Lee, C. C. (2003). The global and the national of the Chinese media: Discourses, market, technology, and ideology. In C. C. Lee (ed.), *Chinese Media, Global Contexts* (pp. 1–31). London: Routledge,

Lee, C. C. (2004). *Chaoyue xifang baoquan: chuanmei yu wenhua zhongguo* (Beyond Western hegemony: Media and Chinese modernity). Hong Kong: Oxford University Press.

Lee, C. C. (2010). Bound to rise: Chinese media discourses on the new global order. In M. Curtin and H. Shah (eds.), *Reorienting global communication: Indian and Chinese media beyond borders* (pp. 260–283). Urbana: University of Illinois Press.

Lee, C. C. (2011). Voices from Asia and beyond: Centre for Communication Research at City University of Hong Kong. *Journalism Studies*, 12(6):826–836.

Lee, C. C., Chan, J. M. Pan, Z. D., and So, C.Y.K. (2002). *Global media spectacle*. Albany, NY: State University of New York Press.

Lee, C. C., Chan, J. M., Pan, Z. D., and So, C.Y.K. (2005). National prisms of a global "media event." In J. Curran and M. Gurevitch (eds.), *Mass media and society*, 4th ed. London: Hodder Arnold.

Lee, C. C., He, Z., and Huang, Y. (2006). Chinese Party Publicity Inc. conglomerated: The case of the Shenzhen Press Group. *Media, Culture and Society*, 28(5), 581–602.

Lee, C. C., He, Z., and Huang, Y. (2007). Party-market corporatism, clientelism, and media in Shanghai. *Harvard International Journal of Press/Politics*, 12, 21–42.

Lee, C. C., Li, H. T., and Lee, F.L.F. (2011). Symbolic use of decisive events: Tiananmen as a news icon in the editorials of the elite U.S. press. *International Journal of Press/Politics*, 16, 335–356.

Lee, C. C., and Li, H. T. (in press). Remembering Tiananmen and Berlin Wall: The elite U.S. press's anniversary journalism, 1989–2010, *Media, Culture and Society*.

Lee, F. L. F. (2006). Cultural discount and cross culture performance predictability: Examining box office performance of American movies in Hong Kong. *Journal of Media Economics*, 19(4), 259–278.

Lee, F.L.F. (2008). Hollywood movies in East Asia: Examining cultural discount and performance predictability at the box office. *Asian Journal of Communication*, 18(2), 117–136.

Lee, F.L.F. (2009). Cultural discount of cinematic achievement: The Academy Awards and U.S. movies' East Asian box office. *Journal of Cultural Economics*, 33(4), 239–262.

Lee, F.L.F., and Chan, J. M. (2005). Political attitudes, political participation, and Hong Kong identities after 1997. *Issues and Studies*, 41(2), 1–35.

Lee, F.L.F., and Chan, J. M. (2009). The political consequences of ambivalence: The case of democratic reform in Hong Kong. *International Journal of Public Opinion Research*, 21(1), 47–64.

Lee, F.L.F., Chan, J.M., and Zhou, B.H. (2011). National lenses on a global news event: Determinants of politicization and domestication of the prelude to the Beijing Olympics. *Chinese Journal of Communication*, 5(3), 274–292.

Lee, F.L.F., He, Z., Lee, C. C., Lin, W. Y., & Yao, M. Z. (2009). Urban Chinese's attitudes towards globalization: A survey study of media influence. *Pacific Affairs*, 82(2), 211–230.

Lee, F.L.F., Lee, C.C., Yao, M.Z., He, Z., & Lin, W.Y. (2010). Foreign media in China: From political economy to media effects. In J.Y.S. Cheng (ed.). *Democratization in China*. Hong Kong: City University of Hong Kong Press.

Lee, S. N. (1994). Mass-communication and national-development in China—Media roles reconsidered. *Journal of Communication*, 44(3), 22–37.

Lerner, D. (1958). *The passing of traditional society: Modernizing the Middle East.* Glencoe, IL: The Free Press.

Li, L. and Shen, L. (1995). On the duality of journalism in China. *Journalism University*, 2, 18–20.

Li, Y., and Hao, D. H. (2004). Three steps in sampling and error analysis. In Y. J. Bian, L. L. Li, and H. Cai (eds.), Social survey research in practice: Chinese experience and analysis (pp. 85–110). Hong Kong: Oxford University Press (in Chinese).

Liebe, T., and Katz, E. (1988). *The export of meaning.* Cambridge, MA: Harvard University Press.

Lin, M. (2004). Changes and consistency: China's media market after WTO entry. *Journal of Media Economics*, 17(3), 177–192.

Lin, W. Y., Song, H., and Ball-Rokeach, S. (2010). Localizing the global: Exploring the transnational ties that bind in new immigrant communities. *Journal of Communication*, 60(3), 205–229.

Lin, Y. (1935). *My country and my people.* New York: Reynal and Hitchcock.

Lippmann, W. (1922). *Public opinion.* New York: Harcourt Brace.

Liu, Y. (2006). Liu Yunshan's speech on Chinese Journalism Changjiang and Taofen Awards Conferring Ceremony (Liu Yunshan zai Zhongguo Xinwenjiang Changjiang Taofenjiang Banjiang Wanhui Shang de Jianghua). Accessed at: http://politics.people.com.cn/GB/1024/5018223.html

Lukes, S. (1974). *Power: A radical view.* London: Macmillan Press.

Ma, E.K.W. (1999). Media, cultural identity and the state: The case of Hong Kong. In J. Curran (ed.), *Media Organisations* (pp. 252–272). London: Edward Arnold.

Ma, E.K.W. (2011). *Desiring Hong Kong, consuming South China.* Hong Kong: Hong Kong University Press.

Macrae, C. N., Milne, A. B., and Bodenhausen, G. V. (1994). Stereotypes as energy-saving devices: A peek inside the cognitive toolbox. *Journal of Personality and Social Psychology*, 66, 37–47.

Mannheim, K. (1936). *Ideology & utopia: An introduction to the sociology of knowledge.* San Diego, CA: Harvest.

Martinez, M. D., Craig, S. C., and Kane, J. G. (2005). Pros and cons: Ambivalence and public opinion. In S. C. Craig and M. D. Martinez (eds.), *Ambivalence and the structure of political opinion* (pp. 1–14). New York: McMillan.

Mathews, G., Ma, E., and Lui, T. L. (2007). *Hong Kong, China: Learning to belong to a nation.* New York: Routledge.

McGraw, K. M., Hasecke, E., and Conger, K. (2003). Ambivalence, uncertainty, and processes of candidate evaluation. *Political Psychology*, 24(3), 421–448.

McLuhan, M. (1964). *Understanding Media: The Extensions of Man.* New York: McGraw-Hill.

Meng, B. C. (2009). Who needs democracy if we can pick our favorite girl? *Super Girl* as media spectacle. *Chinese Journal of Communication*, 2(3), 257–272.

Meng, B. C. (2011). From steamed bun to grass mud horse: E-gao as alternative political discourse on the Chinese Internet. *Global Media and Communication*, 7(1), 33–51.

Merton, R. K. (1957). *Social theory and social structure.* Glencoe, Ill.: Free Press.

Micklethwaite, J., and Wooldridge, A. (2001). The globalization backlash. *Foreign Policy*, 126,16–26.

Miller, T., Govil, N., McMurria, J., Maxwell, R., and Wang, T. (2005). *Global Hollywood 2.* London: British Film Institute.

Mills, C. W. (2000). *The sociological imagination*, 40th anniversary edition. Oxford, UK: Oxford University Press.

Moran, A. (2009). Global franchising, local customizing: The cultural economy of TV program formats. *Continuum: Journal of Media and Cultural Studies, 23*(2), 115–125.

Morton, T. A., and Duck, J. M. (2001). Communication and health beliefs: Mass and interpersonal influences on perceptions of risk to self and others. *Communication Research, 28*(5), 602–626.

Mutz, D. C. (1998). *Impersonal influence.* New York: Cambridge University Press.

Mutz, D. C. (1992). Mass media and the depoliticization of personal experience. *American Journal of Political Science, 36*(2), 483–508.

Mutz, D. C. (1994). Contextualizing personal experience: The role of mass media. *Journal of Politics, 56*(3), 689–714.

Nincic, M., and Russett, B. (1979). The effect of similarity and interest on attitudes toward foreign countries. *The Public Opinion Quarterly, 43*, 1, 68–78.

Nisbet, E. C., Nisbet, M. C., Scheufele, D. A., and Shanahan, J. E. (2004). Public diplomacy, television news, and Muslim opinion. *Harvard International Journal of Press/Politics, 9*(2), 11–37.

Noelle-Neumann, E. (1983). *Spiral of silence.* Chicago: University of Chicago Press.

Nolan, M. (2005). Anti-Americanism and Americanization in Germany. *Politics and Society, 33*(1), 88–122.

Norris, P. (2001). *Digital divide.* Cambridge, UK: Cambridge University Press.

Norris, P., and Inglehart, R. (2009). *Cosmopolitan communications: Cultural diversity in a globalized world.* Cambridge, UK: Cambridge University Press.

Nye, J. S. (1990). *Bound to lead: The changing nature of American power.* New York: Basic Books.

Nye, J. S. (2001). Asia's first globalizer. *The Washington Quarterly, 23*(4), 121–124.

Ong, A. (1999). *Flexible citizenship: the cultural logics of transnationality.* Durham, NC: Duke University Press.

Ong, A. (2006). *Neoliberalism as exception.* Durham, NC: Duke University Press.

OpenNet (2005). *Country profile: China (including Hong Kong)* . Available at: http://opennet.net/country/china

Ortner, S. B. (1994). Theory in anthropology since the Sixties. In N. B. Dirks, G. Eley, and S. Ortner (eds.), *Culture/Power/History* (pp. 371–411). Princeton, NJ: Princeton University Press.

Pan, L. (2011). English language ideologies in the Chinese foreign language education policies: A world-system perspective. *Language Policy, 10*(3), 245–263.

Pan, Z. D. (2000). Improvising reform activities: The changing reality of journalistic practice in China. In C. C. Lee (ed.), *Power, money, and media: Communication patterns and bureaucratic control in cultural China* (pp. 68–111). Evanston, IL: Northwestern University Press.

Pan, Z. D., and Chan, J. M. (2000). Building a market-based party organ: Television and national integration in China. In D. French and M. Richards (eds.), *Television in contemporary Asia* (pp. 233–263). London: Sage.

Pan, Z. D., and Kosicki, G. M. (1993). Framing analysis: An approach to news discourse. *Political Communication, 10*(1), 55–75.

Park, R. E. (1922). *The immigrant press and its control.* NY: Harper and Brothers.

Parker, R. P. (1988). Anti-American attitudes in the Arab world. *Annals of the American Academy of Political and Social Science, 497*, 46–57.

Pennycook, A. (1994). *The cultural politics of English as an international language.* London; New York: Longman.

People's Daily (1989). Jiang Zemin Qinqie Jiyu Gongqingtuan Ganbu. July 17, p. 1.
People's Daily (1990a). Jiang Zemin Tong "Fendouzhe de Zuji" Baogaotuan Zuotan. April 5, p. 1.
People's Daily (1990b). Budui Zhishifenzi Xuexi Jiang Zemin Zhongyao Jianghua. May 11, p. 3.
People's Daily (1991). Zhongxuanbu deng Lianhe Fachu Tongzhi Yaoqiu, Yunyong Wenwu Jinxing Aiguo Zhuyi he Gemin Chuantong Jiaoyu. September 15, p. 4.
People's Daily (1995). Kongzi Jiaxiang hua Chuantong Xuanyuan Guli lun Aiguo. June 15, p. 10.
Perry, D. K. (1990). News reading, knowledge about, and attitudes toward foreign countries. *Journalism Quarterly*, 67(2), 353–358.
Phillipson, R. (1992). *Linguistic imperialism*. Oxford, UK, and New York: Oxford University Press.
Polanyi, M. (1958). *Personal knowledge: Towards a post-critical philosophy*. Chicago: University of Chicago Press.
Polumbaum, J. (1990). The tribulations of China's journalism after a decade of reform. In C. C. Lee (eds.), *Voices of China: The interplay of politics and journalism* (pp. 33–68). New York: Guilford Press.
Price, V., Nir, L., and Capella, J. N. (2005). Framing public discussion of gay civil unions. *Public Opinion Quarterly*, 69(2), 179–212.
Priester J. R., and Petty R. E. (1996). The gradual threshold model of ambivalence: Relating the positive and negative bases of attitudes to subjective ambivalence. *Journal of Personality and Social Psychology, 71*, 431–449.
Reid, E., and Steele, J. (2009). Free trade: What is it good for/Globalization, deregulation, and "public opinion." *Journal of Law and Society, 36*(1), 11–31.
Ricento, T. (2006). *An introduction to language policy: Theory and method*. Malden, MA: Blackwell.
Ridout, T. N., Grosse, A. C., & Appleton, A. M. (2008). News media use and Americans' perceptions of global threat. *British Journal of Political Science, 38*, 575–593.
Robertson, R. (1992). *Globalization: Social theory and global culture*. London: Sage.
Robertson, R. (1997). Mapping the global condition. In A. Sreberny-Mohammadi, D. Winseck, J. McKenna and O. Boyd-Barrett (eds.), *Media in global context: A reader* (pp. 1–10). London: Arnold.
Rogers, E. M. (1995). *Diffusion of innovations*, 4th ed. New York: Free Press.
Rogers, E. M. (2003). *Diffusion of innovations*, 5th ed. New York: Free Press.
Rogowski, R. (1989). *Commerce and coalitions*. Princeton, NJ: Princeton University Press.
Rokeach, M. (1973). *The nature of human values*. New York: Free Press.
Rosen, S. (2003). Chinese media and youth: attitudes toward nationalism and internationalism. In C. C. Lee (ed.), *Chinese media, global contexts* (pp. 97–118). London: Routledge Curzon.
Rubenstein, A., and Smith, D. (eds.) (1985). *Anti-Americanism in the third world: Implications for U.S. foreign policy*. New York: Praeger.
Rudolph, T. J., and Popp, E. (2007). An information processing theory of ambivalence. *Political Psychology, 28*(5), 563–585.
Salwen, M. B. (1991). Cultural imperialism: A media effects approach. *Critical Studies in Mass Communication, 8*(1), 29–38.
Salwen, M. B. (1998). Perceptions of media influence and support for censorship: The third-person effect in the 1996 presidential election. *Communication Research*, 25, 259–285.
Salwen, M. B., and Driscoll, P. D. (1995). Feeling informed? The "assurance function" of the mass media. *International Journal of Public Opinion Research, 7*, 270–275.
Sassen, S. (1991). *The global city*. Princeton, NJ: Princeton University Press.

Scannell, P. (2006). Personal influence and the end of the masses. *Annals of the American Academy of Political and Social Science, 608*, 115–129.

Scheufele, D. A. (1999). Framing as a theory of media effects. *Journal of Communication, 49*(1), 103–122.

Schiller, H. I. (1976). *Communication and cultural domination.* New York: International Arts and Sciences Press.

Schiller, H. I. (1989). *Culture, Inc.: The corporate takeover of public expression.* New York: Oxford University Press.

Schiller, H. I. (1991). Not yet the post-imperialist era. *Critical Studies in Mass Communication, 8*(1), 13–28.

Schramm, W. (1964). *Mass media and national development.* Stanford, CA: Stanford University Press.

Semetko, H. A., Brzinski, J. B., Weaver, D., and Willnat, L. (1992). TV news and U.S. public opinion about foreign countries: The impact of exposure and attention. *International Journal of Public Opinion Research, 4*, 18–36.

Severin, W. J. (1994). The new cultural revolution: the spread of satellite dishes in China. *International Journal of Public Opinion Research, 6*(72–76).

Shambaugh, D. (1991). *The beautiful imperialist: China perceives America.* Princeton, NJ: Princeton University Press.

Shen, S. (2011). "Obamania" in China and its yielding to nationalism: Quantitative responses from elitist Chinese students in Beijing toward the 2008 U.S. election and structural analysis. *China Review, 11*(2), 183–209.

Shi, T. J., and Lu, J. (2010). The shadow of Confucianism. *Journal of Democracy, 21*(4), 123–130.

Shih, C. Y. (2003). Consuming part-time nationalism: China as an immigrant in the global society. *New Political Science, 25*(3), 365–384.

Simonson, P., and Weimann, G. (2003). Critical research at Columbia: Lazarsfeld's and Merton's "mass communication, popular taste, and organized social action In E. Katz, J. O. Peters, T. Liebes, and A. Orloff (eds.), *Canonic texts in media research.* London: Polity.

Sinnott, R. (2008). Determinants of mass attitudes to globalization. In T. Inoguchi and I. Marsh (eds.), *Globalisation, public opinion and the state* (pp. 223–254). London: Routledge.

Sklair, L. (2002). Democracy and the transnational capitalist class. *Annals of the American Academy of Political and Social Sciences, 581*(1), 144–157.

Smith, A. D. (1993). *National Identity.* Reno: University of Nevada Press.

Tajfel, H. (1974). Social identity and intergroup behavior. *Social Science Information, 13*, 65–93.

Tajfel, H. (1981*). Human groups and social categories.* Cambridge, UK: Cambridge University Press.

Tajfel, H. (1982a). *Social identity and intergroup relations.* Cambridge, UK: Cambridge University Press.

Tajfel, H. (1982b). Social psychology of intergroup relations. *Annual Review of Psychology, 33*, 1–39.

Tarrow, S. (2005). *The new transnational activism.* Cambridge, UK: Cambridge University Press.

Thompson, J. B. (1995). *The media and modernity.* Stanford, CA: Stanford University Press.

Thompson, M., Zanna, M. P., and Griffin, D. W. (1995). Let's not be indifferent about (attitudinal) ambivalence. In R. E. Petty and J. Krosnick (eds.), *Attitude strength: Antecedents and consequences* (pp. 361–386). Mahwah: N.J.: LEA.

Thornton, J. L. (2008). Long time coming: The prospects for democracy in China. *Foreign Affairs, 87*(1), January/February 2008. Available at: http://www.foreignaffairs.com/articles/63041/john-l-thornton/long-time-coming

Thussu, D. K. (2007). Mapping global media flow and contra-flow. In D. Thussu (ed.) *Media on the move* (pp. 10–29). London: Routledge.

Thussu, D. K. (2007). *News as entertainment: The rise of global infotainment.* London: Sage.

Tichenor, P. J., Donohue, G. A., and Olien, C. N. (1970). Mass media flow and differential growth in knowledge. *Public Opinion Quarterly. 34,* 159–170.

Tian, C., and Nathan, J. A. (2001). The polls-trends: American ambivalence toward China. *Public Opinion Quarterly, 65,* 124–138.

Tims, A. R., and Miller, M. M. (1986). Determinants of attitudes toward foreign countries. *International Journal of Intercultural Relations,* 10, 471–484.

To, Y., and Yep, R. (2008). Global capital and media control: A case of joint venture in China's media market before WTO. *East Asia: An International Quarterly, 25,* 167–185.

Tomlinson, J. (1991). *Cultural imperialism: A critical introduction.* New York: John Hopkins University Press.

Tomlinson, J. (1999). *Globalization and culture.* Chicago: University of Chicago Press.

Townsend, J. (1996). Chinese nationalism. In Jonathan Unger (ed.), *Chinese Nationalism.* New York: M. E. Sharpe.

Tunstall, J. (1977). *The media are American: Anglo-American media in the world.* London: Constable.

Unger, J. (ed.) (1996). *Chinese nationalism.* New York: M. E. Sharpe.

Van Dijk, T. A. (1988). *News as discourse.* Hillsdale, NJ: LEA.

Wallerstein, I. (1974). *The modern world-system I.* Waltham, MA: Academic Press.

Wallerstein, I. (1999). *The end of the world as we know it: social science for the twenty-first century.* Minneapolis: University of Minnesota Press.

Wallis, C. (2011). New media practices in China: Youth patterns, processes, and politics. *International Journal of Communication,* 5, 406–436.

Wang, J., and Chang, T. K. (1996). From class ideologue to state manager: TV programming and foreign imports in China, 1970–1990. *Journal of Broadcasting and Electronic Media,* 40(2), 196–207.

Wang, H. Y., Lee, F. L. F., and Wang B. (2013). Foreign news as marketable power display: Reporting foreign disasters in the Chinese local media. *International Journal of Communication,* 7, 884-902.

Wang, W. F., and Lam, A. (2009). The English language curriculum for senior secondary school in China: its evolution from 1949. *RELC Journal,* 40(1), 65–82.

Wasser, F. (1995). Is Hollywood America: The transnationalization of the American film industry. *Critical Studies in Mass Communication,* 12(4), 423–437.

Waters, M. (2001). *Globalization.* London: Routledge.

Wei, R., and Pan, Z. (1999). Mass media and consumerist values in the People's Republic of China. *International Journal of Public Opinion Research,* 11(1), 75–96.

Wildman, S. and Siwek, S. (1988). *International trade in films and television programs.* Cambridge, MA: Ballinger.

Williams, R. (1958). *Culture and society, 1780–1950.* New York: Columbia University Press.

Willnat, L., He, Z., and Hao, X. M. (1997). Foreign media exposure and perceptions of Americans in Hong Kong, Shenzhen, and Singapore. *Journalism and Mass Communication Quarterly,* 74(4), 738–756.

Willnat, L., He, Z., Takeshita, T., and Lopez-Escobar, E. (2002). Perceptions of foreign media influence in Asia and Europe: The third-person effect and media imperialism. *International Journal of Public Opinion Research, 14*(2), 175–192.

Wolfe, R., and Mendelsohn, M. (2005). Values and interests in attitudes toward trade and globalization: The continuing compromise of embedded liberalism. *Canadian Journal of Political Science, 38*(1), 45–68.

World Bank. (2011). *Migration and remittances factbook 2011*. Washington DC: The World Bank.

Womack, B. (1990). The dilemma of centricity and internationalism. In C.C. Lee (ed.), *Voices of China: The Interplay of Politics and Journalism* (pp.229–242). New York: Guilford Press.

Woodward, I., Skrbis, Z., and Bean, C. (2008). Attitudes towards globalization and cosmopolitanism: Cultural diversity, personal consumption and the national economy. *British Journal of Sociology, 59*(2), 207–226.

Wu, H. T., and Chan, J. M. (2007). Globalizing Chinese martial arts cinema: The global-local alliance and the production of *Crouching Tiger, Hidden Dragon*. *Media, Culture and Society, 29*(2), 195–214.

Xin, X. (2010). Xinhua News Agency in the context of the "crisis of news agencies." In O. Boyd-Barrett (ed.), *News agencies in the turbulent era of the Internet* (pp. 283–303). Generalitat de Catalunya: Col-leccio Lexikon.

Yeoh, B. S. A., Huang, S., and Lam, T. (2005). Transnationalizing the "Asian" family: Imaginaries, intimacies and strategic intents. *Global Networks—A Journal of Transnational Affairs, 5*(4), 307–315.

Yu, T. (1993). The conduct of post-Tiananmen U.S. China policy: Domestic constraints, systemic change, and value incompatibility. *Asian Affairs, 19*(4), 229–247.

Yu, Z., and Zhao, D. (2006). Differential participation and the nature of a movement: a study of the 1999 anti-U.S. Beijing student demonstrations. *Social Forces, 84*(3), 1755–1777.

Zhang, W. (2003). "Zhongguoren kan meiguo: shiyong zuyi+bentuhua qingjie." *Horizon Research*. Available at: http://www.horizonkey.com/c/cn/news/2003–08/12/news_248.html

Zhang, Y. B., and Harwood, J. (2002). Television viewing and perceptions of traditional Chinese values among Chinese college students. *Journal of Broadcasting and Electronic Media, 46*(2), 245–264.

Zhao, D. X. (2002) An angle on nationalism in China today: Attitudes among Beijing students after the Belgrade 1999. *The China Quarterly, 172*, 885–905.

Zhao, S. (2004). *A nation-state by construction*. Stanford, CA: Stanford University Press.

Zhao, S. (2005). China's pragmatic nationalism: Is it manageable? *The Washington Quarterly, 29*(1), 131–44.

Zhao, Y. Z. (1998). *Media, market, and democracy in China: Between the Party Line and the Bottom Line*. Urbana and Chicago: University of Illinois Press.

Zhao, Y. Z. (2000). Caught in the Web: the Public interest and the battle for control of China's information superhighway. *The Journal of Policy, Regulation and Strategy for Telecommunication Information and Media, 2*(1), 41–66.

Zhao, Y. Z. (2000). From commercialization to conglomeration: The transformation of the Chinese press within the orbit of the party state. *Journal of Communication, 50*(2), 3–26.

Zhao, Y. Z. (2003). "Enter the world": Neoliberal globalization, the dream for a strong nation, and Chinese press discourses on the WTO. In C. C. Lee (ed.), *Chinese media, global context* (pp. 32–56). London: Routledge.

Zhao, Y. Z. (2003). Transnational capital, the Chinese state, and China's communication industries in a fractured society. *Javnost—the Public, 10*(4), 53–73.

Zhao, Y. Z. (2004). Leaving China: Media, migration, and transnational imagination. *Pacific Affairs, 77*(1), 111–112.

Zhao, Y. Z. (2008). *Communication in China*. Lanham, MD: Rowman and Littlefield.

Zhou, B. (2010). Linkage politics in Chinese TV foreign news: A Study of Xinwen Lianbo of CCTV. *Communication and Society*, 13, 37–74. (in Chinese)

Ziehl, S. (2003). Forging the links: Globalization and family patterns. *Society in Transition*, 34(2), 320–337.

Index